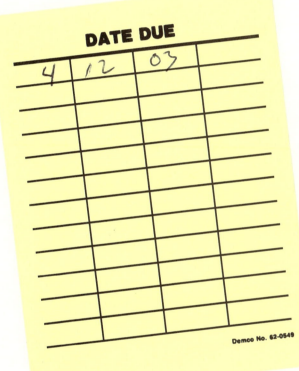

DATE DUE

4	12	03	

ARMED AND CONSIDERED DANGEROUS
A Survey of Felons and Their Firearms

SOCIAL INSTITUTIONS AND SOCIAL CHANGE

EDITED BY

Peter H. Rossi
Michael Useem
James D. Wright

ARMED AND CONSIDERED DANGEROUS
A Survey of Felons and Their Firearms

JAMES D. WRIGHT

PETER H. ROSSI

ALDINE DE GRUYTER
New York

James D. Wright is Professor of Sociology at the University of Massachusetts, Amherst, and Director of the Social and Demographic Research Institute and has published seven books and over fifty scholarly articles and papers on topics ranging from job satisfaction to the state and local politics of natural disasters. He has been studying private ownership of weapons since 1975. His recent books include *The Dissent of the Governed: Alienation and Democracy in America* and a three-volume series on social science and natural hazards, all co-authored with Peter H. Rossi.

Peter H. Rossi is Professor of Sociology at the University of Massachusetts, Amherst, Director of Research at the Social and Demographic Research Institute, and Past President of the American Sociological Association. Widely regarded as one of the most eminent American social scientists, Dr. Rossi has published 21 books and over 125 scholarly papers and articles. His recent books include *Reforming Public Welfare, Measuring Social Judgements,* and *Natural Hazards and Public Choice.* He has pioneered the application of social science research methods to matters of public policy concern.

Aldine de Gruyter (Formerly Aldine Publishing Company)
Division of Walter de Gruyter, Inc.
200 Saw Mill River Road
Hawthorne, New York 10532

Library of Congress Cataloging-in-Publication Data

Wright, James D.
  Armed and considered dangerous.

  Bibliography: p.
  Includes index.
  1. Gun control—United States.   2. Firearm ownership—United States.   3. Crime and criminals—United States.
I. Rossi, Peter Henry, 1921–   .   II. Title.
HV7436.W75   1986   363.3'3   86-3617
ISBN 0-202-30330-6 (lib. bdg.)
ISBN 0-202-30331-4 (pbk.)

Printed in the United States of America
10 9 8 7 6 5 4 3 2 1

CONTENTS

PREFACE

The study reported in this volume is part of a larger research program on criminal violence being undertaken by the Social and Demographic Research Institute of the University of Massachusetts. The focus here is on the acquisition, carrying, and use of guns (and other weapons) in the commission of criminal acts. Data consist of questionnaires administered to nearly 2000 convicted felons serving time in state prisons all around the country. While many other large surveys of the prison population have been done, none have focused so exclusively or exhaustively on the firearms aspect of the crime problem.

The design and contents of this survey evolved out of a comprehensive review of the extant literature on "weapons, crime, and violence in America" (Wright, Rossi, and Daly, 1983). Although vast reams have been written on these topics, many important questions have not been thoroughly researched, and some of the most important have barely been researched at all. In the latter category we would include the question of how, where, and why criminals acquire, carry, and use firearms. Indeed, prior to the study whose results are reported here, nearly everything that was known about these topics was based on samples of firearms confiscated by the police in the course of criminal investigations, an approach known to be fraught with problems.

Information obtained from convicted felons in self-administered questionnaires is also fraught with problems that we are happy to acknowledge. We do not believe that these survey data constitute the final word on any of the topics discussed in this volume. The states where this survey was conducted were chosen mainly because of their willingness to cooperate and, therefore, do not constitute a probability sample of states; the prisons within states were also selected mainly for their willingness to cooperate and therefore do not constitute a probability sample of prisons; finally, since participation in the survey was voluntary, specific respondents were also self-selected and therefore do not constitute a probability sample of convicted felons. The data we have assembled are national in scope and, we hope, in implications, but in no sense are they "nationally generalizable" in the strict statistical sense of the word.

Sampling issues aside, there are also formidable problems of measurement in a survey of this sort. There is obviously no guarantee that prisoners answered our questions truthfully or completely; indeed, given their strong felonious inclinations, there is ample reason to be skeptical of everything they have to say. Already in prison, they run no additional risk in reporting honestly on their backgrounds, behaviors, and criminal histories; but at the same time, there is very little positive motivation for them to report the truth either. In the few cases where we could inquire about the correspondence between what was reported in the questionnaire and what was known about the felon through his criminal justice records, the correspondence was comfortingly close (see Chapter Two), but there is no guarantee that this convenient pattern generalizes throughout the data.

Finally, it bears emphasis (here and throughout the volume) that a sample of convicted felons doing time in state prisons is *not*, by any means, a representative sample of the criminal population at large. Juvenile offenders are rarely sent to the kinds of facilities where we conducted this study and they are therefore grossly underrepresented in our data. Likewise, first-time adult offenders are rarely imprisoned and are also underrepresented here. In general, the kinds of men we studied are older, more hardened, more violent, and have longer criminal records than the population of criminals at large would be. Their firearms behavior may, therefore, not be indicative of the firearms behaviors of the larger criminal population. All the findings reported here must be interpreted with this fact very much in mind.

Because this study grew out of a very detailed and comprehensive review of the literature on guns, crime, and violence, our review of pertinent literature here is rather cursory; reference is usually made to the literature review rather than to the primary sources. We have, however, made an effort to cite the most important studies that have appeared in the literature since our earlier review was completed. The relative brevity of our reference list results not from academic solipsism but from a desire to avoid redundant labor.

Our purpose in undertaking this study was primarily to *describe* the weapons behavior of the felon population, not to test specific hypotheses or theories of crime, and most assuredly not to evaluate the relative wisdom of this or that approach to "gun control." We have, of course, addressed both theoretical issues and policy implications whenever it seemed appropriate to do so; but this was in all cases subsidiary to our more fundamental descriptive task. We therefore plead guilty in advance to the (inevitable) charge that this work is largely atheoretical. But, on the other hand, where is the criminological theory that says *anything at all* about the role of firearms in the lives and activities of the criminal population?

This study was originally funded in the Spring of 1981; data collection began in earnest the following August and continued through December. A preliminary research report (running well in excess of six hundred pages) was submitted to the study sponsor in the Spring of 1984, whereupon we were informed that the National Institute of Justice could no longer publish such massive reports and that a 100-page version would be more suitable for their needs. This much-condensed version of the study results was subsequently published by the Institute (Wright and Rossi, 1985); the present volume, in turn, is a much revised (and somewhat abridged) version of the initial research report.

The initial research report contained two appendixes, both of which have been omitted from this volume. The first was simply a reproduction of the study questionnaire (the questionnaire itself ran to 75 pages). Since the present volume does not contain a copy of the questionnaire, we have made every effort to give exact question wordings in the tables or in the associated text. Readers seeking more information about the exact study contents and formats can obtain a copy of the study codebook (and a copy of the data themselves) from the Interuniversity Consortium for Political and Social Research (PO Box 1248, Ann Arbor, MI 48106), where the data and documentation have been archived.

The second appendix was a long, detailed, and rather tedious blow-by-blow description of how the sample was sorted into the categories of the "Armed Criminals" typology that is introduced in Chapter Three. For nearly 90% of the sample, this sorting-out was completely straightforward (as described in the chapter), but for the remaining tenth, it was not. The detailed description of how this tenth was handled is available directly from us upon request.

James D. Wright
Peter H. Rossi

ACKNOWLEDGMENTS

A research project such as the one reported here only succeeds if it enjoys the cooperation and assistance of any number of people who, through obligation or courtesy, make themselves and their expertise available to the research staff. Whether this project has in fact succeeded is for readers, not us, to decide; such failings as it may contain, however, are not for lack of the enthusiastic cooperation and capable assistance of the following individuals, for whose contributions we are most grateful:

Our first and largest debt is to the National Institute of Justice, who provided the funds to undertake this research and who has supported the Social and Demographic Research Institute's violent crime research program for the past seven years. Officials at NIJ who have been involved in varying degrees with the project include the Institute Director, James K. Stewart, and the Associate Director, Robert Burkhardt; Fred Heinzelmann, Director of the Institute's Community Crime Prevention Division; and Dr. Lois Mock, who served as project monitor for the study.

We note a special gratitude to Dr. Mock for her patience in seeing the project through to completion, her assistance in winning the initial grant, her many valuable suggestions as the research proceeded, and her detailed and helpful comments on earlier drafts.

We are also grateful for the time and advice of the scholars and practitioners who constituted the project's Advisory Committee: Mr. Al Andrews, Chief of Police of Peoria, Illinois; Dr. Marcia Chaiken of the National Institute for Sentencing Alternatives; Dr. Phillip Cook of Duke University; Dr. Mark Moore of Harvard University; and Mr. William Wilkie of the National Institute of Corrections. The members of the Advisory Committee met formally to review the project pretest results and to brainstorm over the contents of the questionnnaire; most of them were also pestered by mail or phone periodically throughout the study for advice and counsel.

Mr. Wilkie is owed a special note of thanks for his assistance in arranging our access to the state prison systems where we eventually interviewed. A day on the phone in behalf of a research project not of his own making saved us what would have otherwise been several months of work.

The project was also blessed with an extraordinarily resourceful and talented field team who traveled to prisons all over the United States gathering the data on which this study is based. For services dramatically in excess of the rate of pay—for countless hours in coach class, endless nights in Holiday Inns, fifteen- and sixteen-hour working days, and infinite patience (and good research judgment) in the face of wary administrators and hostile inmates—we thank Jeff Segal, Joe Pereira, and Tommy Joyner.

Additional thanks are owed Mr. Pereira for having undertaken the data quality analysis reported in the text and for assisting in the translation of the Spanish version of the questionnaire; and also to Mr. Segal, who undertook the data analyses and first drafts of the material on stolen firearms.

Data entry, analysis, and management were under the general direction of SADRI's Director of Software Development and Data Base Management, Ms. Eleanor Weber-Burdin, whose talents on the computer are exceeded only by her commitment to the people and projects of "the shop." Her assistant, Ms. Marianne Geronimo, provided supervision of the data entry staff and much assistance to the principal investigators in the data analysis. Special thanks to both of them for yet another job well done.

Gratitude is also owed the several undergraduate and graduate students at the University of Massachusetts who entered the data from the raw questionnaires onto the computer quickly and with remarkably few errors: Rachael Angeline, Matthew Archibald, Denise Furlong, Michael Hanrahan, Amy Kopel, Lisa Lorant, Mary Ellen Madaio, and Aida Rodriguez. Ms. Rodriguez also assisted in preparing the Spanish version of the questionnaire.

Our presence in the ten research sites, and therefore our ability to gather the project data, was only possible because of the cooperation and assistance of each state's corrections administration—from the State Commissioner of Corrections down to and including the security staff who were assigned to watch over the field team while we were in the site. None of the following people had any obligation to render, or stood to profit from, the help which was, nonetheless, freely given:

In Michigan: Mr. Perry M. Johnson, Director, Michigan Department of Corrections; Mr. William Kime, Deputy Director of Research; Mr. Robert Richardson, Chief of Research in the Program Bureau; Warden John Jabe and Deputy Warden Gach, Michigan Reformatory; Mr. Jabe's Administrative Assistant, Mr. Joe Cross; Mr. Robert Heriford; and Officers Bernard Clark, Richard Signs, Don Gostenell, and Bradley Harris.

In Missouri: Dr. Lee Roy Black, Director, Department of Corrections and Human Resources; Mr. Dale Riley, Acting Director, Division of Adult Institutions; Mr. Gerard Frey, Superintendent, and Mr. Don Cabana, Assistant Superintendent, Missouri Eastern Correctional Center; and at the Center, Ms. Micki Andrews.

In Minnesota: Mr. Jack G. Young, Commissioner, Mr. Orville Pung, Deputy Commissioner, and Mr. Gerry Strathman, Research Director, Minnesota Department of Corrections; Mr. Frank Wood, Superintendent, and Mr. Dennis Benson, Residential Program Manager, Minnesota Corrections Facility at Oak Park Heights; at the Oak Park Heights facility, Lt. Lou Stender, Mr. David Crist, and Mr. Rick Hillengass; Mr. James Hulburt, Superintendent, Minnesota Corrections Facility at Lino Lake; and at the Lino Lakes facility, Mr. William McGrath, Ms. Delores Redfield, Ms. Toby Larson, and Officer Pat Clemens.

In Oklahoma: Mr. Larry R. Meachum, Director, and Mr. Clifton Sandel, Supervisor of Planning and Research, Oklahoma Department of Corrections; Mr. Larry Fields, Warden, Joe Harp Correctional Center; and at the Center, Mr. Larry Thornton, Medical Director; Mr. Sam Preston, Programs Director; and Officers Stephen D. Moore, Terry W. Ragsdale, Jerome L. Carson, Keith Hall, and John Y. Brown.

In Florida: Mr. Louis L. Wainwright, Secretary, Dr. John H. Dale, Jr., Chief, Bureau of Planning, Research, and Statistics, and Mr. Bob Kriegner, Florida Department of Corrections; Superintendent Raymond D. Massey and Mr. Paul V. Gunning, Assistant Superintendent for Operations, Union Correctional Institution; and at the Institution, Colonel Jackson, Major Tomlinson, Lieutenant Rayburn, and Sergeant Newman of the Security Staff; Mr. Cunningham, Chief of Classification; Mr. J. L. Pitcher, Business Manager; Mr. Chuck Davis, Director of the educational unit; and Officer Robbie Watson.

In Georgia: Mr. David C. Evans, Commissioner, Mr. Ben Wyckoff, Director of Research and Evaluation, and Ms. Meg Updycke, Office of Public Affairs, Georgia Department of Corrections; Mr. Bob Francis, Warden, Georgia Diagnostic and Classification Center; and at the Center, Mr. Parrish, Assistant Superintendent for Security, Mr. David Fields, Assistant Superintendent for Operations, and Mr. Steve Phillips, Assistant Superintendent for Care and Treatment; Mr. Dave Cawthon; and Officers Wesley Baker and Tommy Lee Williamson.

In Nevada: Mr. Vernon Housewright, Director, Nevada Department of Prisons; Mr. George Sumner, Superintendent, Nevada State Prison; and at the Prison, Counsellor Robin Bates and Lt. Roger Belleville.

In Arizona: Mr. Ellis MacDougall, Director, Mr. Jerry Thompson, Deputy Director, and Mr. Bob Anderson, Head of Research, Arizona Department of Corrections; Mr. Don Wawrzaszek, Chief Administrator, Arizona State Prison; Mr. Bob Goldsmith, Warden, and Mr. Al

Grijalva, Assistant Warden, Central Unit; and at the Unit, Major Herndon, Chief of Security, and Officers Becky Blanco, Myron B. Fristad, Gary E. Peterson, Rickey Garrett, and John A. Nielson.

In Maryland: Mr. John P. Galley, Commissioner, and Mr. Bruce Stout, Executive Assistant, Maryland Division of Correction; Mr. Marlin Bachtell, Warden, Maryland Correctional Training Center; and at the Center, Mr. Terrie Chavis, Assistant Superintendent for Treatment, and his assistant, Mr. Bernard Burnes; Mr. Brewer, Security Officer; Lt. Nelson Baker; and Officers John Mills, Charles Turner, and Daniel Sirbaugh.

In Massachusetts: Mr. Michael V. Fair, Commissioner, Mr. Dennis Humphrey, Associate Commissioner, and Mr. Frank Carney, Director of Research, Massachusetts Department of Correction; Superintendent Terence Holbrook and Deputy Superintendent Michael Maloney, Massachusetts Correctional Institution at Norfolk; and at the Institution, Mr. Carlos Geromini, Principal of the Education Unit, and Officer James Butler.

The next-to-final draft of the survey questionnaire was pretested on 18 men serving sentences in the Berkshire County House of Corrections, a county jail in Western Massachusetts. We are grateful to Sheriff Carmen C. Massimiano and Officer Paul Therrien of the Pittsfield Police Department for arranging our access to the pretest site.

Over the course of this project, SADRI was well-served by an able and cheerful secretarial pool consisting at various times of Ms. Cindy Coffman, Mr. Ken Forfia, Ms. Jeanne Reinle, Ms. Kathy Moore, and Ms. Jane Karp, all of whom contributed to the production of this manuscript or to one (or more) of its several predecessors.

Previous drafts of the study report (or its component parts) profitted immensely from the careful reading and critical commentary of Dr. Lois Mock, Dr. Phillip Cook, Dr. Paul Blackman, Mr. Mark Benenson, Dr. Gary Kleck, Dr. Marcia Chaiken, Dr. Alan Lizotte, Mr. Don Kates, Dr. Colin Loftin, several of our colleagues at the University of Massachusetts, numerous participants at various meetings and symposia where preliminary findings were presented, and others who have asked not to be identified. We are grateful indeed to these people for having prevented many factual errors and interpretive excesses from seeing the light of print.

Finally, we express our gratitude to the nearly 2000 prisoners all over the United States who agreed to participate in this study and complete a survey questionnaire.

Despite the considerable assistance just acknowledged, none of the persons and institutions identified above, nor the National Institute of Justice, nor the United States government, bears any responsibility whatsoever for any of the findings, interpretations, conclusions, or implications expressed in this volume, all of which remain our own.

1

THE CRIMINAL ACQUISITION AND USE OF FIREARMS

INTRODUCTION

How and why criminals acquire, carry, and use firearms are the central topics of this volume. Almost all of the information presented here was obtained from a survey of men serving sentences for felony offenses in 11 state prisons scattered throughout the country. However uncertain one may be about their reliability as sources, convicted criminals are about the only source of empirical information on this topic that can be tapped at reasonable cost. (We also show later that convicted felons are not totally unreliable informants.)

The research effort that generated our data was supported by a grant from the National Institute of Justice.[1] There are many compelling reasons to devote public funds and scholarly effort to obtaining empirical information on the criminal acquisition and use of firearms. The first and most compelling reason is that by any standard, the level of damage to persons and property through the criminal use of firearms is unacceptably high in the United States. Crime is a major social problem, and violent crime, where firearms play a critical role, is an especially troublesome aspect of the problem.

Second, the question of how social order is maintained is at the very heart of social science concerns. Crime constitutes one of the major forms of social disorder, one to whose understanding social scientists have devoted much attention. In addition, the possession of firearms is so widespread among Americans that an adequate interpretation of American culture requires some understanding of how guns fit into the larger society. The devotion of many Americans to the ownership and use of firearms clearly

[1] NIJ Grant #82-NIJ-CX-0001 (James D. Wright, Principal Investigator, and Peter H. Rossi, Co-Principal Investigator). A highly abbreviated version of the materials reported in this volume is contained in Wright and Rossi, *The Armed Criminal in America* (Washington, D.C.: The National Institute of Justice, 1985). The survey data themselves are available through the Inter-University Consortium for Political and Social Research (PO Box 1248, Ann Arbor, Michigan 48106).

conditions, perhaps strongly, the actions that can be taken to reduce the criminal use of guns.[2]

Third, there is a clear policy interest in understanding how firearms, crime, and American culture are related. Effective social policy aimed at reducing crime, in general, and gun-related crime, in particular, depends on a sound understanding of these relationships and the limits they set on various policy initiatives.

These three sets of concerns form the background of this monograph in the sense that they constitute the origins of the research effort whose results are described in the following chapters. These three concerns also represent our major goals. If this volume advances our understanding of the social problem of crime, or helps to reveal the structural foundations of social order, or illuminates ways that policy might reduce gun crime, then the aspirations that fueled its writing will have been fulfilled.

GUN CRIME AS A SOCIAL PROBLEM

Violent crime that threatens or abuses the physical safety of its victims lies at the heart of the crime problem in America today. In turn, the use of firearms to commit crime constitutes a major portion of the violent crime problem. Each year, approximately 30,000 American citizens die through the suicidal, homicidal, or accidental abuse of guns; several hundreds of thousands are injured (intentionally or accidentally); hundreds of thousands more are victimized by gun crimes (Wright, Rossi, and Daly, 1983).

Crime of all sorts impacts on a major portion of the nation's households: Victimization surveys show that one out of five households is victimized by crime annually (Rossi, 1983). Although violent crime per se constitutes only about one-tenth of all crime, the remainder being property crimes in which firearms ostensibly played no role, it contributes considerably more than its share to the fear of crime and to the public's sense of crime as a serious problem. Indeed, it can be argued that violent crime is *the* crime problem and that its reduction should be a matter of the highest priority on the law enforcement and criminal justice policy agendas of the Nation.

The line between "violent" and "nonviolent" crimes is clear in some instances but hazy and indistinct in others. Homicide, manslaughter, assault, and robbery are, by definition, clearly violent crimes in which physical harm is either inflicted or threatened. But a burglary, ordinarily a nonviolent crime, can easily become violent if the burglar (or his victim) is carrying a gun. Similarly, a minor argument that would otherwise be no

---

[2] Research on the general phenomenon of gun ownership in American society is reviewed in Wright, Rossi, and Daly (1983). Also useful in this connection is Tonso (1982). Surveys dating to 1959 have consistently shown that about one-half of all U.S. households possesses a firearm.

more serious than a disturbance of the peace can be transformed into an aggravated assault if one of the parties attempts to emphasize his or her views by brandishing or using a weapon.

In a very real sense, most felonies either are or have the potential to become violent crimes. All that is needed is the inclination and means to inflict physical harm on a victim. And while it is obviously possible to inflict a great deal of harm with almost any object, it is both easier and potentially more damaging with firearms than with other weapons. Moreover, guns can be used at a distance, thus keeping the perpetrator safely beyond the reach of the victim; they are easily concealed about the person so that potential victims may be unaware of the danger they are about to confront; perhaps of greatest significance, guns are very intimidating weapons that make for compliant victims and easy pickings.

The main dimensions of the social problem of gun crime are often said to be the obvious consequences of these characteristics of firearms. Gun crimes cause more physical damage to victims; guns make crimes easier to commit, thereby increasing the crime rate; guns make it possible to undertake larger scale crimes, thereby increasing the overall social cost. Clearly, or so it is argued, if guns could somehow be abolished, both the scale of our crime problem and the physical damages associated with crime would decrease.

Or would they?

One of the principal lessons of this volume is that the connection between guns and crime, while seemingly obvious and clear, is actually quite complex and rife with potentially counterbalancing interactions. It is, for example, true that many crimes are committed with guns, but it does not follow that if there were no guns (or fewer guns), there would be no (or less) crime. Guns may only increase the efficiency of the criminal and have no consequence for his rate of criminal activity. A gunless society might still have as much crime; indeed, if criminals compensated for decreased efficiency with an increase in the number of crimes committed, a newly gunless society might find its crime rate going up, *not down*.

Likewise, it is certain that guns are used by criminals to inflict physical harm upon their victims. But again, it does not follow that fewer guns in criminal hands would mean less physical harm. Indeed, according to some researchers, the use of guns in crime actually *lowers* the level of harm since victims are less inclined to resist—and thereby less likely to be injured—when confronted with a gun.

In the same vein, guns enable larger scale crimes, for instance, they make possible the robbing of banks. But it does not follow that the elimination of these larger scale crimes would, *ipso facto,* reduce the overall social cost. Cook (1976) has stressed that criminals carry guns in part because guns allow them to "hit" more lucrative targets; in the absence of such opportunities, they may decide to rob less lucrative (and less resistant) targets instead— the young, the old, and the infirm. And it is *not at all clear* that a reduction in bank robberies won at the cost of an increased rate of robbery against, for example, the elderly represents a genuine reduction in the social cost of crime.

Another extremely important and often underappreciated dimension of the gun crime problem is that gun ownership and use are so widespread among the American population. There are approximately 120–140 million firearms in private hands in the United States. Sample surveys show that about one-half of all American households possess at least one firearm, and that about one in three or four possess a handgun (see Wright, Rossi, and Daly, 1983). It is also clear that only a very small fraction of these privately owned firearms are ever involved in crime or interpersonal violence, the vast bulk of them being owned and used more or less exclusively for sport and recreational purposes, or for self-protection.

This pattern of widespread firearms possession and use places strong constraints on social policies aimed at the control of criminal weapons abuse. At one extreme, a policy aimed at removing all weapons from private hands is rendered completely unthinkable: Firearms are as American as automobiles and apple pie. At the other extreme, any policy that facilitates easy access to firearms among legitimate gun owners also makes firearms readily available for criminal use as well. Of course, neither of these extremes is currently at issue. Rather, current controversies center around policies advanced as either necessary to control gun crime, despite any inconvenience to the legitimate gun owner, or as directed solely at the criminal or negligent use of guns. The same policies are, in turn, opposed as being either unacceptably restrictive, based on the constitutionally guaranteed "right to keep and bear arms," or as symbolic but largely ineffectual barriers to criminal gun abuse.

Although the formation and adoption of social policies are not guided exclusively by empirical knowledge of the problem in question (nor should they be), policies based on inaccurate or incomplete knowledge are bound to be of limited effectiveness. Hence, the role of scientific knowledge in the formation of social policy is primarily that of showing the characteristics of the problem to which policy must be attentive. For example, a policy that calls for the registration of all handguns in the United States must reckon with the fact that there are 30–50 million handguns already in private hands. Legislation that seeks to prohibit the ownership of handguns by convicted felons must come to grips with the unfortunate fact that there is no easy way to enforce such laws.

Clearly, the findings presented in this volume are relevant to policy concerns. How felons obtain their guns and why they use them in crime bear directly on strategies designed to intervene in the processes that lead to firearms abuse. Not that the "fit" between findings and criminal justice policy is a perfect one: The facts presented here are consistent with a variety of policy initiatives. But these findings also show, at least to our satisfaction, that some of the more commonly proposed policy strategies could well prove ineffective or even strongly counterproductive, possibilities that policymakers will ignore only at considerable peril.

SOCIAL SCIENCE IMPLICATIONS

All the social sciences address themselves to an understanding of crime and more general patterns of human behavior that contravene societal values and norms. Economists are inclined to regard crime as a matter of rational choice in which the benefits and costs of crime are weighed, at least implicitly, by all. Psychologists may see crime as a generalized response of persons who are imperfectly socialized to patterns of conformity or as aggression born of frustration. Sociologists have paid primary attention to the links between socioeconomic status and crime, noting that both victims and offenders are drawn disproportionately from the lower strata of the society.

Although firearms do not figure prominently in any criminological theories, any investigation of the role of firearms in crime *per force* must take into account what the social sciences have had to say about criminal behavior. Correspondingly, what we learn about the role of firearms in crime casts light on the nature of that activity and, hence, contributes to the scientific understanding of crime.

There are several theoretical frameworks in the social sciences that are relevant to the criminal use of firearms. Microeconomic theories of crime are perhaps most directly applicable. (For examples of this general approach, see Anderson, Harris, and Miller, 1983; Becker, 1968; Cook, 1976; Fleisher, 1966.) In barest outline, the microeconomic framework conceptualizes crime as the outcome of decisions constantly being made by persons faced with the choice between committing crime and pursuing legitimate ways to obtain resources. In such decisions, the individual weighs the benefits against the costs and acts accordingly. The role of firearms in such decisions is presumably to alter both the anticipated benefits and the anticipated costs. Thus, using a firearm to commit a robbery enhances the probability of success: A potential victim is not likely to put up much resistance when faced with an armed robber. The use of firearms in crime might also alter the costs, since some jurisdictions explicitly enhance sentences for the use of firearms in crime. From the microeconomic viewpoint, the decision to commit gun crime is clearly instrumental. Although this approach does not state whether the anticipated benefits of gun use exceed the incurred additional costs, it does direct the researcher to include measures of benefits and costs in studying the motivations of armed criminals. Our research, accordingly, measures the benefits and costs of the instrumental use of firearms in crime.

The microeconomic framework is most useful in studying criminal activity that is directed toward economic gain. It is less useful in understanding crimes that do not have obvious economic payoffs. For example, assaults that are unaccompanied by attempts at economic gain are difficult to interpret within the microeconomic framework. Clearly, *some* benefits are presumably gained from assaulting someone in the course of a dispute, but it is difficult to envisage the measurement of such benefits in metrics that would make them commensurate with the costs of engaging in alternative approaches to settling disputes.[3]

Deterrence theory, a variant of the microeconomic approach, is also relevant (see, for example, Zimring and Hawkins, 1973). Deterrence theory directs attention to the cost side of crime commission and particularly to the punishments meted out by the criminal justice system. According to this theory, crimes generally are deterred (thwarted, prevented) to the extent that the expected punishment for crimes is certain, quick, and harsh. Of course, to some extent deterrence theory is irrelevant to understanding *convicted* felons of the sort studied here, these being persons who clearly were *not* deterred from committing the crimes for which they were incarcerated. Nonetheless, this theoretical framework also points to investigating the role played by anticipated punishments in the decision to commit crimes and, for gun crimes in particular, the role played by explicit legislative provisions or informal sentencing practices that threaten gun criminals with enhanced sanctions.

Sociologists tend to pay attention to the microsocial contexts of criminal activity, viewing crime as both a *learned* activity acquired in the social milieu surrounding the individual and a *social* activity supported by that milieu. [Notable examples of this approach include Miller, 1958; Suttles, 1968; and, of course, the entire "Chicago School" of criminological ethnographies produced in the 1920s and 1930s (e.g., Thrasher, 1927).] Here, the role played by families and peers of criminals is critical. As far as the general American population is concerned, social research has shown that the best predictor of gun ownership among adults is having grown up in a family where guns were owned and used (see, Caetano, 1979; Lizotte and Bordua, 1980; Marks and Stokes, 1976). In such environments, males are instructed in the use of guns and perhaps even given guns as gifts at an early age. Using guns *in crime* likewise may be regarded as learned behavior reinforced in friendship groups in which peers are themselves armed and use guns in crime. This viewpoint directs the researcher to inquire into patterns of gun possession and use among family, friends, and acquaintances of gun criminals. As detailed in Chapter Five, we gave considerable attention to such issues in this study.

---

[3] The so-called crimes of passion are, virtually by definition, those that cannot be described in simple cost-benefit terms, unless expiation or catharsis is included among the presumed benefits.

There are, to be sure, many social science theories of crime that, in our view, contribute little or nothing to the understanding of *gun* crime. We include in this category the so-called *social control theories* (theories stressing the restraining effects of firm and consistent disciplinary regimens within households and schools as the key to crime prevention), *conflict theories* (theories that depict crime as the inevitable consequence of social inequalities or as inherent in the structure of capitalist societies), and *labeling theories* (theories that explain deviant behavior as the outcome of the social affixing of deviant labels). Each of these theories may well contribute to an understanding of crime in a broad sense, but none of them seems directly pertinent to the study of gun crimes or gun criminals.

It should be noted, finally, that theories of crime were mainly useful in alerting us to the kinds of information we should attempt to obtain from the felons we studied. No specific hypotheses were formulated on the basis of these theories, although, as the reader will note, many of our more important observations on gun crime and gun criminals were suggested by these theoretical orientations.

POLICYMAKING CONSIDERATIONS

Perhaps the most important influence on the design of this research was a desire to make contributions to the formation of policies that might alleviate the problem of gun crime in America. As indicated above, our conception of the proper role of research in policymaking is a rather modest one. We do not believe that policy should be dictated by research, but rather that research should make its contribution by providing data that policymakers can use in deciding among various alternatives. As such, our principal goal in this volume is to describe the gun crime problem in policy-relevant terms.

To be relevant to policy formation, research has to be designed around the existing "policy space," that is, around those policy alternatives that are either actively being considered or at least lie within the range of the politically acceptable. Using this rule, it would make relatively little sense to consider such (currently) unacceptable policies as (at the one extreme) forced confiscation of all firearms in private hands or (at the other extreme) policies that would require all adults to acquire and carry guns.[4]

[4]Although these options may appear at first glance to be way beyond the existing American "policy space," both have in fact made appearances in the recent past. A recent ordinance passed in Morton Grove, Illinois, has outlawed the possession of handguns within the town; an outright ban on handguns is also a principal aim of the National Coalition to Ban Handguns; the new gun legislation enacted in Washington D.C. in 1975 (see Jones, 1981) also amounts, for all practical purposes, to a ban on handgun ownership within the District. At the opposite extreme, the city fathers of Kennesaw, Georgia, in apparent response to the Morton Grove ordinance, have passed a law *requiring* every (noncriminal) head of household to keep a gun, this for the common defense of the community.

Most existing approaches to the control of criminal gun use can be seen as variations on one of two basic strategies: (1) attempts to interdict the acquisition of handguns (and other firearms) by persons with criminal backgrounds or tendencies; and, (2) attempts to deter criminals from using handguns by raising the costs of doing so. Correspondingly, our research focuses heavily on the empirical questions relevant to these two strategies.

Interdicting the acquisition of handguns by criminals requires some knowledge of how criminals typically obtain guns. It would make a considerable difference in the policies to be considered and adopted if criminals were found to obtain most of their handguns from registered firearms dealers and obtained guns in other ways only rarely or with great difficulty. Under such circumstances, policy efforts might profitably be directed at regulating registered firearms dealers and their transactions, as, indeed, we currently attempt to do under provisions of the Gun Control Act of 1968. On the other hand, if criminals were found to be only minimally connected to the legitimate retail market, then interdiction becomes more difficult, our likely success depending critically on the actual means of acquisition employed.

The second mode of attack on the gun crime problem is to provide strong incentives for criminals not to use guns in committing their crimes. In this connection, several empirical questions arise: What motivates criminals to carry and use guns? Are guns used instrumentally to increase the efficiency of crime? Are guns carried for other reasons and used more or less incidentally in crimes? If the former, increasing penalties for gun crimes might deter some criminals from criminal gun abuse. If the latter, then the reduction of gun crime may have to take other directions.

AN OVERVIEW OF PRIOR LITERATURE AND OUR FINDINGS

The study reported in this volume evolved from our earlier review of the existing scholarly literature on weapons, crime, and violence in the United States (Wright, Rossi, and Daly, 1983). Given the seriousness of the gun crime problem and a long-standing tradition of criminological research, we expected to discover a rich array of information on topics such as how and why criminals acquire, carry, and use firearms. This, however, proved not to be the case. "Remarkably, no nationally representative data [on these topics] are available" (Wright, Rossi, and Daly, 1983: 16).

Most of what has been learned to date about the uses of firearms in crimes has been based either on samples of confiscated weapons or on surveys of crime victims. Neither of these is an entirely adequate source of data for the purpose. The confiscation studies encounter formidable methodological and interpretative problems that render them of dubious utility (see, e.g., Brill, 1977, or Wright, Rossi, and Daly, 1983: Ch. 9, for extensive discussions). And clearly, the victims of crime possess relatively little information about the more general motives, habits, or tendencies of their assailants. Aside from a well-demonstrated criminal preference for handguns rather than shoulder arms, not much has been learned from either of these sources about the "hows" and "whys" of criminal firearms abuse.

Our literature review did uncover one study that took an entirely different approach to the problem. Burr (1977) attempted to study these issues through direct surveys of incarcerated offenders. Although the survey results were intriguing, they were based on a rather small sample, restricted to a single state (Florida), and covered a very narrow range of topics. The study reported in this volume is largely an effort to extend Burr's approach to a larger sample drawn from a number of states, covering a much wider set of issues.

Burr's findings have been reviewed in some detail elsewhere (Wright, Rossi, and Daly, 1983: 183–187); similarities and differences between his results and ours are noted consistently throughout this volume. Where pertinent, we also compare and contrast our findings with those reported from the confiscation and victimization studies.

Since the completion of our earlier literature review, a number of new studies have appeared that we have drawn on either in the design of the data collection effort or in the interpretation of our results.

We note first in this connection the continuing research effort directed toward evaluating the effects of gun laws on the incidence of violent crime. By far the most heavily studied of these laws is the Massachusetts Bartley–Fox Amendment, which provides a mandatory 1-year prison sentence for unlicensed carrying of firearms (see, for example, Beha, 1977; Deutsch and Alt, 1977; Pierce and Bowers, 1981). The Detroit mandatory sentence enhancement law (Loftin and MacDowell, 1981), the Washington, D.C. gun law (Jones, 1981), and the federal Gun Control Act of 1968 (Magaddino and Medoff, 1984) have also received recent attention. And there is a continuing effort to examine state firearms laws as a possible explanation of state-to-state differences in crime rates (e.g., Geisel, Roll, and Wettick, 1969; Murray, 1975; and most recently DeZee, 1983).

The principal generalization to be made from these evaluation studies is that guns laws have at best modest effects, and at worst no effects, on the incidence of criminal violence. In a phrase, "gun laws do not appear to affect gun crimes" (DeZee, 1983: 374). Far more intriguing (to us, in any case) than the finding itself is DeZee's interpretation of the finding: "[T]he possible reason for such ineffectiveness is not necessarily the nature of the solutions (laws) but rather the misunderstanding of the problem (gun violence) by policy implementers" (1983: 367). What is being claimed here is that we do not yet know enough about why and how criminals acquire and use guns to design effective policies to make them stop it. Clearly, extant legislation is based on inadequate models of criminal firearms acquisition and use; otherwise, it would presumably be more effective than it demonstrably is. Exploring the inadequacies of these models is a leading goal of this volume.

We have also profited from on-going research on the so-called "career criminal," particularly the recent RAND study of "Criminal Careers" (Chaiken and Chaiken, 1982) which is also based on a large survey of incarcerated felons. These studies have shown (1) that juvenile criminality is a strong predictor of adult criminality (i.e., that crime can be considered as a "career"); (2) that a small fraction of the criminal population commits a large fraction of the total crime; and (3) that criminals, particularly the high-rate criminals (RAND's "violent predators"), rarely specialize in one particular crime type (they are, rather, opportunists who commit many kinds of crime, depending on the opportunities presented to them). All of these findings are replicated in the present study; as such, comparisons between our and RAND's findings are noted throughout the volume.

The archetypical predatory armed crime is, of course, robbery, and in this regard we call attention to the recent series of studies by Cook (1981, 1982, 1983, 1984, 1985), which are nearly encyclopedic in their coverage. Cook's description of the apparently wanton and needless slaughter of defenseless robbery victims first suggested to us the need to consider weapons ownership and use among criminals as something perhaps more fundamental than a simple desire for criminal efficiency or quick intimidation of the victim.[5]

We have conceived this study, loosely, as an analysis of the illicit firearms market, a market like any other in that it consists of transactions between suppliers and consumers. For a more general "market analysis" of handguns, see Balkin and MacDonald (1984). Based on the results of Burr's survey and the confiscation studies, we had prior reason to expect that stolen handguns would figure prominently in the criminal firearms market [as, indeed, they do (Chapter Ten)]; Moore (1981) has provided a useful, if rather speculative, account of the nature of the problem of gun theft. Moore also hypothesizes that the licit and illicit firearms markets will be largely indistinguishable in fundamental ways, a point confirmed in several of the following analyses.

A long- and hotly debated issue in the area of firearms and crime concerns the protective efficacy of private gun ownership. Here the issue is whether armed citizens represent any deterrent to the commission of crim-

[5] That much of the violence associated with armed robbery *appears* wanton and needless is clearly not proof that this violence serves no instrumental purpose; it only raises the possibility that at least some robbers may be motivated by factors other than a desire for simple and quick intimidation of the victim. There has been a concern for several years now that robberies are becoming "more violent," i.e., more likely to involve what appears to be gratuitous harm to the victim. In fact, according to Cook (1984), robbery-connected violence has been declining since about 1981.

inal acts. The assumption that they do *not* has long been an article of faith in the conventional wisdom about guns and gun control; considerable evidence that they *do* has recently been published by Kleck and Bordua (1983, 1984). There is evidence, for example, that the odds to a felon of confronting an armed victim are approximately as great as the odds of being apprehended, convicted, and sentenced for the crime; there is also evidence (from FBI data on justifiable homicides) that a felon is at least as likely to be shot to death by a civilian as he is to be slain by the police. These and other findings raise the question of how felons themselves assess the various risks they face in going about their criminal activities and of the felons' own experiences with and feelings about encounters with armed victims, topics considered in some detail later in this volume (see especially Chapter Seven).

Other research by Kleck (1984a) has also raised a question of particular policy interest, namely, the kinds of weapons criminals would substitute for handguns in the face of various partial or total handgun bans. This is of particular interest because much of the gun control legislation currently being urged on legislative bodies stipulates a ban on all handguns or on certain classes of handguns (e.g., small, cheap ones); handgun bans, whether partial or total, are, in short, apparently viable policy options in the current environment.

All would agree, as Kleck (1984) points out, that in the complete absence of handguns, *some* criminals would shift "downward" to less lethal weapons (for example, knives and clubs) and that *some* criminals would shift "upward" to more lethal weapons (for example, shoulder arms, appropriately modified, if need be, to make them concealable). Kleck further points out that the net effect on the death rate from crime that would result from a total handgun ban would therefore strictly depend on two variables: the "relative deadliness" of the substitute weapon and the "substitution fraction"—the fraction of criminals currently using handguns that would substitute some other weapon instead (Kleck, 1984). The relative deadliness of rifles and shotguns versus handguns is on the order of three or four to one (shoulder arms, that is, are some three or four times more lethal than handguns, on the average). What remains largely unknown is the substitution fraction. In order to explore likely values of this fraction under different hypothetical conditions, we asked a number of questions in the survey on how felons thought they might respond to various partial or total handgun bans; results from these questions are discussed in Chapter Eleven.

Although the studies cited above have contributed important information to the study of firearms violence, major gaps in our knowledge clearly remain. In order to fill those gaps dealing specifically with the acquisition and use of guns by criminals, we designed and conducted a survey of prisoners who had been incarcerated for felony offenses and were serving time in a sample of state prisons all around the country. We questioned them about their acquisition and use of guns in the period of time before their imprisonment. Self-administered questionnaires were filled out by 1874 felons in state prisons in Michigan, Missouri, Oklahoma, Minnesota, Nevada, Arizona, Florida, Georgia, Maryland, and Massachusetts. The procedures by which these states were chosen are discussed in Chapter Two.

Eligibility criteria for participation in the survey were fairly minimal: We interviewed only men who were in prison on a felony conviction and who had been sentenced to their current term on or after 1 January 1979. We did not attempt to restrict the sample only to men who had committed crimes with guns, on the grounds that it was important to have a group of unarmed criminals to serve as a comparison group. About two-fifths of the final sample claimed never to have committed any crime armed with any weapons; the remainder had.

CHARACTERISTICS OF THE PRISONER SAMPLE

The sample obtained for this study closely resembles the state prisoner population in the United States as a whole (Chapter Two), being predominantly young, poorly educated, and disproportionately nonwhite. The men in this sample also tend to have grown up around guns and to have owned and used guns for most of their lives. About three-quarters report that their fathers owned guns; about one-half report that they were taught how to shoot guns by their fathers. The average man in the sample first fired a gun at age 13.

A TYPOLOGY OF CRIMINAL GUN USE

The felons in the sample evidenced wide variability in their prior criminal weapons behavior (Chapter Three). About 40% of the sample claimed never to have committed any crime armed with any kind of weapons; these men constitute the Unarmed Criminals who are used for comparison purposes throughout the analysis. Another one-tenth had committed armed crime, some of them rather frequently, but never with a gun; based on the customary weapon of choice, this one-tenth is further divided into Knife Criminals (7% of the sample) and Improvisors (4%).

The remaining half of the sample had committed at least one gun crime; these are the Gun Criminals who are further divided into four groups, depending on the weapon used most frequently (handgun versus shoulder weapon) and the frequency of use. The One-Timers are men who had committed one but only one gun crime; they represent about 28% of the Gun Criminals and 14% of the total sample. Sporadics are men who had committed "a few" gun crimes; there are just about as many of them as there are One-Timers. The remainder, 44% of the Gun Criminals and 22% of the total sample, had committed more (and often much more) than a few gun crimes; these men are the truly predatory felons and are classified as

Handgun Predators (17% of the total sample) or Shotgun Predators (5% of the total sample), depending on the type of firearm they said they used most frequently in committing their crimes. The foregoing seven-category typology is used for descriptive purposes throughout the analysis.

As one would expect, there were sharp differences across these seven groups in their patterns of criminality. The modal conviction offense for the Unarmed Criminals was burglary; for the Improvisors, homicide (by a small margin); for the Knife Criminals, burglary; and among all categories of Gun Criminals, robbery. With the exception of rape, the Predators were in fact the most likely to have committed each and every crime we asked about and to have committed them at a higher than average rate. Calculations reported in Chapter Three suggest that the Predators, representing only about 20% of the sample, account for nearly one-half of the total criminal violence perpetrated by the men in this sample.

FIREARMS OWNERSHIP AND USE

Three-quarters of the men in the sample reported having owned at least one gun in their lives; more than three-quarters of the gun owners had owned handguns (Chapter Four). Since only one-half of the sample had ever committed a gun crime, it is clear that not every gun-owning felon commits crimes with his guns. Still, the tendency ever to have committed a gun crime was higher among felons who had owned guns than among those who had not; and among the gun-owning felons, the tendency to have committed a gun crime increased with the number of guns ever owned.

Felons who had ever owned guns appear to have owned them in fairly large numbers, although the absence of appropriate comparative data makes this an uncertain conclusion. They are also much more likely than gun owners in general to have owned *handguns*. They tended in the majority to keep their guns loaded at all times and to fire them, in our opinion, at a rather high rate.

Most of the men who were armed during their conviction crime reported having used their weapon in some way in the course of the crime, most frequently to intimidate the victim. Nearly two-fifths of those armed with a gun during the conviction crime reported that the gun was fired during the incident. Most of these firings were said to be unplanned.

Most (57%) of the Gun Criminals in the sample also said they had fired a gun at least once in the course of a crime at some point in their criminal careers.

Evidence on carrying behavior shows that about 30% of the Gun Criminals made it a practice to carry a gun more or less all the time. Another 50% carried in "certain situations," namely, whenever they felt that they might need to protect themselves. One in five carried only when they intended to commit a crime. Thus, most of the weapons that are used to

commit crimes are not carried exclusively for that purpose. The best predictor of the tendency to carry more or less all the time is associating with
others who carried guns.

GROWING UP WITH GUNS

Prisoners in our sample became acquainted with firearms early in their
lives (Chapter Five). As among gun owners in general, early socialization
appears to be a relevant factor, at least insofar as the clearly legitimate aspects of weapons behavior are concerned (e.g., ever owning a gun, numbers of guns owned). Men raised by gun owning fathers, in other words,
were distinctively more likely to have owned guns themselves than men
whose fathers did not own guns.

In contrast, the clearly illegitimate aspects of weapons ownership (e.g.,
whether armed with a gun during the conviction offense, the tendency to
carry on a regular basis) were only weakly predicted by parental socialization and were much more strongly predicted by peer influences and, in particular, by the number of friends who themselves owned and carried guns.

WHY DO CRIMINALS CARRY GUNS?

Why do felons bother to carry guns in the first place? What, in short, is
"the motivation to go armed" (Chapter Six)? Our data suggest that the possibility of using one's gun to commit a crime is not the only motive for
carrying one. Most Gun Criminals appear to have acquired and carried guns
also for their own self-protection in what is clearly a hostile and violent
environment.

To illustrate, a principal reason for acquiring one's most recent handgun
was self-protection in 58% of the cases; "to use in my crimes," in only
28% of the cases. In general, self-protection motives were even more important to the Predators than to other Gun Criminals. In short, as with the
carrying patterns discussed earlier, most of the guns that are actually used
in crimes are not exclusively acquired for criminal purposes but for self-
defense as well. (Of course, the line between self-defense and instrumental
use in crime is blurred when a criminal claims that his purpose in carrying
a gun is to "protect" himself from his victims and the police, which was
frequently the case.)

All the Gun Criminals were given a list of reasons why they might carry
a gun and were asked how important each reason was to them. As it happens, every reason listed was stated to be more important by the Predators
than by the other groups, which suggests that they are considerably more
serious about their gun carrying than other felons are. Among the Predators, the single most important reason to carry a gun was that "when you
have a gun, you are prepared for anything that might happen."

Evidence from several lines of analysis converges, therefore, on the conclusion that predatory felons acquire and carry guns as much to protect themselves against the uncertainties of an unfriendly environment as to prey upon the larger population. The potential criminal applications of firearms share importance with these other, more defensive purposes.

ARMED VICTIMS

Among the reasons given for why one might carry a gun during crime was that "there's always a chance my victim would be armed." This was cited as a very important reason by 50% of the Gun Criminals. Chapter Seven presents evidence from the survey on felons' attitudes about and experiences with armed-victim encounters. The attitudinal results show clearly that these felons were made nervous by the prospect of such encounters. Four-fifths agreed that "a smart criminal always tries to find out if his victim is armed," and three-fifths agreed that "most criminals are more worried about meeting an armed victim than they are about running into the police."

The experiential data also show that armed victim encounters were fairly frequent among these men. About two-fifths of the sample reported at least one armed-victim encounter at some time in their careers; just over one-third said that they had personally been "scared off, shot at, wounded, or captured by an armed victim." About two-fifths reported having decided at least once in their lives not to commit a crime because they had reason to suspect that the intended victim was armed. This result makes it clear that at least some crimes are prevented by gun-wielding victims.

One must, of course, be cautious in interpreting the above results. Many of these men's "victims" are in all likelihood other men much like themselves. The armed-victim encounters reported by this sample may well be confrontations between two men with equally felonious histories and motives as between hard-core perpetrators and total innocents.

WHAT FELONS LOOK FOR IN FIREARMS

What do felons look for in a handgun? What characteristics are important to them? What kinds of handguns do they actually own and carry? The often-assumed criminal preference for small, cheap handguns is not confirmed in our data (Chapter Eight). When asked what kinds of traits would be important to them in a handgun, accuracy, untraceability, and quality of construction were much more frequent responses than price, low caliber, and so on. In general, the characteristics of the so-called "Saturday Night Special" did not emerge as being particularly important to these men; the preference, in contrast, seems to have been for well-made, large-caliber handguns.

Analysis of the preference questions according to criminal type revealed a rather interesting and straightforward pattern: The preference for small, cheap handguns was concentrated among felons who did not use guns in committing crimes; the preference for large, well-made handguns was likewise strongest in the more predatory categories of the typology. Preference for the bigger and better made handguns was also stronger among gun owners than among nonowners. The principal generalization to surface in this analysis is that serious criminals prefer serious equipment.

Evidence on the most recent handguns actually owned by the sample tends to confirm the results from the preference questions. On the average, these "most recent" handguns were relatively expensive (two-thirds worth $100 or more), large barreled (70% with barrel lengths of 4 inches or more), and large caliber (70% larger than .32 caliber). Not more than about 15% of them would qualify as Saturday Night Specials, even with a somewhat inclusive definition of the term, and likewise, not more than one-third would qualify as "snubbies" (barrel length of 3 inches or less). In general, criminals both prefer to carry, and actually carry, bigger and better handguns than has been suggested in most previous studies.

THE MARKET FOR CRIMINALS' GUNS

Where and how do criminals obtain their guns (Chapter Nine)? As others have suggested, informal, off-the-record sources predominate in the illicit-handgun market. The principal mode of acquisition for the most recent handguns owned by our sample was outright cash purchase, typically from friends or family members; following cash purchase was theft. About 43% of the sample's most recent handguns were bought for cash; just under one-third were stolen directly by the felons themselves. Gifts (8%), borrowing (8%), and swaps and trades (7%) were also of some importance.

All told, 40% of the sample's most recent handguns were obtained from friends. "Off the street" was a distant second, mentioned by 14%, followed by gun shops (11%), pawnshops (6%), fences (5%), family members (4%), and drug dealers (4%). Combining categories in obvious ways, friends and family were the most important source of supply (44%), followed by various gray and black market sources (26%), followed, finally, by customary retail outlets (21%), with the remaining one-tenth acquired from a variety of odd-lot sources.

The cross-tabulation of the "where" and "how" questions revealed that friends and family were the most common source of supply whatever the means of acquisition, including theft. Indeed, 31% of the directly stolen handguns were reported to have been stolen from friends or family members. Another 30% of them were stolen from various gray- and black-market sources; about one-tenth were stolen directly from retail outlets; the remainder (29%) were stolen from the homes, apartments, and automobiles of strangers.

The Gun Control Act of 1968 attempts to interdict the criminal acquisition of guns at the point of retail exchange through the provision that forbids the sale of guns to persons with a felony conviction. It is, therefore, of some interest to inquire about the fraction of our sample's most recent handguns that were obtained via outright cash purchase from a customary retail outlet. As it happens, that fraction is 16%. About one criminal handgun in six is obtained through methods and sources likely to be concerned about the legality of the transaction; about five in six are not. The illicit firearms market is heavily dominated by informal, off-the-record transactions.

Perhaps the most surprising of our results concerning the methods and sources of handgun acquisition is the fraction (32%) that were obtained through direct theft by the criminal himself (Chapter Ten). In addition, one must consider that many of the other handgun transactions these men undertook (i.e., a swap with a friend, a cash purchase from one's drug dealer) would have also involved stolen guns. To tap what we refer to as the secondary market in stolen guns, we asked all the handgun owners who said they had obtained their most recent handgun in some way other than by a direct theft whether, to the best of their knowledge, the gun was stolen or not. If we add the handguns reported as "definitely stolen" to those that had been directly stolen by the felons themselves, the fraction of stolen guns among this sample's most recent handguns increases to 46%; and if we include the guns reported as "probably stolen," it increases to 70%. Thus, stolen firearms are a much more important source of supply to the illicit gun market than has been suggested in previous studies.

Stealing firearms was by no means uncommon among the prisoners in the sample. Just under one-half had stolen at least one gun at some time; men who had stolen any guns tended to have done so in fairly large numbers. Gun theft was quite common in all categories of the typology, even among criminals who themselves did not use guns in committing their crimes, but theft was more frequent among the Predators than other groups. A few gun thieves reported having looked specifically for guns to steal; most, however, stole guns whenever they came across them. Typically, the point in stealing a gun was apparently the same as stealing television sets or other items—namely, to fence or swap for cash, drugs, or other goods. Gun theft, in other words, is predominantly an opportunity crime much like any other theft. Still, most of the men who had ever stolen a gun also reported having kept at least one stolen gun for their own use at some time. When asked the reason for this, the most common answer was that "it was a nice piece."

Stolen firearms appear to circulate widely and freely through all the mechanisms of exchange exploited by these men. About one-half the cash purchases involved stolen guns, as did the majority of transactions involving fences, drug dealers, etc. Given the importance of untraceability (Chapter Eight), it is obvious that stolen firearms, especially stolen handguns, are highly desirable commodities among the criminal population and represent a major source of the criminal handgun supply.

"GUN CONTROL" AND CRIMINAL GUN USE

Chapter Eleven raises the question of how felons might respond to various handgun control measures. Every man in this sample has at least one felony conviction and is therefore legally prohibited from acquiring a handgun upon release; interestingly, about three-quarters of the sample were aware of this provision in the Gun Control Act of 1968. This aside, three-quarters also reported that it would be little or no trouble for them to obtain a handgun once they were released from prison, that they could arm themselves in a matter of a few hours or, at most, a few days, and that the out-of-pocket cost to do so would be approximately $100. Since the sample averages three prior imprisonments, one may assume that many of these men will have been in the same situation in question at some prior time; we suspect, therefore, that these data reflect prior experience as much as judgments about future possibilities.

We also asked the sample hypothetical questions concerning their likely response to various kinds of handgun measures that might be enacted in the future (e.g., a "pricing strategy" that greatly increased the cost of the cheapest handguns available, a ban on small, cheap handguns, and a complete ban on all handguns). Without belaboring the details, the majority of the Gun Criminals in the sample said they would circumvent the first option by borrowing or stealing an appropriate gun, the second by obtaining bigger and more expensive handguns, and the third by carrying sawed-off shotguns and rifles. If these responses can be taken at face value (admittedly a big "if"), then all the options considered in the question sequence would appear to produce a net shift toward more lethal rather than less lethal equipment.

POLICY IMPLICATIONS

The concluding chapter considers the policy implications of the study results. As is often the case in research of this sort, the data are very useful in describing the problem in great detail and rather less useful in suggesting appropriate solutions. What to do about the problem of gun crime is a topic that has been considered by intelligent people for decades, and no one has yet conjured up a completely effective and workable solution, at least not one that was also politically acceptable. It may well be that no effective and workable solution exists, or that all potentially workable solutions are

politically unacceptable for one or another reason. The "policy implications" considered in the final chapter are thus descriptions of the constraints within which any firearms control policy will have to operate more
than they are specific legislative recommendations.

Still, five potentially important policy implications are suggested by our
results.

First, because criminals acquire and use guns as much for self-protection in a social world where many of their associates go armed as they do
for instrumental uses in committing crimes, viable social policies have to
address the issue of reducing the violence and routine carrying of guns that
appear to be endemic to many impoverished urban neighborhoods. The
reduction of crime in such neighborhoods has to be as much in the center
of law enforcement concern as protecting middle-class citizens from the
incursions of violent criminals. That criminals prey upon each other and
upon others of similar background and circumstance as much as (or more
than) they prey on the suburban middle class should not be a matter of
indifference to criminal-justice policy.

Second, a major source of supply to the illicit firearms market is via theft
from persons who own and use firearms legally. Cutting down on the theft
of firearms ought to be, therefore, a second goal of social policy. Whether
this means better security measures for gun-owning households, more
elaborate antitheft measures for gun merchants and manufacturers, strict and
mandatory penalties for the crime of gun theft, mandatory reporting of stolen guns by their owners, or special insurance provisions cannot be decided by our data alone. In all probability, given the frequency of gun theft
as reported by our sample, all of these ultimately may prove necessary.

Third, gun control measures that attempt to interdict the retail sale of
weapons to criminals through legitimate channels miss perhaps as many as
five-sixths of the criminal firearms transactions. Customary retail outlets appear to have almost no role in an illicit market dominated by informal purchases, swaps, and trades. In addition to interdiction at the point of retail
sale, methods must be found that successfully interdict the much larger and
more important informal market as well.

Fourth, sentence-enhancement policies that would punish more heavily
crimes in which guns are used appear to be largely irrelevant to the more
predatory gun users, for whom guns are useful in a variety of ways, not the
least being their own survival. These men are apparently insensitive to
punishment deterrence in any event and often own and carry guns because
they fear the prospects of life without them. Mandatory penalties for criminal gun use may well be advisable for other reasons, but they are not likely
to have much effect on the firearms practices of truly predatory felons.

Finally, some of the more frequently discussed "gun control" measures,
such as a ban on small, cheap handguns, may well prove to have counterproductive consequences. Most observers would agree that many of these

measures would probably result in at least some felons switching to more, rather than less, lethal firearms, but the precise fraction who actually would do so has been a matter of considerable dispute. So that the findings from our study are not mistaken, let us stress that this fraction is still not known. The fraction of the felons in our sample who *said* that this was what they would do, however, was well more than one-half.

2

THE FELON SURVEY: METHODS, PROCEDURES, DESCRIPTIVE DATA

RESEARCH GOALS

Any attempt to control the acquisition of guns by criminals, much less control their use, has to be based on accurate knowledge of the extent of gun usage among that population and of how guns are typically acquired by criminals. Our review of the existing literature (Wright, Rossi, and Daly, 1983) had shown that relatively little was known about why and how criminals acquire, carry, and use guns (and other weapons). Knowledge of the topic had been derived mostly from samples of weapons confiscated by the police, an approach with acknowledged limitations (Brill, 1977).

Ideally, a study of how criminals obtain and use their weapons should be based on a sample of persons currently active in crime. For quite obvious reasons, this direct approach is impractical since it is impossible to identify with certainty who might currently be a criminal. Rather, it is necessary to approach the problem somewhat indirectly, for example, by studies of persons known to have criminal pasts.

Our literature review uncovered a promising study by Burr (1977), who had obtained some very intriguing data on felons and their firearms by interviewing a sample of prisoners. Burr found that they were quite willing to talk about their previous criminal careers and about their acquisition and use of guns. However, since Burr's sample was based on Florida felons only, his findings were of limited generality.

The study reported in this volume extends Burr's method to a nationwide sample of state-prison inmates. Although convicted felons are to some unknown degree a selected group of criminals, a strong case can be made on several grounds that a study based on a large sample of prisoners might produce much interesting and policy-relevant information on the criminal use and abuse of guns.

First, state prisoners are accessible for study at relatively low cost. Second, although first offenders often are not imprisoned, and as a consequence would be seriously underrepresented in any sample of prisoners, repeat offenders (those most likely to be imprisoned) apparently constitute the source of much criminal behavior and often of its more serious forms (Chaiken and Chaiken, 1982). Hence, the crimes committed by men most likely to be found in prison constitute a considerable portion of the overall crime problem. Third, men who are already in prison for their crimes would not be at any further peril in cooperating with the researchers and could therefore be expected to provide reasonably truthful information. Fourth, prisons are an obvious place to find criminal gun abusers in large numbers. Finally, although juveniles by definition are excluded from such a study, many felons have long careers of crime extending back into their adolesence and perhaps even earlier. Hence, juvenile crime can be included in part by considering the crime careers of current prisoners. Such, in any case, were the principal rationales for the use of inmates of state prisons as sources of information for this study.

There are also some fairly serious limitations that derive from this decision. No sample of prisoners, for example, will contain any criminals who consistently, by luck or talent, evade apprehension and imprisonment. Of course, no one knows how large this group is, nor how much of the total crime problem is generated by their criminal activities. The prevailing opinion among criminologists is that most reasonably active criminals spend time in prison sooner or later.

A second and probably more serious limitation is the substantial under-representation of juveniles, who are heavy contributors to crime rates. Since many juvenile criminals may never persist in their criminality into adulthood, the juvenile careers of those who do may be unrepresentative. A consequence is that this study has relatively little to say about the firearms behavior of men who have yet to reach the age of majority, except in the form of recall information from those whose criminality persisted into their adult years.

Third, there is the serious issue of the validity of prisoners' answers to questions concerning their criminal activities. Although there may not be much motivation for prisoners to distort their accounts of their criminal careers, neither is there much motivation for truthfulness. Previous research on this issue, however, has reported that comparisons between information given by the prisoners and information in their official records show little evidence of systematic distortion (e.g., Marquis, 1981).

Finally, first offenders are often not sent to prison, even if convicted, and are clearly underrepresented in any prison sample. It is conceivable, perhaps even likely, that their patterns of firearms use are quite different from those who have longer records.

In sum, any sample of incarcerated felons probably differs from the total population of criminals in the following ways: State prisoners are probably older and have longer and more sustained involvements in criminality and in the criminal justice system. They are also more likely to have been more violent in their crime than criminals in general and to have committed more serious offenses. Moreover, prisoners may have been less skillful (or careful) in committing their crimes and hence more likely to have been imprisoned. In addition, prisoners' responses are of unknown and suspect validity. Finally, prisoners may be less responsive to the risks encountered in a criminal career since, obviously, they were *not* deterred by the risks of imprisonment. Hence, prisoners probably overrepresent the "hard-core" persistent criminals. All the findings reported in this volume should be interpreted in light of the above facts.

SURVEY DESIGN AND METHOD

The data presented in this volume consist of answers to self-administered questionnaires filled out by a sample of 1982 inmates who were serving time in state prisons. The prisons were selected from 10 states, a "sample" that was designed to provide a range across the major regions of the United States.

Fully aware of both the inherent limitations described above and the absence of a better approach that was also practical, work began on the project in December 1981. The first 6 months were spent in negotiations for access to a set of prisons and in developing a pretest draft of the survey protocol. A draft questionnaire was pretested in June 1982 in a county jail in Massachusetts. Data collection started in August 1982 and continued through January 1983.

SELECTION OF RESEARCH SITES

Since prisoners are located in clusters (i.e. prisons), an efficient and relatively inexpensive sampling strategy, cluster sampling, can be employed to obtain a sample of prisoners. "Site selection" was therefore a two-stage process: first, choosing states, and second, choosing specific prisons within states.

The number of sites to be included in the study was constrained by the project budget; assuming some 200 cases per site, available resources allowed for a total of 8 to 12 sites. In the end, data were collected in 11 prisons in 10 states: Two prisons in Minnesota were included and one prison each in Michigan, Missouri, Oklahoma, Nevada, Arizona, Florida, Georgia, Maryland, and Massachusetts.

Initially, we proposed to select states on the basis of two state characteristics that we anticipated might be relevant to the weapons behavior of the felon population: (1) the density of private gun ownership in the state and (2) the stringency of state firearms regulations. The rather strong and well-known correlation of both these factors with region, however, suggested that our purposes would be adequately served if the ultimate sample of states had a reasonable geographical spread, as, indeed, it does.

Other than regional spread, the primary constraint on the selection of states was the willingness of a state's prison system to cooperate in the research. We were counselled by members of the Advisory Committee that some states would flatly refuse to cooperate, that others would be at best highly suspicious, and that other states had a prior record of enthusiastic cooperation in research of this general sort. We chose states to approach accordingly. In the end, every state that we approached agreed to participate, but we only approached states where we had reason to believe that this would be the outcome.

Our initial hope was to obtain access to the main maximum security facility in each of the selected states, on the grounds that hard-core gun-using felons would be housed primarily in such institutions. In fact, in almost every case, the decision as to which prison we were allowed to study was made by state corrections officials. In most states, we were not granted access to the main maximum-security prison, often because the safety of the field team could not be assured. Ultimately, four maximum-security prisons, three medium- to maximum-security prisons, and three medium-security prisons were included. Except for Minnesota, we interviewed in only one prison per state; in Minnesota, we interviewed in two facilities and have combined these data in all subsequent analyses. In general, men housed in less than maximum-security facilities have shorter records and fewer previous arrests; for the most part, these men are further from "hard-core" status than the men housed in stricter facilities.

It is also worth noting that, despite the security classifications, prison systems in many states now make it a practice to move their men around rather frequently, such that at any one time, the population in any facility is a reasonably good "mix" of the total. These points notwithstanding, there are some strong differences across sites in the proportions of "hard-core" felons in the samples, the proportions being generally higher in maximum-security facilities than elsewhere.[1]

---

[1] Having interviewed in only one prison per state, prison differences and state differences are perfectly confounded in these data, which further implies that these data are *not* well suited for the examination of the effects of state-level variables (e.g., stringency of gun laws) on criminal firearms behavior. Observed differences across states, in other words, *might* result from the effects of state-level variables, but they *might* result only from the unique characteristics of prisoners who happen to have been housed in the facility where we interviewed.

Had we interviewed in "equivalent" prisons in each state, this problem would not exist (at least not to the same degree), but in fact there are very large differences across the 10 states in the kinds of prisons where we interviewed (see below, "Site Descriptions and Characteristics"). As a consequence, we do not know whether the differences between, say, Arizona felons and Missouri felons reflect a difference between Arizona and Missouri or whether they only reflect that our Arizona respondents were housed in a maximum-security facility whereas the Missouri respondents were not.

The general procedures followed for gaining access to the prisons were very similar in all 10 states. Negotiations commenced with the state Commissioner of Corrections and were often referred thereafter to a Deputy Commissioner. Some states had elaborate "application" procedures (e.g., requiring that a proposal be submitted, that assurances of anonymity be made); others were run on a much more informal basis. In all cases, the outcome of our negotiations at the Commissioner's level was permission to negotiate directly with the warden or superintendent of whatever prison the Commissioner (or his Deputy) had decided we could enter.

In the prisons themselves, we were often referred by the warden to an assistant or deputy to hammer out the actual details of our visit. All officials at the prison were given a brief description of the study and its purposes. We agreed, of course, to abide by any restrictions the prison officials saw fit to impose. Much initial anxiety disappeared when we made it clear that we were studying prisoners, not prisons, and that we were more than willing to "bend" our preferred procedures to accommodate local site preferences and needs.

Every prison imposed at least some restrictions on which men we could interview. In most cases, this meant we could not question men in protective custody, in disciplinary confinement, in psychiatric wards, or on death row. We made no effort in any prison to dissuade local officials from these constraints. Each prison also had set procedures by which the inducements to respondents would be dispensed, and these too were accepted without complaint in every case.

In the preliminary negotiations with local prison officials, we made it clear that the project was autonomous and required little extra work on the prison's part: We required (1) official permission to enter the prison and conduct interviews, and (2) a room (or rooms) to set up the survey operation. In exchange, we agreed to pay the overtime salaries of two guards for each day we were at the site, who assisted us in transporting prisoners and who provided security for the field staff. This, in essence, was a small "chit" that the warden or superintendent could use to reward his favorite security personnel with a little overtime work. As a further inducement, we also volunteered a $200 donation to the prison library fund. All the wardens with whom we negotiated seemed pleased with this "package."

Given the above discussion, it is clear that the 10 states included in this analysis do not constitute a probability sample of states, and that the 11 prisons where we interviewed do not constitute a probability sample of correctional institutions. However, it must be stated that the nature of the sample does not necessarily invalidate our findings. A probability sample of prisoners and of prisons would certainly give greater plausibility to our findings, but there are ample indications in the findings themselves that the prisoners studied are not atypical of the population of convicted felons in the United States as a whole.

CHOOSING RESPONDENTS WITHIN PRISONS

Once having gained access to a particular prison, we next faced the task of sampling felons within prisons and inducing them to participate in the study. Since felons are overwhelmingly male, and few prisons are "co-ed," we decided to interview male prisoners only. Misdemeanants were also excluded; only men with a felony conviction were eligible. Finally, on the reasoning that a man in the twenty-fifth year of a life sentence would have little to tell us about the illicit firearms market of today, we restricted the study to felons who had been out "on the street" recently enough to possess useful, current information; operationally, this meant a restriction to men who began their current prison term on or after 1 January 1979.

We did not impose any restrictions based on conviction offenses; we did not seek a sample composed exclusively of gun criminals. Indeed, recent research on criminal careers showed how difficult it would be to construct an adequate measure of being a "gun criminal" since so many criminals commit a wide variety of crimes, only a portion of which would be reflected in their official record (Chaiken and Chaiken, 1982). Also, given the project aims, we felt it was as important to understand why some criminals did not use guns as to understand why others did, and so we were concerned with obtaining adequate numbers of both groups for the final sample. On this point, at least, we were quite successful: about one-half the final sample had done at least one gun crime, about two-fifths had never committed any armed crime, and the remaining one-tenth had committed armed crimes but never with a gun (see Chapter Three). This distribution, incidentally, is quite consistent with what we had originally expected, based on results obtained in the RAND "Criminal Careers" survey.

Given the above restrictions, the selection of actual respondents was straightforward. We attempted, in preliminary negotiations with prison officials, to get a crude estimate of the likely number of men in the site who would meet our eligibility criteria. If this number were fewer than about 400 eligibles, we interviewed every man in the prison who agreed to participate. If the likely number of eligibles were greater than about 400, we obtained a current prisoner census and drew a simple random sample. In the end, it proved necessary to use a random sample in only three sites; in the remaining seven sties, every willing participant was included.

In most sites where every eligible felon could participate, notification of the study was made through public sources (e.g., announcements on bulletin boards and in prison newsletters). In sites where only a sample was eligible, each man in the sample was sent a personalized advance letter inviting his participation. In both cases, the notification contained a brief description of the project, assurances of confidentiality and anonymity, and an offer of a carton of cigarettes (or the cash equivalent) as an incentive for participating. In most sites, this was a more than ample inducement.

FIELD OPERATIONS

Personal interviews were originally proposed for this data collection but were rejected in favor of self-administered questionnaires for a variety of reasons. Self-administration would provide for greater anonymity and would be substantially less intrusive at the site than face-to-face interviewing would have been. Self-administered questionnaires were also considerably less expensive; personal interviews with samples of the contemplated size would have required being at each site for periods of 10 days to 2 weeks each; with group administration of the sort finally employed, we were not in any site for more than 4 days. Further, our pretest results showed clearly that prisoners could readily "handle" even a fairly complicated self-administered questionnaire.

Field visits at each site varied from 2 to 4 days. The sampled prisoners were given questionnaires to fill out in groups that ranged from 10 to more than 100 men but that averaged about 30 each. A Spanish-language version of the questionnaire was available for Spanish-dominant respondents; functional illiterates were given the protocol as an oral interview. Every man signed a "written consent form" prior to starting the actual questionnaire.[2]

Survey sessions averaged about 2 hours each. One or more members of the field staff were present in the survey room at all times to answer questions or clarify instructions. Virtually all the survey sessions went smoothly. As reported by others who have surveyed prisoners, most respondents appeared to look on the protocol as a "test" and made an obvious effort to complete it accurately and well. For many of our respondents, the questionnaire was the longest single piece of text (75 pages) they had ever read. Frequently, men showed up at the survey room carrying their own pencils, "just in case." Questions about words, meanings, and instructions were fairly common. With the occasional surly exception, most respondents appeared eager and cooperative—even grateful in many cases for the carton of cigarettes and the break from prison routine.

The field staff consisted of three men: one white, one black, and one Hispanic. All three had considerable prior experience dealing with prisoners or those in conflict with the law.

Local security for the staff was supplied by prison guards being paid from project funds. Guards were seldom in the survey room itself, but were present just outside the door. No genuine security problems were encountered in any site, although as a condition of access at one site, the field staff signed an agreement that in the event they were taken hostage, prison officials were not obligated to negotiate for their release.

[2] The contents of the survey questionnaire are contained within the codebook for the data that is available through the ICPSR; see Chapter 1, note 1.

RESPONSE RATES

Given the sampling and selection procedures followed, precise response rates for the survey are difficult to calculate. There is, first, considerable ambiguity about the actual number of persons eligible to participate. In most sites, in fact, we obtained no more than rough estimates of the total number of eligibles present. More precise estimates were impossible to obtain because of the frequency with which prisoners are moved around among prisons. Often, men who were otherwise eligible were disallowed as respondents by the prison officials for one or another reason (e.g., protective or disciplinary custody).

Still, despite the ambiguities, it is clear that the response rate was remarkably good in some sites and very poor in others. In one site where a precise response rate could be calculated, we achieved the cooperation of 96%; in another, only 22%. In general, however, the response rates were respectable: Across the eight sites where a reasonable estimate of the response rate could be made, we interviewed two-thirds or more of the eligible respondents in five; in three sites, the response rate exceeded 80%.

Response rates across sites were, as one might expect, highly sensitive to the incentives offered for participation. In one state where we were not allowed to offer inmates *any* inducement for participation, our response rate was 24%. In another, inducements were allowed, but virtually all the men in this site worked in a prison factory, made a respectable wage, and were allowed to carry cash with them inside the prison, so a carton of cigarettes was substantially less meaningful there than elsewhere. In this site, the response rate was 40%. In sites where we were allowed to implement our preferred inducement scheme and where there were no peculiar local problems, the response rates were usually quite good, ranging upward from about 70%.

QUESTIONNAIRE DEVELOPMENT AND DISPOSITION

The study questionnaire was drafted and redrafted through roughly six iterations and was then pretested on about 20 men serving time in a county jail in western Massachusetts. The then-current draft and the pretest results were discussed in detail at a subsequent meeting of the project advisory committee. Based on these discussions and the pretest experience, a final draft was prepared.

The final survey protocol ran to 75 pages and contained a large number of dependent questions (i.e., questions to be answered by only some respondents, depending on answers to previous questions). Our concerns that felons might have trouble coping with the resulting skip patterns were allayed considerably by the pretest results. In fact, failure to follow the skip logic correctly was quite rare in the full sample as well. Our explanation for the (to us) surprising success rate in following the skip patterns is that men in prison are accustomed to following precise instructions and doing exactly what they are told.

As indicated previously, a total of 1982 questionnaires were ultimately administered, of which 108 were discarded for one or another reason. Most of the discards were duplicate questionnaires turned in by men who had managed to attend two (or more) of the survey sessions; larcenous tendencies run deep. Other cases were discarded if only a small portion of the total questionnaire had been completed or if the questionnaire contained obviously frivolous (and usually rather hostile) responses.

The remaining 1874 usable questionnaires constitute the data for this project. Of these, 54 (3%) were administered as oral interviews. Another sizable fraction (129 cases, 7% of the usable total) are partial "break-offs" (i.e., the respondent simply quit partway through the questionnaire, providing some but not all the desired information). Finally, there are 292 additional questionnaires (16% of the usable total) that, in the coders' judgments, contain "a lot" of missing data. These, of course, are not break-offs but rather are questionnaires with substantial amounts of intermittently missing information (e.g., entire interior sections left blank). One result is that rates of missing data for any particular question in the survey run upward of about 10%.

SITE DESCRIPTIONS AND CHARACTERISTICS

Michigan

The Michigan site was a high-medium-security facility housing predominantly youthful offenders (ages 16–24). The prison census showed 943 eligible felons; a sample of 404 was drawn. Of these, 74 had become ineligible by the time we arrived: Some men in the initial sample had since been transferred elsewhere, others had been paroled or had completed their sentence, still others had been locked up in disciplinary segregation, leaving a net eligible sample of 330, of whom 265 showed up for the survey and completed a usable questionnaire (response rate = 80%).

Missouri

The Missouri site was a medium-security, "cottage plan" facility housing a total population of 628, the only obvious "Country Club" prison in our sample. Officials at the prison estimated that about 125 of these were old-timers who would not meet our cut-off date; another 30–45 were unavailable to us for various administrative reasons. Survey sessions averaged about 25 men each; however, the men housed here had free movement around the compound, and so many showed up for the survey session twice.

All told, there were 450–500 eligibles at the site; 435 questionnaires were filled out. However, 73 of these proved fraudulent or otherwise unusable, leaving a net of 362 at this site.

Oklahoma

The Oklahoma site was a new, medium-security facility that included a factory and a large psychiatric unit, housing a total of 610 men. Of these, 174 were administratively ineligible, leaving a total of 436 men. Of these, prison officials determined that 323 met our date cutoff and were eligible for participation. The names of these 323 were posted on bulletin boards; no other advance communication with the sample was allowed at this site. Further, no incentives of any kind were permitted. Survey sessions were held in the visiting room. Because of the posting procedure, it appeared that relatively few of the eligibles even knew of the survey; other than relief of boredom, there was no incentive for those who knew about it to partic-ipate. Only 78 completed questionnaires were obtained at this site, 24% of the eligible total.

Minnesota

Interviews were conducted in two Minnesota prisons. The first was a medium-security, industrial program where all inmates are required to work in the prison factory; because of this, they are relatively well paid and have minimal free time available. Thus, our incentive was generally ineffective in this site. The total population at the site was 205 men; 136 of these were eligible to participate, but only 44 actually did. All 44 were run in a single session. The second Minnesota site was a new maximum security facility housing only about 100 men: 67 eligibles were identified, of whom 29 ac-tually participated. Over the two Minnesota sites, the response rate was therefore only about 40%.

Florida

The Florida site was a large "camp" compound designated as high-me-dium, housing about 2600 men. A sample of 430 was drawn from the prison census; of these, 40 were administratively ineligible, leaving a net sample of 390, of whom 260 (67%) actually completed questionnaires.

Georgia

The Georgia sample was interviewed at a recently constructed maxi-mum-security intake and classification center; men are held in this center (for about 4 weeks on the average) pending security classifications and per-manent assignment to an institution. The total prison census count was about

1600, all obviously meeting the date cut-off. However, the project had access only to the "exiting" cohort, which numbered about 400 men from whom volunteers were solicited by "our" guards. Men were interviewed in groups of about 35 in a prison classroom; 301 questionnaires were completed, of which 293 were usable. There was more discernible nervousness about confidentiality in this site than in any other, apparently because volunteers feared that their answers would influence their security classification and assignment; some also expressed the belief (clearly mistaken) that noncooperation with the survey might also influence their assignment. Literacy was also a more serious problem here than in any of the other sites.

Nevada

The Nevada site was a maximum-security state prison housing a total of 540 men, of whom 390 met the date cut-off. Of these, 166 were "locked down" (disciplinary segregation) and administratively unavailable, leaving a net sample of 224, of whom 215 completed questionnaires. Sessions of about 25 men each were run in a large room in an abandoned wing of the prison; prison guards were in the survey room during the sessions.

Arizona

This site was the maximum-security section of the state prison, housing 922 men. Of these, 330 were administratively ineligible, and 165 failed to meet the date cut-off, leaving a net sample of 427 men. Only 96 completed questionnaires (94 usables) were obtained. Two factors apparently contributed to the low response rate. First, our project had been preceded a few weeks earlier by another research project, the inmate response to which had been extremely negative. Second, the project did not enjoy the cooperation of a tough, suspicious prison gang whose manifest hostility toward us made it very difficult to persuade the residents to participate.

Maryland

The Maryland site was a medium-security, vocational-training facility housing mainly younger prisoners (16–25) and first offenders. A sample of 406 was drawn from the census list of 1639; of the 406 sampled felons, 135 were unavailable for interviewing. This left a net sample of 271, from whom 212 completed questionnaires were obtained.

Massachusetts

The Massachusetts site was a high-medium facility used to house inmates from the maximum-security prison as they approached their release dates. Based on discussions with local officials, we anticipated as many as

500 eligibles in this site. An advance letter announcing the project was sent to every resident; volunteers were required by the prison officials to sign up for their sessions. Only 89 volunteers ever signed up, and of these, only 48 appeared for their survey session. An evening "recruiting session" proved fruitless. Based on oral debriefings with the few men who did show up, we learned that many residents in this facility believed that results from a prior survey had been used in certain security classification decisions, and as such, they were not willing to cooperate with our project.[3]

DATA QUALITY

Concerns about data quality arise easily when dealing with self-administered questionnaires and a sample of this general sort. What confidence can one have that felons report honestly and reliably on their criminal activities? That they have made no systematic effort simply to bamboozle a research project to which they are, at best, indifferent? In short, what reason do we have to believe anything that these men have told us about themselves and their criminal pasts?

The definitive study of the quality of prisoner self-report data is Marquis (1981), a data quality analysis of the RAND "Criminal Careers" survey. In this study, data quality was assessed by comparing prisoners' self-reports with information contained in official criminal justice records. Since the format and procedures of the RAND survey were very similar to those followed in our survey, it is reasonable to assume that Marquis' findings generalize. Summarizing briefly, Marquis found:

1. There is no evidence that prisoners attempt to deny salient aspects of their criminal past. Indeed, numbers of prior arrests and convictions reported in the survey generally exceeded the numbers that appeared in a man's official criminal justice record.
2. Comparisons of self-reported conviction-offense data with official records showed that "on a general level, the data are close to unbiased" (Marquis, 1981: 32). Moderate biases were found on some items, but in general, reliability of the self-report data was "moderately high."

[3] The security classifications given in the above discussion are the "official" ones that appear in the American Correctional Association's 1982 Directory. In fact, there are considerable state to state differences in what phrases such as "medium" or "maximum" security actually mean, and in this sense, the official designations can be misleading. Based on actual security provisions inside the walls, the judgment of the field staff is that we ended up interviewing in four clearly "maximum-security" facilities: Michigan, Florida, Nevada, and Arizona. Three additional sites are best considered "medium-to-maximum-security" facilities: Minnesota, Maryland, and Massachusetts. Security provisions in these sites were clearly less restrictive than in the four sites already noted but much more restrictive than those that obtained in the remaining three sites—Missouri, Oklahoma, and Georgia, all three of which are best considered as "medium-security" facilities, whatever their formal designations.

3. Discrepancies between survey and official data were not well predicted by verbal ability, memory, or demographic characteristics, which is to say that reporting errors were, in essence, randomly distributed over the survey population.

Comparisons between "official" and survey data, of course, are not comparisons between "true" and "measured" values but are rather comparisons between two measured values, both subject to error. In general, data base management procedures within the criminal justice system leave much to be desired (e.g., Weber-Burdin, Rossi, Wright, and Daly, 1981; Rossi, Berk, and Lenihan, 1980); as such, there is no guarantee that the official data are somehow "truer" or less error-prone than the self-reported data are. This point in mind, one is necessarily much more impressed by the convergence between official and survey data reported in Marquis' study than by the occasional discrepancy.

Following Marquis, we also have undertaken some limited comparisons between official and survey data. It is perhaps a pertinent comment that most of the prison systems involved in our study were not in a position to supply machine-readable data on our sample without extraordinary, expensive, and time-consuming efforts. Indeed, in the end, we negotiated in details with only two sites for release of official data, and obtained these data only for one site, Michigan. This is not to imply that other states do not keep the appropriate records, only that the records are kept in ways that do not facilitate research use. Even the Michigan data, as we see shortly, are not ideally suited for the use to which we have put them.

In Michigan, we drew an initial sample of 404 men, from whom 265 usable cases were obtained. We received from the Data Processing Division at the Michigan Department of Corrections a computer tape with complete criminal record data for 400 of the original 404 cases. (Four men had either died or left the prison system by the time our tape request was processed.) These circumstances therefore allow for two types of comparisons relevant to our present concerns: (1) We can compare the 265 men from the original sample who completed a usable questionnaire with the 135 who did not; this tells us whether and how respondents differ from nonrespondents and is therefore a measure of self-selection bias; and (2) we can compare survey data with official data for the 265 men for whom we have both, a direct measure of the reliability of the self-reported information.

The "official" data on the Michigan inmates are rather limited in scope, consisting of birth date, marital status, number of dependents, education, race, occupation, drug use, alcohol use, and some details on conviction offenses. Rates of missing data are distressingly high on many of the variables: Birth date, race, occupation, and marital status are present for nearly all men, but 26% of the cases are missing information on educational level, 59% are missing information on drug use, 76% are missing information on alcohol use, and 83% are missing information on number of dependents. As an aside on general issues of data quality, it is worth a note that all these values greatly exceed the missing data rates in the survey responses. Whether truthful or not, whether accurate or misleading, at least the survey data are there, which clearly cannot be said for much of the official records data.

Since participation in the survey was voluntary (in Michigan and all other sites), it is certainly possible that respondents differed significantly from nonrespondents in ways that might imperil the generalizability of the research results. In Michigan, however, this was apparently not the case: Respondents and nonrespondents were nearly identical on every point where comparison is possible. (See Table 2.1.) All these data, of course, are derived from the official records, since we have no survey data on the nonrespondent group. The mean age of the respondents was 21.5 years and of the nonrespondents 21.1 years, clearly a trivial difference. About 64% of the Michigan respondents and 68% of the nonrespondents were black, another trivial difference. Nearly all men in each group (96 and 93%, respectively) were single at the point of last arrest; the average respondent had

TABLE 2.1. Characteristics of Respondents and Nonrespondents: Michigan

	Total sample (400)[a]	Respondents (261)[a]	Nonrespondents (139)[a]
Age[b]			
Mean	21.3	21.5	21.1
SD	2.2	2.3	2.1
Median	21.0	21.0	21.0
Race (in percentages)			
White	32.7	34.1	30.2
Black	65.5	64.0	68.3
Native American	0.7	0.8	0.7
Mexican	1.0	1.1	0.7
Marital status (in percentages)			
Married	5.0	4.0	6.8
Single	95.0	96.0	93.2
Percentage "not reported"			
or unknown	4.4	4.6	4.3
Education			
Mean	9.7	9.8	9.5
SD	1.2	1.3	1.2
Percentage distribution			
Ninth grade or less	45.3	44.3	47.2
Tenth–eleventh grade	47.0	45.3	50.0
High school (GED)	7.0	9.4	2.8
Any college	0.7	1.0	0.0
Percentage "not reported" or			
unknown	25.5	26.4	23.7
			(*continued*)

	Total sample (400)[a]	Respondents (261)[a]	Nonrespondents (139)[a]
Number of dependents			
Mean	1.7	1.9	1.5
SD	1.5	1.7	1.0
Median	1.3	1.3	1.2
Mode	1.0	1.0	1.0
Percentage "not reported" or			
unknown	83.2	81.0	82.7
Occupation (in percentages)			
Professional	—	—	—
Clerical	0.5	0.8	0.0
Service work	2.8	3.5	1.4
Farming/mining	1.3	1.6	0.7
Skilled trade	1.8	1.9	1.4
Unskilled	39.0	39.4	38.1
Structural	2.3	2.7	1.4
Student	3.8	4.7	2.2
None	48.3	45.3	54.7
Known drug use (in percentages)			
Episodic	40.7	40.3	41.0
Unknown	59.2	59.0	59.9
Known alcohol use (in percentages)			
Episodic	23.5	23.4	23.7
Unknown	76.5	76.6	76.3
Sentenced from Detroit			
Percentage from Detroit	34.5	32.9	39.6

[a] Base number.
[b] Age was calculated by subtracting year of birth from 1982.

received 9.8 years of education and the average nonrespondent, 9.5 years. In terms of general social profile, in short, the responding and nonresponding groups were effectively identical. The same is true of the criminal profiles: The distribution of conviction offenses was very nearly identical, as was the fraction reporting a conviction offense in which a weapon was probably present (24 and 23%, respectively, for respondents and nonrespondents).

Another way to express the lack of differences between responders and nonresponders is to regress response status (0 = responder; 1 = nonresponder) on all the available variables. This regression (Table 2.2) produces 13 statistically insignificant coefficients and an overall R^2 (= .05) that is also statistically indistinguishable from zero. In Michigan, then, we can conclude with considerable confidence that respondents and nonrespondents did not differ with respect to any variable maintained in the official criminal justice records of that state. There is, in short, no evidence of self-selection bias, at least in this one site.

Comparisons between official and survey data among the 265 men for

TABLE 2.2. Regression of Response Status on Selected Official Prison Record Data: Michigan[a]

Selected variable	b	S. E.	t
Age	−.0169	(.0141)	.233
Detroit[b]	.0840	(.0677)	.216
White[c]	−.0514	(.0699)	.463
Other ethnicity[c]	.0037	(.2170)	.986
Education[d]	−.0390	(.0234)	.096
Married[e]	.1977	(.1327)	.138
Years incarcerated	.00175	(.0249)	.994
Assault[f]	−.0298	(.0809)	.713
Breaking and entering[f]	.0244	(.0701)	.728
Rape/sex offense[f]	−.0827	(.0776)	.287
Robbery[f]	−.0609	(.0689)	.377
Larceny[f]	.0676	(.0933)	.469
Murder/manslaughter[f]	−.1403	(.8230)	.089
Intercept	1.111	(.3442)	.001
R^2 =	.046	$F = (1.036)$	$p = .416$
(N) =	(400)		

[a] Dependent variable is 0 for respondents and 1 for nonrespondents
[b] Deleted category: "all other sentencing counties."
[c] Deleted category: "black."
[d] Education in years.
[e] Deleted category: "single."
[f] Deleted category: "all other offenses."

whom we have both show an extremely high correspondence on most variables. The correlation between the two marital status variables is .84; between the two race variables, .85; and between the two age variables, .91. Since all these correlations are short of perfect, there is clearly some error in the data (either or both sets); the magnitude of these correlations, however, implies a generally high reliability in the self-reports of major demographic characteristics.

The intercorrelation of the two education variables is somewhat weaker: .50. Cross-tabular analysis suggests that much of the "error" in this case may reflect real changes—that is, having received some additional schooling since coming to prison (e.g., through a Graduate Equivalency Degree (GED) program of the sort found in the Michigan site and in most other state prisons). In any case, where there are disagreements between the survey measure of education and the "official" measure, the nature of the disagreement is more years of schooling reported in the survey than show in the official record; only 6 men (of 188 in this analysis, or 3%) reported fewer years of schooling in the survey than appear in the official record.

Analysis of the self-reported data on criminal activities is restricted to information about the conviction offense and is complicated by (1) multiple conviction offenses (in both records) for much of the sample and (2) the inherently ambiguous meaning of many crime categories. In general, it can be assumed that the self-reported conviction offense is an account in colloquial language of what the felon actually did; the "official" conviction offense is a label from the wording used in the state Criminal Code that is the official designation of the crime of which the felon was convicted (or to which he pleaded guilty).

There are, thus, many legitimate reasons other than reporting error or bias that would cause the self-reported and "official" conviction offenses to disagree. Not every felon, to illustrate, would necessarily be sensitive to the distinction between burglary and robbery; he might report "robbery" as the conviction crime when the official charge was breaking and entering, or larceny, or theft. Plea bargaining might also produce some disparities: A man who is in prison because he stole a car would presumably report "auto theft" as the conviction offense, even if this charge had been plea-bargained down to a lesser offense during court proceedings. In like fashion, a man who had actually attempted a murder might report "attempted homicide" as the conviction crime even though the "official" record shows an aggravated assault.

Of course, discrepancies might also result from systematic exaggeration or denial on the part of the prisoners; they might conceivably claim to have done crimes that they in fact had not done to make themselves appear "bad" to the field staff, or they might deny committing crimes that they had actually committed to make themselves appear "good." We admit both of these as real possibilities that cannot be tested in the data.

The preceding points in mind, it is perhaps remarkable that the conviction offense data are as consistent as they are. The measure of consistency employed in this analysis is the proportion of cases in which the official and survey data agree on the conviction offense. To illustrate, a man who told us he was in prison for rape is considered a "consistent case" if there is at least one "official" conviction offense that is a rape, no matter what other conviction offenses are also present in the official record. The man is also considered a consistent case if he does not give rape as a conviction offense and there is no rape charge to be found within the official record. Obviously, given the simplicity of the response format provided in the survey for the conviction offense question, and the complexity of the criminal codes from which the official conviction offenses are derived, one has to be reasonably charitable in deciding what amounts to a "consistency" and what does not. (Our category of "aggravated assault," for instance, would encompass several dozen specific criminal code charges.)

All told, the 261 Michigan felons for whom we have survey data had 459 official conviction offenses in their records. "Consistency rates" by type of crime are as follows: robbery, 79%; burglary or breaking and entering, 82%; larceny, 84%; assault, 84%; rape, 90%; auto theft, 92%; murder 92%.

All of these, obviously, are large proportions of consistent responses and reflect a comforting degree of convergence between the official and self-reported data. In general, if a man told us he was in prison for a certain crime, we would find the same crime listed as one of the official conviction offenses; and alternatively, if he gave no indication of being in prison for a certain crime, we would find no evidence of that crime among the listed conviction offenses. As indicated, this pattern was observed in some 79–92% of the cases, depending on the crime type.

The (relatively few) inconsistent cases reveal an interesting pattern that merits some comment. Overwhelmingly, these inconsistencies result from prisoners reporting conviction offenses to us that did not appear in the official record (versus offenses appearing in the record that were not reported in the questionnaire). This pattern characterized between 60 and 90% of the inconsistencies that we observed. We believe that in most of these cases, the discrepancy results from the difference between crime as an actual behavior and crime as an official charge: The "inconsistency" is between what the felon actually did (and is now in prison for) and the official charge under which he was sentenced. Which of these is the "truer" or "more correct" record is entirely a matter of judgment and the purposes to which the information is to be put.

The principal conclusions to be derived from the foregoing limited analysis of data quality are straightforward: In the one site where we were in a position to inquire, we found no systematic differences between respondents and nonrespondents (no selection bias); likewise, for the few variables where a comparison was possible, the agreement between self-reported and official data was acceptably close (no obvious reporting bias). It is not certain by any means that these patterns would generalize to sites other than Michigan; in fairness, Michigan was undoubtedly one of our more successful sites, most of all in regard to the response rate. And likewise, there is no guarantee that the general pattern of consistency that we find on a few variables (those that can be compared to the official record) would also be observed on all the variables contained within the questionnaire. Accurate reporting of, say, age or conviction offense does not necessarily imply equally accurate reporting of criminal histories, drug abuse, gun ownership and use, or other potentially sensitive topics. To the extent that the topic can be investigated, however, we find no reason to suspect the overall quality of the survey data. Most of the patterns revealed in this analysis are in accord with those reported by Marquis (1981).

SALIENT SAMPLE CHARACTERISTICS

Comparisons with U.S. State-Prison Population

The general profile of the state-prison population in America is reasonably well-known: In the aggregate, prisoners tend to be young males from socioeconomically disadvantaged backgrounds. In these regards, our sample is not exceptional. More than two-thirds of the sample (69%) were under age 30, just about one-half (50%) were white, fewer than two-fifths (39%) had completed as much as 12 years of schooling, and, when employed, most tended to have held down jobs that were close to the bottom in wages and skill levels.

Selected sociodemographic characteristics of the total U.S. state-prison population are given in the *1981 Sourcebook of Criminal Justice Statistics* (Flanagan, van Alstyne, and Gottfredson, 1981: 485–486). Table 2.3 compares our sample to the data contained in this source for all variables where direct comparisons are possible.

The sample closely resembles the total of U.S. state-prison population on most variables. The most serious '"disparity" that surfaces concerns age: In the total state-prison population, the percentage of men under 30 years is 63%, whereas in the sample, it was 69% (mean age = 27.8 years). This anomaly results almost entirely from the inclusion of the Michigan State Reformatory in the sample, a facility restricted mainly to young men ages 16–24.[4]

Most of the other differences shown are in the direction one would expect given the age difference just discussed. For example, our sample was somewhat more likely to have seen military service (28%) than U.S. state prisoners as a whole (24%); they were also less likely to be married, widowed, or divorced, and more likely never to have been married. The sample's conviction crimes showed the same tendency, showing fewer murders (possibly because murderers draw long sentences and may have been ineligible for our sample for that reason) but more auto thefts and drug crimes than the overall state-prisoner population. Again, however, the differences are generally quite minor, amounting to only a few percentage points in most cases.

One final "disparity" of note concerns race: While the percentage of whites in the sample was almost exactly the same as that shown for the U.S. total, the percentage of blacks was about 7–8 points "too low," and correspondingly, the percentage of "others" was about 7 points "too high." The explanation for the slightly skewed racial composition of the sample is fairly straightforward: Most of the excess "all others" were Native Americans, and their disproportionate presence in the sample resulted from Minnesota, Oklahoma, and Missouri having been among the 10 states where we interviewed, all three states having quite large Native American populations. A second and less important factor is that in one of our sites (and, to a much lesser extent, in a second site), access to the survey room was under the *de facto* control of the Aryan Brotherhood, a white prison gang,

---

[4] With the Michigan cases excluded, the percentage of the remaining sample under age 30 was 64% (mean age = 28.9 years), virtually identical to the age distribution shown in the table for all state inmates.

TABLE 2.3. Comparisons between Prisoner Sample and Known Characteristics of Total U.S. State-Prisoner Population (%)[a]

Characteristic	Sample	U.S. state-prison inmates
Age		
Younger than 30	68.8	63.0
30 and older	31.2	37.0
Race		
White[b]	49.9	49.6
Black	40.3	47.8
All other	9.8	2.5
Hispanic	7.2	9.4
Education		
Fewer than 12 years	61.2	58.0
12 or more years	38.8	42.0
Military service	28.5	23.8
Marital status[c]		
Married	19.8	24.0
Widowed	1.6	3.0
Divorced	10.0	17.0
Separated	5.8	8.0
Never married	37.4	48.0
Living with girlfriend	25.3	—
Conviction offense[d]		
Murder	9.3	15.1
Manslaughter	2.0	4.4
Sexual assault	6.7	6.9
Robbery	23.1	27.7
Assault	12.7	7.1
Burglary	19.4	20.1
Larceny, theft	8.0	5.3
Auto theft	5.1	2.1
Forgery, fraud	4.4	4.9
Drug dealing, sales	9.4	6.3

[a]The source for information on "All State Inmates" is the *1981 Sourcebook of Criminal Justice Statistics*, pp. 485–486 (Flanagan et al., 1981).

[b]Includes persons of Hispanic origin. Hispanics shown separately below.

[c]Marital status is not shown in the 1981 *Sourcebook*. Data given in this panel are from the 1977 *Sourcebook*, p. 616.

[d]The comparison of conviction offenses is not precise. Data reported in the *Sourcebook* are constrained to sum to 100%, whereas the sample could give multiple responses for their conviction offense. The percentage distributions shown here were constructed as follows: (1) The *Sourcebook* gives a final residual "all other" category which contained 10% of the cases. This one-tenth was dropped and the distribution recomputed. (2) For the 10 crimes shown in the *Sourcebook* presentation, the percentage of the sample responding "yes" to that crime as their conviction offense was computed; these percentages were then summed (they added up to 130%) and finally divided through by that sum to constrain the final distribution to add up to 100%.

and in both these sites, the reluctance of black inmates to appear for the interview was quite obvious.

The major message to be found in Table 2.3 is that our sample closely resembles the total United States state-prisoner population on most of the standard background variables, the major exceptions being that the sample is somewhat younger and contains fewer blacks (both differences resulting from local peculiarities in the sites available to us for the research).

Marriage and Family Status

As shown in Table 2.3, most (63%) of the prisoners in the sample had never been married; among the roughly two-fifths who had been married at one or another time, nearly one-half experienced a marital breakup, through divorce, separation, or death. At the time of the survey, the married proportion of the sample was just under one-fifth.[5] Considering that the median age of the sample was 26.0 years, it is apparent that these men "lagged behind" their age peers in the general population, a substantial majority of whom would currently be married. Similar findings have been reported by Rossi, Berk, and Lenihan (1980) for prisoners in Georgia and Texas.

Although fewer than two-fifths of the sample had ever been married, and fewer than one-fifth were actually married at the point of incarceration, over three-fifths (62%) claimed to have fathered a child, a rather high level of fertility considering their ages and marital status.

Families of Origin

The men in the sample tended to have come from rather large families, a characteristic which they share with other persons of low socioeconomic origins. A mere 2% claimed to have had no brothers or sisters, and the median number of siblings reported was 5.0. On average, then, the men in the sample were 1 of 6 children in their family of origin; about 14% were 1 of 10 or more children. The size of the family of origin for the sample was thus about twice the average for all U.S. families.

The siblings of our sample are of some interest (Table 2.4). Over one-half the sample (54%) reported having a brother or sister who was arrested at one or another time; nearly two-fifths (39%) had brothers or sisters who also served prison or jail sentences. Also of considerable interest: One-half the respondents (52%) reported having siblings who owned rifles or shotguns, and nearly as many (44%) reported siblings who owned handguns.

[5] About one-quarter of the sample was "living with a girlfriend" prior to their incarceration, but if one adds the cohabitors to the marrieds, the total proportion of the sample with a regular, monogamous relationship prior to incarceration remains less than one-half.

TABLE 2.4. Siblings of the Prisoners (in Percentages)[a]

Number of siblings	Percentage of prisoners
0	2.3
1	6.1
2	11.7
3	11.6
4	12.0
5	11.9
6	8.3
7	7.7
8	7.0
9	6.2
10 or more	13.7
Yes only[a]	1.4
(N) =	(1823)

Has any of them ever . . .

	Yes	No	(N)[b]
Committed a serious crime?	37.3	62.7	(1660)
Been arrested?	53.5	46.5	(1671)
Served time?	39.1	60.9	(1674)
Beaten up someone?	22.5	77.5	(1568)
Owned a shoulder weapon?	51.5	48.5	(1574)
Owned a handgun?	43.9	56.1	(1541)
Shown you how to shoot?	18.2	81.8	(1696)

[a] Respondent indicated he had at least one sibling but gave no answer to "how many."
[b] Missing data omitted item by item.

About one-fifth of the sample (18%) had a brother or sister who showed them how to shoot a gun. (Effects of early exposure to guns on the sample's own firearms behavior are analyzed in Chapter Five.)

Most (about 84%) of the sample grew up in a home with the father (or, at minimum, a "man of the house") present. Those with a father or father-figure present in the home during the formative years (ages 10–16) were asked a series of questions about that person (Table 2.5).

As is apparent from the table, many of the fathers of the men in the sample themselves lived "outside the law." About one-quarter of the fathers were reported as having been arrested at some point in their lives; just under one-fifth (18%) had served prison time. Interestingly, only 13% of the respondents reported that their fathers ever committed a serious crime, about one-half the number who reported their fathers as having been arrested. Clearly, the prisoners' fathers had relatively frequent contacts with the law: Overall, 28% of the sample with a father present in the home ($N = 1584$) responded "yes" to one or more of these three questions.

TABLE 2.5. The Fathers (or Father-Substitutes) of the Prisoners (in Percentages)

Was there a father or "man of the house" when R was 10–16 years old?	Yes	No	(N)[a]
	84.5	15.5	(1874)
If yes: Did he ever . . .			
Commit a serious crime?	12.7	87.3	(1420)
Get arrested?	24.5	75.5	(1459)
Serve time?	18.5	81.5	(1500)
Beat up or try to kill someone?	23.8	76.2	(1420)
Beat you up?	26.7	73.3	(1582)
Beat up your mother?	31.2	68.8	(1535)
Beat up your brothers/sisters?	22.6	77.4	(1569)
Own a rifle or shotgun?	69.6	30.4	(1509)
Own a handgun?	56.8	43.2	(1471)
Carry a handgun outside home?	36.3	63.7	(1431)
Show you how to shoot a gun?	47.7	52.3	(1575)
Give you a gun of your own?	45.5	54.5	(1460)

[a] Missing data omitted item by item.

Many of the fathers also had violent tendencies. Over one-quarter of the sample reported having been beaten up by their fathers; nearly one-third, that their fathers had beaten up their mothers; and so on. Overall, about one-half (48%) of the sample with a father present responded "yes" to one or more of the four questions about their father's violence. One must take care not to exaggerate these results: It bears emphasis that one-half the men in the sample did not have a violent father (by these standards), and more than two-thirds did not have a criminal father. Still, it is also clear that many of these men were raised in an environment where brutality and crime were very much a part of the ordinary routines of life.

Early Experiences with Guns

It is equally clear that many were raised in homes with firearms present. About 70% of the fathers were reported as having owned a shoulder weapon; well over one-half (57%), as having owned a handgun; more than one-third (35%), as having carried his handgun with him outside the home. Among those with a father present and with nonmissing data on both relevant questions (N = 1441), 75% answered "yes" to either the rifle/shotgun or the handgun question, or both. Since only about one-half of all U.S. households possess a firearm of any sort (Wright, Rossi, and Daly, 1983: Ch. 5), it is therefore fairly obvious that the sample originates disproportionately in social groups in which gun ownership is higher than average.

The Timing of Significant Life Events

Some appreciation of the childhood and adolescent experiences of the prisoners in the sample can be gleaned from Table 2.6, where data are reported from a series of questions asking about the ages at which certain significant experiences occurred. To give a sense of the life chronologies involved, the events in the table are arranged from youngest to oldest mean ages of occurrence.[6]

The questionnaire asked about 18 significant life events. In the average life of our respondents, the first of the 18 to have occurred was firing a gun, which happened on average early in the thirteenth year. During the same year, the average respondent also had sex with a woman for the first time; about midway through the fourteenth year, the average respondent got drunk for the first time. Prior to his sixteenth birthday, he had also stolen something worth more than $50, acquired his first shoulder weapon, and smoked marijuana for the first time. The average respondent, in other words, was

TABLE 2.6. The Timing of Significant Life Events

	Mean	SD	Median	(N)[a]	Percentage "never"	Percentage missing
Current age	27.8	8.1	26.0	(1834)	—	2.1
Age when respondent first						
Fired a gun	13.2	4.4	13.0	(1677)	8.6	1.9
Had sex	13.7	2.9	13.8	(1821)	1.0	1.9
Got drunk	14.5	3.5	14.4	(1679)	8.5	1.9
Stole $50+	15.1	4.6	14.7	(1463)	19.1	2.8
Got long gun	15.1	4.6	14.8	(1233)	31.0	3.2
Smoked pot	15.8	5.6	14.7	(1544)	15.0	2.7
Had full-time job	16.4	2.6	16.2	(1729)	6.0	1.7
Got arrested	16.6	5.7	15.8	(1841)	0.9	0.9
Lived on own	16.8	3.1	16.7	(1687)	8.5	1.5
Did hard drugs	17.1	4.5	16.4	(1113)	36.7	3.9
Sawed-off gun	17.8	4.1	16.8	(372)	74.3	5.8
Got hand gun	18.1	5.6	17.1	(1154)	34.7	3.7
Hurt someone	18.8	7.0	17.2	(937)	46.1	3.9
Did felony	19.0	6.8	17.6	(1791)	—	4.4
Convicted	19.2	6.4	17.8	(1831)	1.2	1.2
Sent to prison	19.2	6.4	17.8	(1830)	1.2	1.2
Did armed crime	19.8	7.0	17.9	(1110)	36.8	4.0
Did handgun crime	19.8	7.1	18.0	(819)	51.2	5.1

[a] Sample size for which mean, SD, and median have been computed.

[6] The arrangement of the results in Table 2.6 from lowest to highest mean ages is a presentational convenience to facilitate discussion of the data and should not be interpreted as an invariant causal sequence. Note in particular that the standard deviations around the averages are relatively large.

"into" sex, drugs, guns, and crime before he was even legally eligible to drive in most states.

During the sixteenth year, the average respondent "came of age," that is, obtained his first full-time job, moved out of the parental household, and experienced his first arrest. On average, our respondents were first arrested at age 16.6 years and were living on their own by age 16.8 years. At this point in the experience of a "normal" teenage male, life's biggest worry might well be acne or whom to invite to the high school prom. In contrast, the people in our sample were already working fulltime jobs, paying their own bills, and getting into trouble with the law.

Early in the seventeenth year, our average respondent had also begun experimenting with hard drugs; as we discuss in more detail later, about one-third (31%, $N = 1659$) were destined eventually to become drug addicts, and roughly another one-third (30%, $N = 1665$), to become alcoholics.

Between the eighteenth and twentieth birthdays, the life of our average respondent went from bad to worse: He obtained his first handgun, on average, at age 18.1 years, seriously hurt or tried to kill someone at age 18.8 years, committed his first felony at age 19.0 years, was first convicted and sent to prison or some other correctional facility at age 19.2 years, and committed his first armed crime at age 19.8 years. On the average, our respondents first went to prison at about the same time many "normal" late adolescent males would otherwise be starting college.

The life histories of the sample during its 20s can be summarized rather more quickly: Most of early adulthood was spent in prison. On average, 8.3 years transpired between the first imprisonment and the time of our study. The average respondent spent 5.0 of those years behind bars, typically not all of it in a single stretch: Indeed, the average respondent in the study had been arrested 9.9 times, convicted 4.3 times, and imprisoned 3.1 times by the time we interviewed him. Since, as noted earlier, the average age at first arrest was 16.6 years, and that at first imprisonment, 19.2 years, it is fairly obvious that most of the late teens and 20s of the sample were spent either getting into trouble with the law or serving time for having done so.

Some comments on the Percentage "Never" column of Table 2.6 are also in order. (To avoid confusion, we note that the averages reported in the table and discussed above in the text were computed with the "nevers" and the missing data omitted.) Of the 18 items included in this analysis, only 2 showed a majority giving the "never" response. About three-quarters of our sample (75% of those answering the question) said they had never sawed off a rifle or shotgun; thus, about one in four had, and among that one in four, the average age when it was first done was 17.8 years. (The survey contains considerable detail on sawing off shoulder weapons that is analyzed in Chapter Eleven.) Also, just over one-half the sample (51%) said they had never "committed a crime while armed with a handgun"; thus, just under one-half had (average age at the first handgun crime = 19.8 years).

Some other items of potential interest: only about one-fifth of the sample (19%) had never committed a theft; just under one-third (31%) had never owned a rifle or shotgun; just over one-third (35%) had never owned a handgun; about seven-eighths (85%) had at least tried marijuana; nearly two-thirds (63%) had also tried hard drugs; just under one-half (46%) claimed never to have "seriously hurt or tried to kill somebody"; barely more than one-third (36%) claimed never to have committed a crime armed with any weapon.

The life history of a "typical" felon is often discussed in terms of what might be called "retarded development," especially in regard to late adolescence and early adulthood. At a time in life when most young males are completing their schooling, getting married, starting a family, and launching themselves into adult careers, the "typical" felon is spending most of his time in prison. Since prison provides few or no opportunities to start a family or to accumulate seniority and experience in a "real world" job, the typical felon's life-cycle development is, accordingly, retarded, and as such, at age 30, he tends to resemble more a 20 year old in terms of educational attainment, marital status, and employment history. This pattern is frequently cited as at least part of the explanation for the adjustment difficulties faced by many felons subsequent to their release from prison. As is clear from the above account (and from other materials presented later in this chapter), our sample also showed these same general tendencies.

There is, however, another aspect of the patterning of life events that has not received so much attention, one that might be called "accelerated development" in the early adolescent years. Stated simply, our felons started doing "adult" things—having sex, getting drunk, doing drugs, leaving home—early in their teenage years, much earlier, we suspect, than "normal" teenage males. Thus, while many of these men resembled 20 year olds at age 30, many also resembled 20 year olds at age 14 or 15. It is as though they rushed very quickly into the stage of "late adolescence" and then managed to remain at more or less the same stage well into their early middle age.

Education, Employment, Income

The lack of education and limited employment histories of the felon population have been described in many prior studies and are certainly evident in this sample as well. Details are shown in Table 2.7. On the whole, the prisoners sampled were poorly educated, with the modal respondent having dropped out of high school in the tenth or eleventh grade. About 16% had graduated from high school, and an additional 23% had some education beyond high school. For most, "education beyond high school" consisted of 1 or 2 years of college; only 3% of the sample had actually attained a college degree.

About two-fifths (39%) of the sample were unemployed at the time they were last arrested. Of those unemployed at arrest, about two-thirds had held at least some sort of job in the previous year; thus, about 12% of the sample were unemployed for the entire year prior to arrest. Roughly 70% of those unemployed at the time of arrest said they were also looking for work.[7]

Among those with a job at any time during the year prior to imprisonment, weekly take home pay averaged $226; about two-thirds were taking home $200 per week or less. Most of the men in the sample (54%) felt that they needed more money than they were making "to make ends meet."

TABLE 2.7. Education, Employment, Income

	Percentage
Educational attainment	
No schooling	0.4
6 or fewer years	3.6
7–9 years	24.6
10–11 years	32.7
High school graduate	16.0
Technical school	6.2
Some college	13.7
College graduate	2.8
(N)=	(1842)
Number of dependents	
0	12.9
1	19.9
2	18.0
3	19.4
4	14.0
5	6.5
6	3.5
7	3.0
8 or more	2.8
Mean response	2.67
(N)=	(1831)
Employed at last arrest?	
Yes	58.5
No	38.6
(N)=	(1820)
	(continued)

[7] By Bureau of Labor Statistics conventions, a person who is unemployed and *not* looking for work is not "unemployed," but rather is "out of the labor force." To compare the unemployment figures given in the text with official unemployment figures, this factor must be taken into account. Of those without a job at the time of arrest (39% of the total), 70% were in fact looking for work (at least, so they said); the fraction unemployed is thus $(.39) \times (.70) = .273$. The denominator of the unemployment rate in this sample is the proportion employed (.61) plus those unemployed $(.273) = .883$. We get the estimated unemployment rate for the sample by dividing: $(.273)/(.883) = .31$, or 31%, approximately four times the national unemployment rate (7.6%) in 1981. (We are grateful to Gary Kleck for these calculations.)

TABLE 2.7. Education, Employment, Income (*continued*)

	Percentage
If no: Employed during previous year?	
Yes	68.1
No	31.9
(N) =	(698)
Combined employment data	
Employed when arrested	61.1
Unemployed at arrest, but employed	
during previous year	26.5
Never employed in entire year	12.4
(N) =	(1794)
"At the time you were arrested . . . ,	
were you . . ."	
Unemployed?	
Yes	35.7
No	64.3
(N) =	(1601)
Looking for work?	
Yes	25.3
No	74.7
Weekly take-home pay	
$100 or less	9.5
$101–150	28.2
$151–200	27.3
$201–250	12.7
$251–300	7.8
$301–400	7.3
$401 or more	7.3
(N) =	(1486)
Mean response =	$226
Was it enough money?	
More than enough	20.6
Just enough	25.2
Needed a little more	31.6
Needed a lot more	22.5
(N) =	(1451)
If R "needed more": How much more?	
Mean response	$175
SD	$205
(N) =	(804)

Among those needing more, the average additional income they felt they needed was rather substantial—$175. Presumably, some share of the criminal activities of these men is a function of this apparent "income deficit."

In summary, the education, employment, and income profile of the sample is consistent with the well-known characteristics of the felon population in the United States: On the whole, they are uneducated, unemployed or underemployed, and rather poorly paid.

Juvenile Criminality

Recent studies have strongly suggested that, like diabetes, "early onset" is the fatal form of the criminal disease. That is, high-rate adult criminals usually share the common characteristic of having committed fairly serious and fairly frequent crimes while they were still juveniles.

Our survey obtained several items of information about the juvenile criminality of the sample; see Table 2.8. On the average, as we have already noted, the men in this sample commenced their criminal careers about midway in their teens: By age 15, the average felon had already committed a nontrivial theft, by age 16.5, had already been arrested, and by age 19, had committed his first "pretty serious" crime (listed as "did felony" in Table 2.7).

A follow-up to this latter question asked what the felon's first "pretty serious" crime had been; responses appear in the top panel of Table 2.8. Burglary and robbery were by far the most common "entry" crimes, mentioned by 22 and 20%, respectively. Theft and automobile theft were also

Table 2.8. Juvenile Criminality (in Percentage)

1. "What kind of crime was your
   first pretty serious crime?"

	Percentage
Burglary	22
Robbery	20
Theft, larceny	11
Auto theft	10
Assault	10
Drug related	5
Homicide	6
All others	16
(N) =	(1707)

2. "How often did you do crimes
   before age 18?" (in percentage)

	Never	Once	A few	10–15	Dozens/ hundreds	(N)
Assault (.73)[a]	53	9	24	6	8	(1749)
Burglary (.78)	41	8	24	8	18	(1746)
Drug related (.75)	62	2	13	4	18	(1738)
Murder (.61)	92	5	2	—	1	(1702)
Rape (.60)	94	4	2	—	—	(1697)
Robbery (.68)	67	7	15	4	7	(1727)
Armed robbery (.70)	73	6	11	3	7	(1710)
Theft (.66)	35	9	25	9	22	(1758)

[a] Correlation with corresponding question about adult criminality.

rather frequent, mentioned by 11 and 10%. About one-tenth entered their criminal career with an assault; some 6% entered with a homicide.

Regardless of the response to the "first serious crime" question, each felon was given a list of common crimes and asked how frequently he had committed each crime "before you were 18 years old." Here too, economic crimes lead the list. About two-thirds (65%) had committed at least one nontrivial theft before age 18, about three-fifths had committed at least one burglary, and one-third had committed at least one robbery. Also, just under one-half (47%) had committed at least one assault. Early involvement with drugs is also indicated in these results: about two-fifths had done drug dealing or sales before age 18. The only crimes which large majorities had not done before age 18 are therefore murder and rape (92 and 94% "never," respectively). It is perhaps of some additional interest that only 18% of the men who answered the juvenile crime sequence responded "never" to all eight questions. Thus, more than four-fifths of the men in the sample had committed at least one of these crimes prior to their eighteenth birthday.

Having done any of these crimes once and only once before age 18 is rather uncommon, with the exception of murder and rape. Most of the men who had ever committed these crimes, in short, had done so at least "a few" times. High-rate juvenile criminals clearly tend to "specialize" in theft, burglaries, and drug deals: 22, 18, and 18%, respectively, had done dozens or even hundreds of these kinds of crimes before age 18.

Drug Abuse

We indicated earlier that the men in this sample began experimenting with drugs (including alcohol) at a relatively early age: By age 14.5, the average man in the sample had gotten drunk at least once, by age 16 he had at least tried marijuana, and by age 17, he had also at least tried hard drugs. For many, these early drug experiences were only the opening events in a life-long history of chemical dependence and substance abuse. Data on the drug usage and abusage of the sample are shown in Table 2.9.

About one-third of the sample (29%) had been alcoholics by their own admission; likewise, about one-third (31%) had been drug addicts, and an equivalent portion (29%) had been admitted to a drug or alcohol rehabilitation program at some time. The cross-tabulation of the "alcoholic?" and "drug addict?" questions reveals that 54% ($N = 1649$) claimed never to have been either; 14% had been both. If we take self-admitted dependency on either alcohol or drugs (or both) as the definition of "serious" drug abuse, then 46% of the felon sample would qualify.

Many of the men who did not admit to outright drug addiction did admit to a heavy pattern of drug use. Each man in the sample was presented with a list of 11 commonly used illicit drugs and asked how frequently he had used each of them before coming to prison. Majorities ranging from 51 to 81% claimed never to have used barbiturates (51% "never"), psychedelics (59% "never"), opium (62% "never"), PCP (63% "never"), heroin (66% "never"), and methadone (81% "never"). In the remaining five cases, however, the majority had used the drug at least once.

Unsurprisingly, alcohol and marijuana were the most commonly used drugs among this sample, by far. A mere 7% of the sample claimed never to have used alcohol; 27% used alcohol "almost all of the time." The corresponding percentages for marijuana were 16 and 31%. Hashish, amphetamines, and cocaine are also frequently used, with about one-tenth in all three cases claiming to have used the drug almost all of the time.

As noted above, at minimum, some 46% of the sample was substance-dependent. An upper boundary to the true fraction of drug abusers in the sample can be obtained by defining "serious drug abuse" to mean using any one of the 11 drugs listed in Table 2.9 "many times" or "almost all of the time." As it happens, only 26% of the total sample claimed not to have used any of these drugs many times or all the time; as a percentage of the

TABLE 2.9. Drug Use and Abuse (in Percentages)

Have you ever:

	Yes	No	(N)
Been an alcoholic?	29	71	1665
Been addicted to drugs?	31	69	1659
Been admitted to rehab?	29	71	1661

Before prison, how often
    did you take:

	Never	Once	A few times	Many times	Almost all the time	(N)
Alcohol	7	2	23	41	27	(1659)
Marijuana	16	3	20	30	31	(1648)
Heroin	66	6	14	9	5	(1614)
Methadone	81	3	8	5	2	(1593)
Psychedelics	59	4	18	14	5	(1624)
Hashish	41	4	24	24	8	(1626)
Opium	62	6	19	10	3	(1608)
Barbituates	51	4	24	15	6	(1615)
Amphetamines	45	3	22	20	9	(1614)
Cocaine	44	6	23	19	9	(1622)
PCP	63	9	17	7	3	(1587)

How often did you take drugs?
About every day	39
About every weekend	12
From time to time	17
Never	38
(N) =	(1598)

(continued)

TABLE 2.9. Drug Use and Abuse (in Percentages) (*continued*)

Ever commit crimes because you needed
    money for drugs or alcohol?
No	65
Once	5
A few times	27
Many times	22
(N) =	(1514)

	Mean	SD	(N)
Heroin users only: average weekly heroin costs:	$55	$98	(192)
Alcohol users only: average weekly alcohol costs:	$13	$70	(1297)
Users of other drugs: average weekly drug costs:	$27	$83	(900)

Total sample: weekly drug costs

Amount spent	Percentage
$0	11
$1–49	35
$50–99	16
$100–199	15
$200–299	7
$300+	15
(N) =	(1432)

During conviction crime, were you:

	Yes	No	(N)
Drunk?	41%	59%	(1605)
High on drugs?	37	63	(1596)
Either or both?	57	43	(1562)

subsample who answered at least one of the drug questions, the figure is 16%. Rephrased, somewhere between three-quarters and five-sixths of the sample used one or more of the 11 drugs either frequently or regularly. As a convenient rule of thumb, then, we can conclude that about one-half the felon sample had been substance-dependent and an additional one-quarter had been serious drug abusers. Nearly one-half the sample (46%) claimed to have used three or more of the drugs on the list many times or most of the time.[8]

[8] The drug use patterns discussed in the text are very close to those reported in the RAND survey. Among the RAND respondents, 83% were found to be serious drug users (Chaiken and Chaiken, 1982: 16), compared to about 84% in our sample. This source also remarks that the pattern of drug abuse extends back into adolescence; "indeed, their use of drugs and their criminal careers usually being at about the same time" (1982: 16). The authors add an important *caveat*, however,

The relationships between use and addiction are much as one would expect. Among those who said they used alcohol "almost all of the time" ($N = 445$), 68% had also been alcoholics; among those who used heroin "many times" or "almost all the time" ($N = 216$), 90% had also been drug addicts.

We also asked each man in the sample how often he usually took drugs. Some 22%, the true abstainers, said "never," and 27% said they only took drugs from time to time. A small group, 12%, used drugs only on the weekends; and the remainder, nearly two-fifths, used drugs just about every day. Slightly more than one-third (35%) confessed to having committed at least one property crime because they needed drug money; 13% had done so many times.

The tendency to have committed crimes to obtain drug money is positively and significantly correlated with all 11 usage questions, with the correlation coefficients ranging from .21 to .41. As would be expected, the strongest correlation is for heroin use (.41), followed by methadone use (.38) and barbiturate use (.36).

To get some sense of the financial burdens imposed by these drug-use patterns, we asked the drug users in the sample how much they had been spending for drugs "in the average week." Heroin users in the sample ($N = 192$) were averaging about $55 a week on heroin, but with a high variation around that average; alcohol users ($N = 1297$) were averaging about $13 a week on alcohol; users of all other drugs ($N = 900$) were averaging about $27 per week for drugs of various sorts. To avoid confusion, users who said they were not spending anything for their drugs are omitted from these calculations. (Many heavy heroin users, for example, are also heroin dealers and cover their own habit through sales to others; the out-of-pocket heroin cost for these men is therefore effectively zero.)

Not all men in the sample answered the questions about drug costs; this battery appeared near the end of the questionnaire. Many who did answer gave a nonnumeric response (e.g., "a lot," "not much," "all the money I had"). Excluding both these sources of missing data, there are 1432 men who gave complete numerical information on their drug expenses. Of these, only 11% were spending nothing in the average week for either drugs or alcohol; an additional 35% incurred only modest drug costs ($1–49). The remainder, some 54% of the sample, were spending at least $50 a week on drugs; 37% were spending $100 a week or more. Using the average weekly take-home pay reported earlier ($226) as the standard, about one-third of the sample were spending one-half this amount for drugs, and about one-fifth (19%) were spending at least this amount or more. Among the rel-

---

one that bears repeating here: "This does not indicate that drug use caused them to become criminals. Rather, drug use appears to be just another element of the criminal life-style they have adopted."

atively serious drug users in the sample, in short, drugs would have doubtlessly been the single largest item in their weekly budget.

Finally, we asked each man in the sample if he had been drunk or high
on drugs when he committed the crime for which he was now in prison.
Surprising no one, most had been: 41% said they were drunk, 37% said
they were high; 57% had been either drunk or high (or both); 18% had
been drunk and high. If the conviction crimes of these men represent a reasonable sample of all the crimes that are committed, then the average crime
involves a perpetrator who is pharmacologically impaired when the offense is committed.

SUMMARY OF SAMPLE CHARACTERISTICS

First, the characteristics of the men in this sample are respectably close
to the known characteristics of the U.S. state-prisoner population on almost
all variables where a direct comparison is possible; most of the exceptions
to this pattern result from specific site peculiarities (e.g., age and race). Like
felons in general, the men in our sample are best typified as young males
from socially marginal backgrounds.

Second, most of the men in the sample were exposed to, or experimenting with, drugs, guns, and crime on or before their sixteenth birthday.
Many had fathers who were either violent, or criminal, or both. The general pattern of life cycle development for these men is to have begun doing
"adult" things rather early in life. The late teens of these men were mostly
spent getting into relatively serious trouble with the law; most spent the
largest share of their 20s in prison.

Third, socioeconomically, the average man in the sample left school in
the tenth or eleventh grade and had an uncertain employment history
thereafter. Rates of unemployment among the sample were some four times
the national average. The average (employed) man in the sample was, at
the point of last arrest, taking home $226 a week to support himself, one
or two other people, and, in most cases, a fairly high level of drug consumption as well.

Fourth, most of the felons in the sample grew up around guns and had
owned and used guns for most of their lives. About three-quarters had gun-
owning fathers; about one-half had gun-owning siblings; some 90% had
fired a gun at some time.

Fifth, the average felon in this sample commenced his criminal career
as a juvenile. About 80% had committed at least one felony before the age
of 18; many had committed large numbers of them, property crimes being
by far the most common. As reported in previous studies, juvenile criminality is a strong predictor of adult criminal activity.

Sixth, about one-half the felons in the sample were (or had been) either
alcoholics or drug addicts, or both, at some point. An additional one-quarter

appear to have been rather heavy drug users, if not addicts. The modal usage pattern was to have used drugs nearly every day. Over one-half the sample was spending more than $50 a week on drugs or alcohol at the time of their last arrest; about two-fifths were spending $100 per week or more.

Seventh, the patterns of criminal activity among this sample are not all "of a piece." Between one-third and two-fifths, for example, said they had never committed an armed crime; the remainder had. And likewise, about one-half said they had never committed a handgun crime; the remainder had. Not all the criminals in this sample, in short, are armed criminals; and not all of the armed criminals are armed with guns. These points suggest the need for a typology of criminals to be employed in subsequent analyses based on patterns of weapons use, and this, as it happens, is the topic of the next chapter.

3

VARIETIES OF ARMED CRIMINALS: A DESCRIPTIVE TYPOLOGY

Although compared to the general male population, the men in our sample appear to be quite homogeneous in their socioeconomic backgrounds, they did vary considerably among themselves in the kinds and amounts of their criminal activities and, most importantly for purposes of this volume, in their patterns of weapons use. For instance, so far as we can tell, many of the men in the sample had never committed any kind of crime armed with any kind of weapon. These, in fact, constitute the modal type. Some had used weapons from time to time but never on a sustained or regular basis. And, by their own admission, some, of course, had done literally hundreds, or even thousands, of armed crimes. Even among those who have used weapons regularly, there are differences in the kind of weapons carried and the uses to which they are customarily put.

These differences in mind, the present chapter develops a basic and simple typology of criminal-weapons users, one that proves useful in sorting the sample into relatively homogeneous categories based on patterns of criminal-weapons use. This typology figures prominently in all subsequent analyses reported in this volume.

The weapons usage typology was constructed using information from the questionnaire about (1) the type of weapon most commonly carried or used in the commission of crimes (no weapon, a knife or a club, a handgun, etc.), and (2) for the subset of firearms users specifically, the frequency of criminal weapons use.

The typology was developed using information on weapons use from the questionnaire, classifying men in the sample into one category or another based on evidence derived from questions that obtained information on the use of weapons in the crimes they had committed.[1]

---

[1] Assignment of men to categories of the typology was completely straightforward in approximately 90% of the cases. These assignments were based on (1) the initial filter questions reproduced in the following paragraph of the text; (2) a question asking about the type of weapon used most frequently in committing crime; and (3) for the subset of Gun Criminals, a question asking about the frequency of gun use. Information from elsewhere in the questionnaire was used for purposes of

The essential division into gun criminals versus those who did not use guns in their crimes was accomplished through the answers to two questions, as follows:

1. "Thinking now about all the crimes you have ever done in your life, . . . have you ever used a weapon to commit a crime or had any kind of weapon with you while you were committing a crime?
2. [If "yes"] Still thinking about all the crimes you have ever done, . . . have you ever used a gun to commit a crime or ever had a gun with you while you were committing a crime?"

As can be seen, these two questions sort the sample initially into three groups: (1) the unarmed criminals, those who answered "no" to the first question; (2) the armed-but-not-with-a-gun criminals, those who answered "yes" to the first question but "no" to the second; and (3) the gun criminals, those who answered "yes" to both questions.

Of course, there is some ambiguity in the responses to these questions. First, not everyone answered both these questions, and in these cases (N = 105), we have made use of other relevant information in the questionnaires.

Second, the question sequence clearly gives precedence to gun crime. To illustrate, a man who had done, let us say, hundreds of armed robberies with a butcher knife and one armed robbery with a handgun would, if he followed instructions correctly, be counted here as a "gun criminal." (We discuss later in this chapter the other kinds of weapons used by men in each of the various categories.) In the same vein, many of these men were accustomed to carrying several weapons, a knife and a handgun being the most common combination. In these cases, clearly, the typology again gives precedence to the handgun (or more generally, firearms) use. Given that our central concern in this study was criminal gun usage, this pattern of precedence was justifiable.

Finally, there were some inconsistencies in the responses given to this question that became apparent when other information provided in the questionnaire was taken into account. In particular, some of the men who claimed never to have used weapons in their crimes indicated elsewhere in the questionnaires that they had indeed used weapons of one or another sort. To the extent possible, these inconsistencies were resolved, usually in favor of gun usage.

The information contained in the initial two questions was supplemented with information on the specific types of weapons used and on the

---

assignment only when the felon failed to answer one or more of the above three sequences. Comprehensive details on the assignment of these men to the categories of the typology are available from the authors on request (c/o Social and Demographic Research Institute, Machmer Hall W-35, University of Massachusetts, Amherst, MA 01003).

frequency with which armed crimes had been committed. The end result was the following typology:

Unarmed Criminals: (N = 725 or 39%)
    Prisoners for whom we could find no positive evidence anywhere in the questionnaire that they had ever used any weapons of any sort in committing their crimes.
Improvisers: (N = 79 or 4%)
    Men who had used weapons, but not guns or knives, in their crimes, usually a variety of ready-to-hand weapons.
Knife Criminals: (N = 134 or 7%)
    Men who used predominately knives and never firearms in committing their crimes.
One-Time Firearms Users: (N = 257 or 14%)
    Men who had committed one and only one gun crime (whatever the type of gun they used).
Sporadic Handgun Users: (N = 257 or 14%)
    Men who have used a handgun "a few times" in committing crimes but never a shoulder weapon.
Handgun Predators: (N = 321 or 17%)
    Men who have used handguns "many," "most," or "all" of the time in committing their crimes.
Shotgun Predators: (N = 101 or 5%)
    Men who claimed shoulder weapons as their most frequently used weapons and who committed more than one crime with such weapons. Since most of these persons used sawed-off shotguns, we use the term Shotgun Predators for them. It should be noted, however, that a few of them used other types of shoulder weapons instead.

VALIDATION

Men in the sample had numerous opportunities to tell us about their past weapons use, and only a subset of these items has been used specifically in constructing the typology of armed criminals.[2] It is therefore possible to get some sense of the validity of the typology by analyzing its relationships to some of these other questions.

We stress in advance that there are inherent ambiguities in the concept of armed crime. To carry a weapon as one is committing a crime is clearly a different matter from using that weapon in some way in the course of the crime. A man who is burglarizing a house and who, incidentally, also happens to have a pocket knife along with him is clearly committing a crime while armed with a weapon but is only arguably committing an armed crime.

---

[2] To be sure, depending on the pattern of missing data to the various component items, virtually all of the information available on some of these men was employed in placing them in the typology. All told, however, 89% of the sample had nonmissing data on all relevant component items; and thus, various of the other pieces of information about weapons use contained within the questionnaire were employed in only 11% of the cases.

Other ambiguities also exist. Burglars, for example, might carry buck or sheath knives with them in the course of their burglaries to use as jimmying tools—to pry open windows and doors, to pick locks, etc. In this case, again, it is clear that these men are committing crimes while armed with a weapon and equally clear that they are using the weapon in order to complete the crime successfully. Would we want to say, however, that they are doing armed crime?

Or consider the case of drug dealers. Many dealers, apparently, go about their business heavily armed: Police often find in the glove compartments or trunks of their cars an imposing arsenal of weaponry, "just in case." Imagine, then, the dealer who has made literally hundreds of deals, was heavily armed in each and every one of those deals, but never encountered a situation where the use of any of the weapons was necessary. Again, that crimes were committed while the perpetrator was armed is obvious. Was it, however, an armed crime?

The very notion of armed crime, in short, is intrinsically ambiguous. As becomes apparent in later chapters, many of the men in our sample carried weapons with them as a matter of course, often for their own "protection." Given an average of nearly 10 prior arrests and more than 4 prior convictions, it is also clear that many of the men in the sample had an active criminal life as well. These points in mind, it should be clear that virtually any crime many of these men ever committed was an armed crime in the sense that they were armed when they committed it.

These inherent ambiguities in the concept of armed crime were anticipated during the development of the questionnaire; our hope was to deal with them by being very explicit and all-inclusive in the relevant questions. To illustrate, the initial question (reproduced above) is worded in the broadest possible terms. The idea was to begin with the broadest possible conception of armed crime and then to refine the concept on the basis of later questions; thus, the question was intended to include the case of a weapon possessed but not used and likewise to include every crime the man ever committed, whether he was apprehended for it or not. Whether it was actually interpreted by all respondents in precisely the way it was intended, however, is very much an open issue.[3]

[3] Our field workers reported more queries from respondents about these two filter questions than about any other set of items in the questionnaire. In many cases, the queries were exactly along the lines suggested in the text. For example, a respondent would indicate that he had possessed a weapon in one of his crimes but did not actually use it and then would ask just where in the questionnaire he was supposed to go. In some cases, the respondent would answer the question as it was literally intended, skip to the appropriate section of the questionnaire, and then get confused because most of the questions he encountered there seemed irrelevant to his situation. That the concept of armed crime was much more ambiguous than we initially thought it was going to be was obvious once we had completed data collection at the first site.

We begin our investigation of the utility of the typology by considering the conviction offenses reported by the sample. Conviction offenses were ascertained by presenting respondents with a list of 19 crime types (and a residual "Other" category) and asking them to indicate which of these crimes they were "now serving a sentence for." Multiple responses were obviously possible and, in fact, quite common; indeed, over the total sample, the mean number of conviction offenses reported was 1.51. The cross-tabulation of the conviction offense data and the armed criminals typology is shown below in Table 3.1.

One would not anticipate that the weapons usage typology will be completely predictive of the conviction offenses of the sample. But if the typology is valid, the relationships should be at least moderately strong.

In the total sample (first column of the table), the most frequent conviction offense was robbery (mentioned by 30%), followed by burglary (25%), aggravated assault (assault with a deadly weapon) (13%), and homicide (12%), with all other categories chosen by 10% or fewer. These patterns varied, at times sharply, across the categories of the typology, almost always in the manner one would expect. The firearms criminals (all four types), for example, were substantially more likely than the others to be doing time on a robbery charge. Likewise, the Handgun Predators and Shotgun Predators were about twice as likely to be in on a weapons charge as was the case for the total sample (22 versus 10%). Other findings of note are as follows.

The Unarmed Criminals

The modal conviction offense among the Unarmed Criminals was burglary and breaking and entering, mentioned by 28%, followed in order by robbery (14%), theft (10%), and rape (10%). The robbery percentage for the group was the lowest shown in the table, and they were also much less likely than any other group to be doing time for aggravated assault. Interestingly, about 6% were in for homicide or manslaughter. The latter notwithstanding, the conviction-offense data for the group were broadly consistent with the patterns one would expect given their weapons behavior. Also of some interest, they reported the fewest average number of conviction offenses (mean = 1.21 offenses). These and other data presented later confirm, as one would guess, that Unarmed Criminals were generally among the least violent and least criminally active men in the sample.

The Improvisers

The Improvisers turned out to be quite a distinctive group. First, unlike any other group, the modal conviction offense for the Improvisers was homicide, mentioned by 28%. Indeed, their homicide percentage was the

TABLE 3.1. Self-Reported Conviction Offenses by Gun-Usage Type (in Percentages)

Conviction offense[a]	Total	Gun-usage type						
		Unarmed	Improviser	Knife	One-timer	Sporadic handgun	Handgun predator	Shoulder weapon
(N) =	(1874)	(725)	(79)	(134)	(257)	(257)	(321)	(101)
Arson	1	1	3	4	0	1	1	2
Simple assault	4	4	4	6	3	2	5	5
ADW	13	5	22	18	18	13	16	27
Auto theft	7	6	3	7	6	6	9	11
Burglary	25	28	25	24	12	27	26	28
Counterfeiting	1	1	0	2	0	0	0	1
Drug possession	7	6	4	2	3	7	12	9
Drug sales	6	7	3	4	5	4	6	6
Forgery	5	6	1	3	3	3	4	4
Fraud	1	1	0	2	0	1	1	4
Kidnapping	4	3	5	5	5	3	5	4
Homicide	12	6	28	15	21	9	14	9
Manslaughter	3	2	1	5	6	2	2	3
Stolen property	5	4	5	2	2	5	8	8
Rape	9	10	7	16	7	8	7	4
Other sex crime	6	8	3	6	4	4	4	5
Robbery	30	14	25	22	37	50	44	40
Theft	10	10	12	9	7	9	14	16
Weapons charge	10	3	3	9	13	11	21	23
X̄ Number of conviction offenses	1.51	1.21	1.47	1.57	1.48	1.61	1.99	2.01

Armed at time								
Percentage yes	54	1	62	79	82	71	80	81
(N)=	(1509)	(470)	(69)	(122)	(232)	(231)	(299)	(86)
If armed, with what?								
(in percentage)[b]								
(N)=	(810)	(6)	(43)	(96)	(191)	(165)	(239)	(70)
Handgun	59	—	9	3	70	73	81	34
Any shoulder weapon	25	—	0	5	24	17	24	63
Any knife	41	—	9	88	16	23	34	51
Any "other"	22	—	79	7	3	6	13	23
X̄ Number of weapons mentioned	1.4	—	0.6	1.2	1.2	1.2	1.8	2.4
Percentage carrying two or more weapons	23	—	5	6	12	19	37	53
Other								
X̄ Prior arrests	9.9	6.7	8.9	9.7	7.5	12.3	16.4	14.4
(N)=	(1680)	(650)	(72)	(126)	(229)	(231)	(293)	(79)
X̄ Prior convictions	4.3	3.3	4.4	4.7	3.2	5.0	6.4	4.8
(N)=	(1748)	(672)	(75)	(126)	(238)	(244)	(305)	(88)
X̄ Prior incarcerations	3.1	2.6	3.5	3.7	2.7	3.4	3.8	3.8
(N)=	(1719)	(665)	(74)	(125)	(230)	(240)	(300)	(85)

[a]Missing data omitted item by item.
[b]Multiple responses are possible.

highest shown in the table and was more than twice the percentage registered for the total sample. The group's figure for aggravated assault was also distinctively higher than the average—22 versus 13% in the total sample; it, too, was among the highest values registered in the table. Thus, relative to the rest of the sample, the Improvisers consisted disproportionately of murderers and aggravated assaulters. It would therefore appear likely that our category of Improvisers contains a fair-sized proportion of so-called criminals of passion—men prone to arguments, scuffles, fights, and barroom brawls and apt to pick up anything at hand for the purpose of meting out physical punishment, frequently enough with devastating results. The image one obtains from the conviction offense data on these men is that their aggressive tendencies were on "short-fuses"; they do not appear to be hardened or calculating criminals. Consistent with this depiction, their robbery percentage was among the lowest recorded in the table.

Knife Criminals

As among the Unarmed, the modal conviction offense among the Knife Criminals was burglary (24%), followed closely by robbery (22%), then aggravated assault (18%), rape (16%), and homicide (15%). The Knife Criminals, interestingly, were much more likely to be doing time on a rape charge than any of the other categories shown in the table.

Firearms Criminals

As might be anticipated, the modal conviction offense among all four categories of firearms criminals was robbery, with percentages ranging from 37 to 50%. Among the One-Time Firearms Users, robbery was followed by homicide (21%), then aggravated assault (18%). In the remaining three categories, burglary was the next most frequently mentioned conviction offense, followed in turn by either aggravated assault or some kind of weapons charge. Note finally that the Handgun Predators and Shotgun Predators showed the highest average number of conviction offenses of any group in the table.

In the questionnaire, the series on conviction offense was followed by a short question sequence asking for some details about the incident, specifically, whether the offender had been armed with any kind of weapon when he committed the crime for which he was then doing time. These data are shown in Panel II of Table 3.1. In the total sample, just over one-half (54%) had been armed during their conviction offense, a figure that varied from 1% (of the Unarmed) to 82% (of the One-Timers). In general, the "armed at the time?" question gave results one would expect: About four-fifths of the Handgun Predators, Shotgun Predators, One-Time Firearms Users, and

Knife Criminals had been armed during the conviction crime as had been 71% of the Sporadic Handgun Users and 62% of the Improvisers.

The remainder of the information contained in Table 3.1 can be summarized rather more quickly; all of it is consistent with expectation. Of the 43 Improvisers who had been armed during their conviction offense, for example, 79% had been armed with some sort of improvised weapon.[4] (A few were also armed with something else as well, those carrying multiple weapons amounting to 5% of the total.) Likewise, 88% of the Knife Criminals who had been armed during the conviction offense ($N = 96$) were in fact armed with a knife, although here, too, a few (6%) were also carrying other weapons. It is worth noting, of course, that a few of both the Improvisers and the Knife Criminals said they were carrying some sort of firearm during the conviction offense, which means, by rights, that they should have answered "yes" to both filter questions and subsequently to have been categorized as firearms criminals. The numbers involved are sufficiently small ($N < 15$), however, that any analysis of these inconsistencies is pointless.

Data for the various categories of firearms offenders are equally straightforward: 94% of the One-Time Firearms Users had been armed with a firearm at the conviction offense; 73% of the Sporadic Handgun Users and 81% of the Handgun Predators had been armed with a handgun during the conviction offense; 63% of the Shotgun Predators had been armed with some kind of shoulder weapon (the remainder with handguns). As in previous cases, many of these men also had been armed with other weapons as well, the tendency to carry multiple weapons being by far the most pronounced among the Predator categories (37 and 53%, respectively, carrying more than one kind of weapon during the conviction crime).

PREVIOUS CRIMINAL HISTORIES

We can anticipate that the weapons usage types will vary in the extent to which they have had previous contacts with the police, the courts, and the prisons. It is to be expected that the Handgun Predators will have had the longest records and will have committed more serious crimes than, say, the Unarmed Criminals.

The data on prior arrests, convictions, and incarcerations also proved to

[4] Since data on the conviction offense were employed in assigning men to categories only when there were missing data on the other, more direct, questions, it is clearly not necessary that every "armed criminal" identified in the typology have been armed during the conviction offense. Likewise, assignment to categories in most cases depends on the man's report of the weapon "most frequently used" in committing crimes, which makes it logically possible that an Improviser, say, could have carried a knife during the conviction offense, or, for that matter, that Handgun Predators could have been armed with knives rather than handguns during the conviction offense, etc.

be much as one would expect. (See Panel IV of Table 3.1.) The total sample averaged 10 prior arrests, 4 prior convictions, and 3 prior incarcerations. In each case, the averages for the Unarmed Criminals were substantially lower than the overall averages, and in general, the averages tend to increase as one moves to the more predatory categories of the typology. The only major exception to this pattern is that the One-Time Firearms Users tended to show fewer "priors" than the Knife Criminals, which, under the circumstances, is perhaps not surprising.[5]

Table 3.2 is based on a series of questions asking how often the prisoners had committed each of a series of specific crimes. The answers constitute approximate criminal histories. As was the case with the data on conviction offenses, the data on criminal histories came out much as one would anticipate. In the total sample, the most commonly committed crime was theft (listed as a crime they had done at least once by 80%), followed by burglary and assault (71% each), then robbery and drug dealing (52% each), then murder and rape (13 and 12%, respectively). Results of interest for each of the seven types of crime are as follows.

Assault

The lowest assault percentage in the table (48%) was registered by the Unarmed Criminals, with percentages in all other categories ranging upward from 75%. "Pride of place" (here and, for all practical purposes, everywhere in the table) went to the two more predatory categories, with 91% in each category claiming at least one prior assault. Most of the men who had ever done an assault had only done one or "a few," the percentage who claim more than "a few" amounting to 28% of the total sample. The low figures on "how often?" were found in the Unarmed, Improviser, and One-Time Firearms categories (13–15% of each category having done more than a few assaults); the high figures, of course, were registered by the Predators.

Overall, some two-thirds of the assaults reported by our sample involved some kind of weapon: Among the Unarmed category, the figure was just under a one-third and increased in a generally predictable fashion up

[5] As shown later, the Knife Criminals were generally more active and more violent on all counts than the One-Time Firearms Users. As with the Improvisors, the One-Timers appear to contain a fair-sized number of "criminals of passion," men who have committed only one serious crime. On all scores, of course, the Unarmed Criminals appear to be mainly "soft-core" criminals. The Improvisers and One-Timers are, as noted, often "criminals of passion," the two categories differing, one imagines, mainly in whether there was a firearm available in the "moment of rage." The Knife Criminals and Sporadic Handgun Users constitute yet a third package—more violent than the Improvisors and One-Time Firearms Users, but by no means the hardest of the "hard core." The hard-core violent criminals in the sample are heavily concentrated in the two Predator categories.

TABLE 3.2. Criminal Histories by Type

					Type			
	Total	Unarmed	Improviser	Knife	One-timer	Sporadic handgun	Handgun predator	Shoulder weapon
(N) =	(1874)	(725)	(79)	(134)	(257)	(257)	(321)	(101)
1. Ever do assault?								
Percentage "yes"	71	48	90	88	75	83	91	91
N "yes"	(1270)	(317)	(70)	(113)	(186)	(206)	(290)	(88)
If yes: How often?								
Percentage more than "a few"	28	14	13	25	15	28	54	44
If yes: Ever use weapon?								
Percentage "yes"	67	32	63	76	73	70	88	85
N "yes"	(817)	(94)	(43)	(84)	(131)	(141)	(251)	(73)
If armed: With what? (in percentage)[a]								
Handgun	52	20	2	10	58	56	78	61
Shoulder weapon	36	9	0	13	23	24	59	88
Any knife	67	38	19	99	37	70	83	88
Any "other"	92	73	116	81	45	87	120	111
2. Ever do burglary?								
Percentage "yes"	71	60	74	76	58	82	88	92
N "yes"	(1261)	(407)	(57)	(95)	(137)	(205)	(274)	(86)
If yes: How often?								
Percentage more than "a few"	40	22	33	41	27	46	68	49
If yes: Ever use weapon?								
Percentage "yes"	46	8	30	56	33	60	85	72
N "yes"	(545)	(30)	(16)	(50)	(43)	(119)	(228)	(59)
If armed: With what? (in percentage)[a]								
Handgun	70	41	7	12	49	80	92	57
Shoulder weapon	14	7	6	4	9	7	16	44
Any knife	70	47	25	98	60	69	72	76
Any "other"	28	30	63	42	28	26	22	36
3. Ever deal drugs?								
Percentage "yes"	52	33	47	54	44	60	85	73
N "yes"	(893)	(210)	(34)	(67)	(103)	(148)	(263)	(68)

(continued)

TABLE 3.2. Criminal Histories by Type (continued)

				Type				
	Total	Unarmed	Improviser	Knife	One-timer	Sporadic handgun	Handgun predator	Shoulder weapon
(N) =	(1874)	(725)	(79)	(134)	(257)	(257)	(321)	(101)
If yes: How often?								
Percentage more than "a few times"	59	47	50	60	47	55	74	69
If yes: Ever carry weapon?								
Percentage "yes"	62	21	34	62	46	69	92	85
N "yes"	(532)	(41)	(11)	(40)	(46)	(99)	(240)	(55)
If armed: With what? (in percentage)[a]								
Handgun	88	81	54	28	85	96	100	78
Shoulder weapon	32	17	36	18	8	20	35	69
Any knife	54	44	55	95	48	46	51	65
Any "other"	20	10	45	33	15	12	21	29
4. Ever kill someone?								
Percentage "yes"	13	2	14	11	14	13	33	34
N "yes"	(225)	(12)	(10)	(13)	(34)	(30)	(97)	(29)
If yes: How often?								
Percentage more than "once"	35	8	0	8	15	27	52	48
If yes: With what? (in percentage)[a]								
Handgun	61	46	20	8	71	70	72	46
Shoulder weapon	50	33	0	38	32	27	59	93
Any knife	32	17	10	92	18	47	27	34
Any "other"	30	17	90	46	9	17	33	34
5. Ever do rape?								
Percentage "yes"	12	10	11	20	9	13	17	18
N "yes"	(211)	(63)	(8)	(23)	(21)	(31)	(48)	(17)
If yes: How often?								
Percentage more than "once"	36	29	25	48	43	35	40	41
If yes: Ever use weapon?								
Percentage "yes"	36	7	38	86	50	45	33	53

68

	(73)	(4)	(3)	(19)	(10)	(13)	(16)	(8)
N "yes"								
If armed: With what? (in percentage)[a]								
Handgun	35	—[b]	—	5	40	33	75	—
Shoulder weapon	16	—	—	11	0	0	19	—
Any knife	66	—	—	116	60	54	50	—
Any "other"	23	—	—	16	20	15	6	—
6. Ever do robbery?								
Percentage "yes"	52	17	47	51	57	85	87	83
N "yes"	(907)	(111)	(34)	(62)	(137)	(213)	(274)	(76)
If yes: How often?								
Percentage more than "a few"	23	6	0	10	4	7	53	41
If yes: Ever use weapon?								
Percentage "yes"	87	26	78	82	93	96	98	97
N "yes"	(767)	(25)	(25)	(49)	(125)	(202)	(268)	(73)
If armed: With what? (in percentage)[a]								
Handgun	79	36	4	19	74	94	97	60
Shoulder weapon	38	8	8	8	20	22	55	95
Any knife	37	16	8	92	18	32	41	45
Any "other"	18	36	88	22	6	8	19	32
7. Ever do theft?								
Percentage "yes"	80	68	85	83	72	95	96	95
N "yes"	(1440)	(463)	(63)	(106)	(176)	(237)	(302)	(93)
If yes: How often?								
Percentage more than "a few"	48	31	44	39	30	49	84	66
If yes: Ever carry weapon?								
Percentage "yes"	42	4	32	37	35	62	79	73
N "yes"	(570)	(17)	(19)	(37)	(59)	(140)	(233)	(65)
If armed: With what? (in percentage)[a]								
Handgun	77	35	6	19	68	88	94	62
Shoulder weapon	31	0	11	3	20	16	39	78
Any knife	56	24	16	105	34	47	63	66
Any "other"	24	47	84	30	12	14	24	32

[a] Multiple responses are possible.
[b] N less than 10.

to the high figure, 88%, among Handgun Predators. Among the 725 Unarmed Criminals, there were 94 men (13%) who had committed at least one armed assault, an apparent inconsistency. However, a further check on the types of weapons employed by these 94 showed the distribution to be dominated by the "other weapon" category—beer bottles, two-by-fours, and other "weapons" that happened to be at hand. It would be debatable, therefore, whether these were truly "armed crimes" in the usual sense of the term.

Excepting the result for the Unarmed Criminals, the other data on weapons used in assault came out precisely as one would expect. Essentially, all of the Improvisers who had ever done an armed assault, for example, used some sort of improvised weapon for the purpose. (To be sure, here as in all cases, a few of them had assaulted with other weapons as well.) Likewise, virtually all of the Knife Criminals who had ever done an armed assault used a knife to do so; 78% of the Handgun Predators had done at least one handgun assault; and 88% of the Shotgun Predators had committed at least one shotgun assault. The choice of assault weapons, in other words, was highly consistent with the categories of our typology.

The use of multiple weapon types in committing assault bears a special emphasis, especially among the more predatory categories. Among the Handgun Predators who had ever done an armed assault (and 78% of them had), 78% had, as noted above, used a handgun in at least one of them. About three-fifths, however, had also committed assaults with shoulder weapons, some 83% with a knife, and all of them had done at least one assault with some "other" weapon. In this sense, the phrase, "Handgun Predator," is somewhat misleading: They turn out to be, in essence (here and everywhere else in the table), omnibus weapons abusers. The same, of course, can be said of the Shotgun Predators: Nearly 90% of those who had done any armed assault had done at least one with a shoulder weapon, but 61% had also committed a handgun asault, about 90% had also done at least one knife assault, and virtually all had committed at least one assault with some "other" weapon.[6]

---

[6] The question about ever having done an assault was followed by an extensive series asking for details. Among those who had ever done an assault ($N = 1270$), about 18% had done only one; the modal response to "how often?" was "a few times" (50%); about 3% of the sample had done "hundreds" of them. Just under one-quarter of the assaulters in the sample affirmed that at least one of their assaults had been directed against a family member; 57% affirmed that at least one had involved "friends or acquaintances." The typical victim, however, was a stranger; 81% of the assaulters in the sample reported at least one assault on someone they "didn't really know." These general patterns were roughly the same for the assaulters in each of our seven categories.

We also asked where these assaults occurred. The most common response was "out in public," mentioned by 66%, followed in order by "in a bar or tavern" (59%),

Burglary

Burglary was a fairly common crime in all categories of the typology, the burglary percentages ranging from 60 (among the Unarmed) to 92% (among Shotgun Predators). Except for theft, burglary was the most common crime among the Unarmed Criminals. As always, the highest burglary percentages were registered by the Predators, some 90% of whom had done at least one burglary. They were also the more active burglars: 68% of the Handgun Predators who had ever done burglary had done more than "a few" of them and likewise for 49% of the Shotgun Predators—these being the two highest values shown in the table. Thus, relative to the others, the Predators were more likely to do burglaries and more likely to do lots of them; they were also the most likely, by far, to have been armed while doing them. It would thus appear that many of the burglaries these men committed may have been "burglaries" only accidentally; had anyone been around at the time, they might well have been robberies instead.

The weapons carried during burglaries were much as one would expect. Most armed burglars carried a handgun and a knife, but then, most armed burglars were Handgun Predators by our definition, and their pattern, therefore, dominates the results for the total sample. In general, burglars who went armed carried the weapons they would be expected to carry given their placement within the categories of our typology.

Drug Dealing

One-half the sample had dealt drugs at least once: The Unarmed were the least likely to have done so (33%), and the Handgun Predators were the most likely (85%), followed by the Shotgun Predators (73%). The Predators were also the most likely to have done so more than "a few times" and the most likely to have carried a weapon in the process. About 90% of the Predators who dealt in drugs did so armed, virtually always with one or another firearm.

"in school" (56%), "in somebody else's house or apartment" (46%), and in the respondent's own house or apartment (39%). In all cases, the Predators reported the highest values: Among the Predators who had done at least one assault, for example, over 70% reported at least one of them to have occurred in a bar or tavern. We also asked the assaulters in the sample whether they had ever "seriously hurt anybody" in the course of their assaults. In the total sample, only 18% answered "no." Well over 90% of the Predator assaulters claimed to have seriously hurt someone during one or more of their assaults. About 21% of the assaulters also affirmed that there was "a chance" that someone had died as a result of the assault(s), a figure that varies from 7% of the assaulters in the Unarmed category up to 39% of the assaulters in the Handgun Predator category.

Criminal Homicide

Of the total sample, 13% claimed to have killed somebody at least once in their lives, a figure that varied from 2% of the Unarmed up to one-third of both predator categories. One-half the Predators who had ever killed someone claimed to have done so more than once, by far the highest percentage recorded. Most of the homicide perpetrators in the sample (61%) claimed to have used a handgun for the purpose, but one-half also claimed to have used a shoulder weapon at least once. As in previous cases, the choice of homicide weapons across categories was generally consistent with the typology.

The heavy concentration of homicide within the Predator categories warrants emphasis. By these men's own admission, there were 225 homicide offenders in our sample—men who had killed at least once. Of the 225, 56% were in one of the two Predator categories, and if the Sporadic Handgun Users were added, the figure would rise to about 70%. In the categories in question, homicide, which is often depicted as a unique sort of crime, appears to be merely one more aspect of a generally violent and criminal life.

The multiple homicide offenders in our sample (men who had killed more than once) were also heavily concentrated in the two predatory categories. All told, our sample contained 79 men who claimed to have committed murder more than once, and 81% of them were in these two classes.

Rape

Rape was the only crime among the seven we asked about where the Predators did not lead the field. Overall, 12% of the sample had raped at least once, a figure that varied from 9 (among the One-Time Firearms Users) to 20% (among the Knife Criminals). The concentration of rapists in the knife category was remarked upon earlier in discussing conviction offenses. The rape percentages in the Predator categories were only slightly below that of the Knife Criminals—approximately 17–18%.

In the total sample, 36% of the men who had ever raped had done so more than once; among the Knife Criminal rapists, the figure was 48%, by far the highest value shown. About one-third of the rapes committed by the sample involved some sort of weapon; and again, the Knife Criminal rapists turned out to be a distinctive group, some 90% of them having used a weapon. The tendency of Handgun Predators not to use weapons while committing rape is perhaps a noteworthy finding (only one-third of them reported a weapons involvement), but the sample size at this point is too small to draw any firm conclusions.

Robbery

One-half the sample had done at least one robbery; and of those who had done at least one, about one-quarter had done more than "a few." The Unarmed Criminals were the least likely to have committed robbery and Handgun Predators, the most likely. Predictably, the Predators were also the most active robbers, with 40–50% of them reporting more than "a few" robberies. Excepting the Unarmed, almost everyone in the sample who had committed robbery used a weapon for the purpose, with percentages ranging from 78 to 98%. The weapons used in committing robberies were as one would expect: The Improvisers used improvised weapons (88%), the Knife Criminals used knives (92%), and the Firearms Criminals used firearms primarily but were also more likely than the other catgegories to carry multiple robbery weapons.

Theft

Theft was the most common of the seven crimes asked about; some four-fifths of the total sample had committed at least one theft. (The question asked whether the man had ever stolen something worth more than $50.) As in almost every other case, the Unarmed showed the lowest theft percentage, and the Predators showed the highest. The Predators were also the most active thieves: In the total, about one-half the men who had ever done theft had done more than "a few," while among the Handgun Predators, the figure was 84%. Our Predators also carried weapons while doing thefts, much more so than any other category. In fact, as becomes increasingly obvious, the Predators tended to do every conceivable kind of crime and to be armed more or less constantly.

"Total Criminality"

The detailed criminal history information just summarized is, at best, cumbersome to work with; it proves useful to combine all the information into a single "total criminality" index. The idea, basically, is to convert each man's past criminal activities into a single variable that can be more efficiently analyzed than the item-by-item results.

Obviously, such a variable has to take into account not only the kinds of crimes each man has done in his career, but their relative seriousness and frequency. Under this viewpoint, a man who has killed once is "more criminal" than a man who committed a single theft, and the man who has done two homicides is "more criminal" than the man who has done only one. An obvious approach is to weight each crime type asked about in the criminal history section by its relative seriousness, multiply the relative seriousness by the frequency with which the crime was committed, then, finally, sum the resulting scores across crime types.

As discussed above, the criminal history questions asked about seven major crime types: assault, burglary, drug dealing, homicide, rape, robbery, and theft. Seriousness scores for each of these seven crime types were derived from recent work published by Wolfgang (1980)[7] in which a national sample of Americans was asked to rate the seriousness of a large number of different crimes. Wolfgang's scores were used to weight the frequencies recorded for each of the seven crime types. Table 3.3 shows the

[7] In the Wolfgang study, literally hundreds of "incidents" were included; in our data, questions dealt exclusively with broad categories of crime types. In order to assign seriousness scores to our crime types, we simply took every incident from the Wolfgang list that represented one of the types of crime, then averaged over the seriousness scores reported for all those incidents (see Table 3.3). To illustrate, there were 15 different "incidents" in the Wolfgang list that we determined to be "assaults," with seriousness scores ranging from 135 to 543. Since our question asks only about "assaults," with no further details, we can therefore derive an average "seriousness score" for the crime of assault by averaging the Wolfgang scores for the 15 assault incidents contained in his study. Table 3.3 records the results of this work: For each crime, it shows (1) the number of "incidents" on which the average for the crime type was based; (2) the minimum and maximum seriousness scores within the set of incidents; and (3) the calculated arithmetic average, the latter being the specific numerical weight we used in creating the Total Criminality Index. In general, the resulting averages are quite consistent with most other "crime seriousness" measures.

The next step was to convert the response options used in the criminal history section to numerical frequencies. With the exception of homicide, this conversion was as follows: If the man said he had never done the crime in question or if he simply did not answer the question, he was given a "0" for the frequency measure. If he responded "just once" or if he indicated in the initial question that he had done the crime but was missing data on how often, he was given a frequency score of "1." For the remaining response categories, the conversions were as follows: "a few times" = 5 times; "maybe ten or fifteen times" = 10 times; "dozens of times" = 25 times; and "hundreds of times" = 100 times. The response options for the homicide question were slightly different and were handled as follows: "no, never" or missing data = 0 times; "just once" or "yes" but no answer to the "how often?" question = 1 time; "a few times" = 5 times; and "many times" = 10 times.

The final step was to multiply the seriousness score for each crime type by the frequency with which the man had committed that crime type and then to sum the resulting scores over the seven crime types. Theoretically, the resulting sum can vary from 0 (the score a man would receive if he never committed any of the seven crimes in question) to 166,450 (the score a man would receive if he had done "hundreds" of every crime but homicide and "many" homicides.)

Empirically, 136 "zero" scores were observed, a plausible result since many of the men in the sample will have never committed any of the crimes asked about in the sequence; and the highest score observed for any single man was 129,299—some 78% of the maximum possible value. (Five men obtained scores over 100,000.) To avoid any further dealings with ludicrously large numbers, our final measure of total criminality is the score discussed above divided by 100.

TABLE 3.3. Derived "Seriousness Scores" for Seven Types of Crime[a]

Crime	Number of incidents	Minimum seriousness	Maximum seriousness	Average seriousness
Burglary	14	61	212	125
Theft	15	38	239	128
Robbery	22	112	460	249
Assault	15	135	543	271
Drug dealing	5	187	452	304
Rape	4	369	657	508
Murder	5	611	946	795

[a]See Fn. 7 for details on the entries in this table.

TABLE 3.4. "Total Criminality" by Type

	$\overline{X}$	SD	Sum	Percentage of total sum
Unarmed	61	113	44,011	17
Improvisers	101	140	8,005	3
Knife criminals	109	129	14,560	6
One-timer	84	136	21,677	8
Sporadic	151	158	38,773	15
Handgun predators	332	232	106,453	41
Shotgun predators	265	269	26,807	10
Total	139	190	260,286	100

seriousness scores that were used in weighting the crimes committed by men in the sample.

Table 3.4 shows the means and standard deviations of the resulting Total Criminality Index, first for the total sample then separately for each of the seven categories of the typology. The numbers do not have any intuitively obvious meaning except that the higher the Total Criminality Index, the more serious and more frequent was the total set of crimes admitted by the felon.

The overall sample mean was 139. As would be expected, the lowest category mean was found for the Unarmed Criminals (mean = 61), followed, interestingly, by the One-Time Firearms Users (mean = 84). Judging from the "total criminality" result, these two categories contained mostly "soft-core" felons—men who had committed fewer crimes and less serious crimes than the others.

The Improvisers (mean = 101) and the Knife Criminals (mean = 109) formed a second distinctive cluster—clearly more criminal overall than the Unarmed and the One-Timers, but well below the remaining categories.

Then, about midway between this last set of categories and the truly high-rate felons, one finds the Sporadic Handgun Users (mean = 151).

Finally, there are the Predators, whose scores were sharply higher than the scores obtained in any of the other categories. Among the Shotgun Predators, the mean = 265, and among the Handgun Predators, who are clearly the most active and most violent of them all, the mean = 332. As was apparent in the item-by-item results, the men we have labeled Predators were clearly omnibus felons—men who, one imagines, committed more or less any crime they had the opportunity to commit.

As shown in the third column of the table, the sum of the "total criminality" index over the entire sample was about 260,000. The percentage of this total sum accounted for by each of the seven categories is shown in the fourth column. The Unarmed Criminals amounted to about 39% of the total sample but accounted for only 17% of the total crime this sample has committed. The Predators (handgun and shotgun combined), in contrast, amounted to about 22% of the sample and yet accounted for 51% of the total crime. If one adds the Sporadics in, we are dealing with just over one-third of the total sample and just under two-thirds of the total crime. Thus, when we talk about "controlling crime" in the United States today, we are talking largely about controlling the behavior of these men.

The distinctiveness of the Predators can be seen in yet another way. In the well-known RAND study of criminal careers (Chaiken and Chaiken, 1982), a category of criminal was isolated and given the label "violent predator"—obviously quite similar to our Predator categories. The RAND category was defined by the crimes of assault, robbery, and drug dealing. Response categories to the relevant questions in our study were very different from those employed in the RAND survey, making it impossible to duplicate the RAND typology exactly. However, we can locate the subset of our sample that had done more than "a few" robberies, more than "a few" assaults, and more than "a few" drug deals. As it happens, there were 90 men in our sample who had done more than "a few" of all three types of crime, of whom 84 fell into one of the two Predator categories. (Three of the remaining six were Sporadic Handgun Users by our definition; none of the other categories had more than one apiece.) Among these 90, incidentally, the average score on the Total Criminality Index was 573, and thus, these 90 men alone (representing only 5% of the sample) accounted for nearly 20% of the total crime committed by the sample. It is, we think, fairly obvious that RAND's "violent predators" and our Handgun and Shotgun Predators are, in the main, the same kinds of people.

It is also clear from the materials presented in this chapter that the Predators were not criminal "specialists" in any sense of the word. They were, instead, what we can refer to as omnibus felons—men prone to commit virtually any kind of crime available in the environment for them to commit. Thus, excepting rape, they were the most likely to have done each of the crimes we asked about, the most likely to have done each of them more than a few times, and the most likely to have been armed when they did it. Clearly, these men were criminal "opportunists," the hardest of the hard-core, the so-called career criminals who contribute so disproportionally to the American crime problem.

4

PATTERNS OF WEAPONS OWNERSHIP AND USE: ON THE CIRCUMSTANCES OF CRIMINAL VIOLENCE

Americans use firearms in many ways in the pursuit of a variety of ends. In this respect, felons resemble other Americans, although their mix of purposes tends to be markedly different from that of their fellow citizens. As we see in this chapter, many felons use guns in legitimate as well as illegitimate applications. Although many of the prisoners we interviewed had used guns in their crimes, many gun-owning felons had not. And even those who had used guns in their crimes also used them for other purposes as well. In short, firearms ownership and use are not all "of a piece" even among the criminal population.

It also proves useful to look closely at how weapons are actually used in crimes. In some cases, weapons are used instrumentally, to intimidate prospective victims; in others, weapons may be present "just in case," to be used only if circumstances appear to demand it. The actual patterns of criminal gun use prove to be complicated and diverse. Understanding them will lead, one hopes, to better ideas about how to cope with the policy issues involved.

OVERALL PATTERNS OF OWNERSHIP AND USE

To obtain a proper perspective on prisoners' use of firearms, we begin by describing the general patterns of firearms ownership and use among the overall sample, as background to the more extended discussion of *criminal* aspects of gun ownership and use that follows. Relevant data are shown in Table 4.1. As indicated, three-quarters of the men in the sample had owned one or more firearms at some time in their lives. This amounts to just over 1300 men, the subsample on which all the rest of this section is based. A little more than one-half (57%) owned a gun at the time of their last arrest.[1]

[1] It is worth a note that nearly one-half of the men in the sample who did not own a gun at the time they were last arrested but were armed, nonetheless, during that offense, were armed with some sort of firearm. Clearly, one does not need actually to own a gun in order to carry a gun during one's crimes: In many cases, these firearms would have been borrowed from friends and associates or stolen during the crime, etc.

TABLE 4.1. General Ownership and Use of Firearms: Total Sample
(in Percentages)

1. Have you personally ever owned or possessed any kind of gun?
   No   25
   Yes   75
   (N)   (1732)
2. [If yes] About how many firearms, altogether, have you ever owned or possessed?
   1   (1)[a]   15
   2–3   (2.5)   27
   4–5   (4.5)   15
   6–10 (8)   10
   11+   (13)   33
   (N) =   (1123)
   Mean =   6.6 guns
3. [If yes to (1)] Ever owned a handgun?
   No   13
   Yes   87
   (N) =   (1184)
4. [If yes to (1)]: Did you own a gun when you were last arrested?
   No   43
   Yes   57
   (N) =   (1169)
   What kind was it?

	Yes	*(N)* =
Handgun	78	(659)
Rifle	34	(658)
Shotgun	44	(660)

5. [If yes to (3)]: How many handguns have you ever owned?
   1   (1)[a]   17
   2–3   (2.5)   28
   4–5   (4.5)   14
   6–10 (8)   13
   11+   (13)   29
   (N) =   (951)
   Mean =   6.2 handguns
6. [If yes to (1)]: Ever owned a rifle?
   No   24
   Yes   76
   (N) =   (1176)
   A shotgun?
   No   23
   Yes   77
   (N) =   (1170)
7. [If yes to (1)]: Did you ever register any of your guns with the police or authorities?
   No   75
   Yes   25
   (N) =   (1164)

(continued)

Did you ever apply for a permit to purchase or carry?

No	85
Yes	15
(N)=	(1166)

8. [If yes to (1)]: When you had a gun, did you usually keep it loaded or unloaded?

Loaded	61
Unloaded	39
(N)=	(1172)

9. [If yes to (1)]: Did you ever get a gun specifically for use in crimes?

No	72
Yes	28
(N)=	(1169)

10. [If yes to (1)]: Except during military service, did you ever threaten to shoot someone with any of your guns?

No, never	51
Yes, one time	15
Yes, a few times	27
Yes, many times	6
(N)=	(1152)

11. [If yes to (1)]: Except during military service, have you ever actually fired a gun at somebody?

No, never	50
Yes, one time	21
Yes, a few times	23
Yes, many times	6
(N)=	(1146)

12. [If yes to (1)]: Which of the following best describes the situation(s) in which you fired a gun at somebody?

	Yes	(N)=
During a gang fight	32	(563)
During a family fight	8	(562)
In a bar or tavern	27	(563)
To protect myself	66	(563)
Someone breaking into my home	14	(561)
While committing a crime	39	(561)
While leaving scene of a crime	29	(561)
During a drug deal	29	(561)
Shootout with police	17	(559)
On my job	6	(556)

13. [If yes to (1)]: Did you ever actually wound a person by shooting them with a gun?

No	31
Yes, once	37
Yes, a few times	27
Yes, many times	5
(N)=	(557)

14. [If yes to (13)]: Were you trying to wound them (or kill them) or was it an accident?

Trying	80
Accidental	20
(N)=	(372)

(continued)

TABLE 4.1. General Ownership and Use of Firearms: Total Sample
(in Percentages) (*continued*)

---

15. [If yes to (1)]: Before you came to this prison, about how often would you say
    you fired your gun?

Never	10
Once a year	8
A few times a year	25
About once a month	8
A few times a month	18
About every week	13
More than once a week	18
(N) =	(1099)

16. [If "once a year" or more to (15)]: Which of the following best describes the
    situation in which you *usually* fired your gun?

In self-defense	14
While hunting	17
Target shooting	35
At a gun club, range	3
Multiple "legal" response	19
During a crime	11
(N) =	(974)

---

[a] The numbers in parentheses show the category midpoints used to calculate the
reported averages.

It is difficult to compare this level of gun ownership with existing data
on the general American population. National household surveys have been
the major source of data on civilian gun ownership and have consistently
shown that about one-half of all households own at least one firearm (Wright,
Rossi, and Daly, 1983). Unfortunately, these surveys typically ask about guns
in possession of *households* at the *time of the survey*. In contrast, our prisoners were interviewed as *individuals* and asked whether they had *ever
owned* a firearm *at any time* in their lives. It is certainly conceivable that a
national survey of adult men that asked about gun ownership over entire
lifetimes would also find some three-quarters responding yes.

A possibly more appropriate comparison with the American population
in general can be made by considering the proportion of prisoners who
claimed to have personally owned a firearm at the time of their arrest (57%).
Since 1980, the National Opinion Research Center's General Social Surveys have included an approximately comparable question on individual
(versus household) gun ownership. According to Gary Kleck (personal
communication), these data show a rate of gun ownership of 23% among
black males age 18–39, and a rate of 49% among white males in the same
age categories. (To emphasize, these figures are for *personal*, not household, ownership.) If we weight these ownership figures according to the
racial distribution of the prisoners in the sample, we get a predicted rate of
gun ownership among our felons of 37%, versus the observed rate of 57%.

Based on these comparisons, we would conclude that felons are substantially more likely to own guns than their counterparts in the civilian population. (Even this comparison is, of course, imprecise. A more precise comparison would require further adjustments for city size, social class or income, and possibly other factors. These data, in short, *suggest* a higher than average rate of gun ownership among felons, but the result is by no means definitive.)

There are some ways, however, in which prisoners were inarguably different from the general civilian population. Of those who owned a gun at the point of last arrest, most (78%) owned a handgun, some 34% owned a rifle, and 44% owned a shotgun. Handgun ownership thus appears to be proportionally more widespread among prisoners than among the general population, in which perhaps one-half the households who own any guns own handguns.

In addition, prisoners appear to have owned larger numbers of guns than their civilian counterparts (although this, too, is by no means certain). Men in the sample who had ever owned guns tended to have owned them in what appears to be fairly large numbers. Indeed, the modal number of guns of all types ever owned was "more than 10," and the average (mean) number ever owned among those having owned at least one was 6.6 firearms. This can be loosely contrasted with the average number of guns owned among all U.S. families owning at least one gun, which is about 3.2 firearms (Wright, Rossi, and Daly, 1983: 40). This comparison is only a rough one because the data from national surveys pertain to ownership at the time of the survey and not over the entire lifetime of the household. Nevertheless, it suggests that gun-owning criminals tend to own guns in rather large numbers.[2]

Gun-owning criminals were also much more likely ever to have owned handguns than gun-owning families at large. Available data suggest that about one-quarter of all U.S. families, and thus about one-half of all gun-owning families, possess at least one handgun (Wright, Rossi, and Daly, 1983: Chs. 2–5); among the men in our sample who had ever owned any firearm, 87% had owned at least one handgun.

[2] Our question asks each man how many guns he has ever owned; the survey estimate of 3.2 firearms per gun-owning U.S. household is based on a question about the number of guns presently owned. It is certainly conceivable, and perhaps even rather likely, that the average number of guns ever owned among U.S. families owning at least one of them is on the order of 6 or 7 guns (or possibly more), in which case the average number ever owned among the men in our sample would be about average for gun-owning households. So far as we know, however, no national survey has ever asked gun-owning families about the number of firearms they have ever owned, so no precise comparison between our results and comparable national results is possible. The only safe conclusion would be that gun-owning felons tend to own guns at a rate that is at least as high as the rate among all U.S. gun owners in general.

As with firearms in general, these men also tended to have owned handguns in large numbers: again, the modal response to the "how many handguns" question was "more than 10" and the mean number owned among those ever owning at least 1 was 6.2 handguns. More than three-quarters of those ever owning any firearm had also owned at least 1 shotgun and a similiar proportion had owned at least 1 rifle. The general picture that emerges here is that our prisoners were a heavily armed group; their tendency, clearly, was to have owned all types of firearms and to have owned fairly large numbers of them.[3]

By definition, our prisoners were not law-abiding citizens. Hence, there was little reason to anticipate that their weapons ownership would be "within the law." In at least some of the states in our sample, gun-registration laws were in effect. But few of the prisoners had ever registered their guns with authorities or applied for purchase or ownership permits. Men who had ever owned a gun were asked whether they had ever registered any of their guns with police or other authorities and also whether they had ever applied for a permit to purchase or carry their guns. The strong majority response was "no" in both cases (75% had never registered a gun, and 85% had never applied for a permit to purchase or carry). In general, the tendency not to have done these things was about the same in every state, regardless of state laws mandating one or the other of these measures.

Most of the gun owners in the sample (61%) made it a practice to keep their gun(s) loaded at all times; how this compares with normal practice among legitimate gun owners is unknown. In any event, being armed also meant keeping their guns "at the ready."

Of course, the crucial way in which felons differed from other gun owners is that many of them had used their guns in the commission of crimes. Although only 28% of the gun owners in the felon sample said that they had ever acquired a gun *specifically* for use in crime, it may be assumed that this proportion is much higher than in the general civilian population(!) But this finding also has another and somewhat more interesting implication: Since at least one half of the men in the sample had committed at least one gun crime at some point in their lives, it follows directly that many of the firearms that are ultimately used in crime are not acquired specifically for that purpose.

Whatever the reasons for acquisition, however, we saw in the previous

[3] Again, the comparisons reported in the text are hardly exact. A more exact comparison would be between the rate of handgun ownership observed in our sample and the rate of handgun ownership among a sample of predominantly central city men of equivalent age, background, and social circumstance. So far as we know, the appropriate data for such a comparison have never been published. So here, too, we are left with the *impression* that the rate of handgun ownership among the gun owners in our sample is higher than the norm, but we are unable to confirm this impression.

chapter that many of these men had used their guns to commit crimes. Indeed, many had used them in ways that directly threatened bodily harm to other persons: Almost one-half (49%) of the gun owners admitted to having threatened to shoot someone with one of their guns at some time. Apparently, these were not idle threats either: One-half of the sample also claimed to have actually fired their guns at human targets at some time. A cross-tabulation of these two items showed that among those who had ever threatened to shoot someone, 75% actually did.

Men who indicated that they had actually fired a gun at somebody (military service excluded) were asked about the circumstances in which this took place. The most common response by far, mentioned by 66%, was "to protect myself."[4] What this response actually means is far from clear: It doubtlessly covers diverse circumstances ranging from those in which the felon himself acted with some degree of aggression to those in which he was attacked without provocation by someone else. A robber who fires his weapon at the police in order to prevent his own arrest has most assuredly "protected" himself but certainly not in the usual sense. (On the self-protection theme, see also Chapters 6 and 7.)

The next most common circumstance for firing a gun at somebody was "while committing a crime" (noted by 39%), followed by "during a gang fight" (32%), while leaving the scene of a crime (29%), during a drug deal (29%), and "in a bar or tavern" (27%). All other possibilities were noted by 20% or less.

Men who indicated that they had fired a gun at someone were asked whether they had managed to inflict a wound in the process; most (69%) had. And of those who managed to inflict a wound, 80% said they had intended to do so; accidental woundings were indicated in only 20% of the relevant cases.

In short, although the typical gun-owning criminal in our sample claimed not to have acquired his weapons for the primary purpose of committing crimes with them, he nevertheless managed in many cases to do so, even to the point of threatening or committing felonious assaults. Given the evident lifestyles of the men in this sample and the likely etiology of the as-

---

[4] In contrast, available survey data suggest that the proportion of the entire U.S. adult population that has ever actually fired a gun in self-defense is on the order of 2–6% (Wright, Rossi, and Daly, 1983: 148). Since this is a result for the total adult population, the appropriate comparative figure from our survey is the proportion of our sample who has ever owned a gun (75%) times the proportion of those who have ever fired one at somebody (50%) times the proportion of those who say they fired "to protect myself" (66%), or about 25% of the total sample. (More directly, we have 373 men in the sample who say they have fired a gun at somebody "to protect myself," and this amounts to just 20% of the total sample, all missing data included.) Thus, firing a gun at somebody "in self-defense" is at least 4 times more common, and perhaps as much as 10–12 times more common, among our sample than among the adult population at large.

saults involved, the distinction between aggression and self-protection is obviously muddled.

Finally, we asked our gun owners how often they fired their guns. One-tenth responded "never," and another one-third said only once or a few times a year. On the other hand, the majority (57%) fired their gun(s) once a month or more, on the average; and almost one-fifth fired them several times a week. It would be useful to compare these results with comparable data on legitimate firearms owners, but the relevant data do not exist. Our informal impression is that these men tend to have fired their guns at something more than the average rate, but this is only a conjecture.[5]

It would be wrong to infer from the above results that all or even most of these firings involved some sort of criminal activity. Much if not most of the gun firing that these men did would qualify as sporting or recreational. Indeed, the most common situation in which their guns were fired was "target shooting, plinking" (35%), hunting (17%), or a combination of target shooting and hunting (19%). Adding "at a gun club or shooting range" to the above three responses, sporting and recreational usage accounted for nearly three-quarters of the gun firing in this sample. The remaining one-quarter was divided nearly equally between firing "in self-defense" (14%) and firing during the course of a crime (11%). Like other men of similar age and circumstances, these men clearly used firearms rather frequently in sport and recreational applications; unlike other men, they also sometimes used them for illicit criminal purposes as well, and it is to this latter usage that we now turn attention.

---

[5] Newton and Zimring (1969: 5) report that there were about 4.4 billion rounds of ammunition manufactured in 1967. In the same year, there were about 80–100 million firearms in private hands in the United States. Simple division therefore suggests about 50 rounds fired per weapon per year on the average. This may be a high estimate, since a lot of the manufactured ammunition (exact percentage unknown) would have gone to military or police use. On the other hand, it may be a low estimate since it would include neither surplus military ammunition nor hand-loaded ammunition. In any case, it would not be uncommon to go through 40 or 50 rounds in a single plinking or target-shooting session. Given these numbers, it is therefore conceivable that the "typical" private firearm is taken out and actually fired no more than about once or twice a year on the average. It is also likely that the actual distribution of gun-firings is sharply bimodal, with a large fraction of the total number of guns never being fired and another fraction being fired quite regularly. All this, to emphasize, is sheer speculation.

The rate at which our felons said they fired their guns may seem implausibly high, particularly given results reported later concerning the kinds of guns they tended to own (typically, large caliber, well-made weapons) and the price of ammunition for these firearms. Unfortunately, we did not probe for much detail on this point. As noted below in the text, the most common circumstance for firing a gun was "target shooting." This would presumably include, in addition to the usual things, such practices as firing at road signs from cars or motorcycles and other similar firearms practices that would tend to drive the average rate of firing upward.

PATTERNS OF WEAPONS USE: THE CONVICTION OFFENSE

As indicated in the previous chapter, we asked for considerable details concerning the weapons these men carried during their conviction offense; results from these questions are discussed in this section. As background, we begin with some of the circumstances of the conviction crime itself. According to their own reports (see Chapter 2), about 39% of the men in the sample were unemployed or looking for work at the time of their conviction crime; almost one-half (49%) were either "broke" or "short on money"; and substantially more than one-half (57%) were either drunk, high on drugs, or both. Only about one-quarter were "worried about getting caught."

Although 61% of our sample had committed at least one armed crime at some point in their criminal careers, only 54% were actually armed during the crime for which they were then in prison. This 54% amounts to 810 men who admitted to carrying a weapon during their conviction offense, the subsample on which most of the following analysis is based.

Men who were either drunk or high on drugs during their conviction crime ($N = 840$) were slightly more likely to also have been armed during that crime (57%) than those who were neither high nor drunk ($N = 669$; 50% were armed). On the other hand, among those who were armed during the conviction offense, the pharmacologically impaired were less likely than the others to have been armed with a firearm (67 versus 78%). Further analyses revealed no interesting or significant differences in the uses of the firearm in the conviction crime according to whether the felon was or was not drunk or high on drugs.

Differences in the tendency to have been armed during the conviction offense across the categories of our Armed Criminals typology were discussed briefly in Chapter Three (see Table 3.2). The fraction armed during the conviction crime varied from a low of about three-fifths among the Improvisers to a high of about four-fifths in the more predatory groups.

As we document later, the truly predatory felons in our sample were distinguished from other felons by their habit of carrying a weapon more or less all the time. Clearly, a man who is constantly armed will be armed, by definition, during any offense he commits. The rather higher proportions armed during the conviction crime among the more predatory groups is not, therefore, an indication that they were more likely to have been committing (at the time) a crime for which some weapon was needed, but rather a result of their tendency to have carried weapons on a regular basis, whether they were planning to do crimes or not (see below, "Additional Details on Weapons Carrying Behavior").

Whether a felon was armed during the conviction crime, of course, did depend to some extent on the kind of crime committed: Data on the proportions armed according to conviction offense are shown in Table 4.2.

TABLE 4.2. Percentages Armed during Conviction Offense, by
Conviction Offense (in Percentages)

| | Armed with a weapon | | |
Crime	Yes	No	(N = 100%)
Arson	42	58	(19)
Simple assault	58	42	(52)
Aggravated assault, ADW	85	15	(212)
Auto theft	50	50	(105)
Burglary, B + E	41	59	(369)
Counterfeiting	50	50	(8)
Drug possession	45	55	(101)
Drug dealing	43	57	(80)
Forgery	25	75	(67)
Fraud, swindle	42	58	(12)
Kidnapping	64	36	(66)
Homicide	78	22	(192)
Manslaughter	83	17	(41)
Possession stolen property	52	48	(73)
Rape	42	58	(122)
Other sex offense	21	79	(82)
Robbery	78	22	(478)
Theft, larceny	52	48	(155)
Weapons charge	83	17	(174)

Much of the information contained in the table is almost redundant: We should not be surprised to learn, for example, that 83% of the men in the sample doing time on a weapons charge were armed with a weapon when they committed that offense! (Indeed, what may be surprising is that 17% claimed that they were not armed, a reflection, possibly, of errors in reporting either their conviction charges or their weapons carrying.) The reported percentages for aggravated assault (85%), manslaughter and homicide (83 and 78%, respectively), and robbery (78%) are also to be expected given that so many of these crimes involve the use of weapons.

Table 4.2 also shows, however, a great deal of weapons carrying in crimes that do not necessarily require weapons to complete successfully, for example, auto theft (50% armed at the time), drug possession or sales (43–45% armed at the time), theft (52% armed), receipt of stolen property (52% armed), or burglary (41% armed).

The pattern shown for burglary is of special note and is indicative of the tendency of many of these men to have carried weapons at all times; the result suggests that perhaps two-fifths of all burglaries would have had high probabilities of turning into robberies if anyone had been at home at the time to confront the intruder. It is also worth mentioning that 58% of the men doing time on simple assault had in fact been armed when the assault in question occurred, suggesting a degree of self-restraint (or, possibly, the effects of plea bargaining) among at least some small share of the sample. (On the other hand, the armed "simple assaulters" amount in total to only 30 men.)

The handgun was, by far, the weapon of choice among those armed during the conviction offense. All told, 60% of these men ($N = 796$) were armed with a handgun at the time. About 15% were armed with sawed-off equipment; 11% were armed with regular (not sawed-off) shoulder weapons. About 40% carried a knife during the conviction offense; another 16% were armed with some other weapon (e.g., straight razor, brass knuckles, explosives, martial arts weapons).

As is obvious from the total of the percentages reported above, the carrying of multiple weapons during the conviction offense was a fairly common practice. Of the 789 men who answered all the questions about the kinds of weapons carried during the conviction crime, 25% reported carrying more than one weapon, a handgun and a knife being the most common combination. (Almost 10% reported carrying three or more weapons during the conviction offense.) As would be expected, the tendency to carry multiple weapons was especially pronounced among the Predator groups, among whom 43% were armed with more than one weapon during their conviction crime. (Among the Sporadics, the figure was about 20%; and in the other categories of the typology, on the order of 10% or less.)

Given this pattern of multiple-weapons carrying, there is some ambiguity in sorting the sample out into firearms and non-firearms criminals. If, however, we give precedence to the carrying of a firearm (as in the development of the typology), then about three-quarters (72%) of the men who were armed during the conviction offense were armed with a firearm of one sort or another (even if they were also armed with something else), and the remaining one-quarter (28%) were armed with something other than a firearm. The cross-tabulation of this variable with other items from the conviction offense sequence is shown in Table 4.3.

Men who had been armed with a firearm during the conviction offense were asked whether the gun was actually fired during the crime. Surprisingly, nearly two-fifths (39%) responded "yes," which suggests (among other things) a notable readiness to use the weapon(s) being carried. Details on the actual firing of guns during the conviction offense are discussed later. Of course, these gun firings during the conviction crime may be one of the reasons why these felons appear in our sample in the first place, since the noise of firing might have raised probability of being apprehended, and the act of firing, the probability of being convicted and sent to prison. (The result, in other words, may not generalize to the population of armed crime incidents.)

Another question in the sequence asked whether the felon brought his weapon(s) with him to the scene of the crime or whether the weapon(s) had been acquired at the scene. Indirectly, these findings address, to some

TABLE 4.3. Weapons Use in Conviction Offenses (in Percentages)

	During conviction offense, felon was armed with:	
	Firearm (N = 580)	Something else (N = 230)
1. Was the gun actually fired during the crime?		
No	61	—
Yes	39	—
2. Did you bring your weapon with you . . . or get it at the scene?		
Brought it with me	79	66
Got it at scene	12	23
Both	9	11
3. Did you actually use your weapon . . . in committing that crime or did you just have it with you . . . ?		
Just had it	24	42
Actually used it	76	58
If "actually used it:" How did you use the weapon?		
4. To scare victim:	69	44
(N) =	(407)	(118)
5. To injure victim:	16	26
(N) =	(407)	(117)
6. To kill victim:	18	16
(N) =	(404)	(117)
7. To get away:	26	18
(N) =	(407)	(116)
8. To protect myself:	38	32
(N) =	(406)	(117)
9. Did you plan to use the weapon in the way you did, or was it something that just happened . . . ?		
Planned to use	44	26
Just happened	56	74
(N) =	(346)	(103)

extent, the so-called "crime of passion" scenario, the idea that much criminal violence occurs in a "moment of rage," making use of whatever weapons are available at the time. Somewhat in contrast to this scenario, the large majority of both types of felons brought their weapons with them: The majorities amounted to 79% of those who were armed with a firearm during the conviction crime and 66% of those who were armed with something else. Thus, most armed crime (whether it involves firearms or other types of weaponry) apparently involves at least some degree of premeditation—enough advance thought, at least, to bring one's weapons along. Note also that acquiring "other weapons" at the scene was somewhat more common than acquiring a firearm at the scene; and that in about one-tenth of the cases, the felon both brought weapons to the scene and acquired them while there.[6]

(To be sure, it is possible that the degree of premeditation involved in bringing one's weapon along again raised the probability of conviction, incarceration, and subsequently an appearance in our sample. The true "crime of passion" may as a consequence be underrepresented in these data.)

To have carried a weapon during the conviction offense is not necessarily the same as actually using the weapon to commit the offense. We asked the sample whether they had actually used their weapon in committing the crime or whether they just had it with them. Majorities of both types reported that they actually used the weapon in some way, but the majority was considerably larger (76%) among those armed with a gun than among those armed with "other" weapons (58%). Judging from these results, some three-quarters of the men who committed crimes while armed with a gun actually used the gun in some fashion in the course of that crime.

Felons who indicated that they had in fact used the weapon in some way were then asked, "How did you use the weapon?" "To scare the victim" was by far the most common usage among both types, mentioned by 69% of those armed with a gun and 44% of those armed with other weapons. A principal motive for the use of weapons in crime, and especially for the use of guns in crime, is apparently to intimidate the victim into quick and ready capitulation to the offender's demands. "To protect myself" was the next most frequent response in both categories, noted by 38 and 32%, respectively. The ambiguity of this response was already remarked upon above.

The use of weapons to injure or kill the victim was predictably much less common than the use of weapons for purposes of intimidation; still, 18% of those armed with a gun and 16% of those armed with something else said they used the weapon to kill the victim during their conviction offense. (Lest these figures seem unreasonably high, recall that about 15% of the total sample were doing time on a homicide or manslaughter charge.) Interestingly, the use of the weapon to *injure* the victim was somewhat more frequent among those armed with something else (26%) than among those

[6]For example, a burglar armed with a knife (say, for purposes of jimmying a window) who, in the course of a burglary, stole a gun from a residence would have brought one weapon with him to the scene (the knife) and would have acquired another weapon at the scene. An armed drug dealer who, in one particular trade, exchanged drugs for guns would also have brought weapons to the scene and acquired additional ones at the scene. The pattern, in short, is not inconceivable.

armed with a gun (16%). This pattern is consistent with findings reported by Cook (1980), namely, that in robberies at least, the overall injury rate is higher among nongun robberies than among gun robberies (presumably because people who are being robbed at gun point are less likely to resist).

The final question in the sequence asked those who had used their weapon in some way to commit the crime whether they had planned to use the weapon or whether it "just happened." Advance planning for the use of the weapon was the minority report in both cases. Still, among those armed with a gun, some 44% indicated that they had planned to use the gun in the way that they did. (Among the "something else" group, the figure was 26%.)

TABLE 4.4. Firing Guns in Crime Situations as a Function of Planned Use of the Weapon (in Percentages)[a]

| | Did you plan to use the weapon in the way that you did? | | |
	Yes	No	(Row Ns)
Was the gun actually fired?			
No	72	30	(171)
Yes	28	70	(182)
(N) =	(157)	(196)	

[a]Table is based only on the subsample who were armed with a gun at the conviction offense and who actually used the gun in committing that offense.

All told, there were 156 men in the sample who were armed with a gun during the conviction offense, who also used the gun in some way in committing that offense, and who, finally, indicated that they had planned on using the gun in the way that they did. As one might anticipate, most of these 156 men (73%, to be precise) were in prison on a robbery charge. Some 27% were in on a weapons charge, 22% on an aggravated assault or "assault with a deadly weapon" charge, 15% on a burglary charge, and 10% on a homicide charge. (Given the total of these percentages, many of these men were clearly in prison on more than one charge, a robbery charge and a weapons violation being the most common combination.) Also unsurprisingly, 57% of them fell into the two predatory categories of our typology.

Interestingly, among those who were armed with a gun during the conviction offense and who actually used the gun in committing the offense, the tendency to have fired the weapon was much lower among those who planned on using the gun than among those who did not (Table 4.4). Among those who had planned on using the weapon, 28% reported firing the weapon during the crime; among those who had not "plan(ned) on using the weapon in the way that you did," 70% report having fired the weapon. Percentaging in the other direction, only 24% of those who reported having fired their gun during the conviction offense also reported having planned to use the weapon in that way.

The strong implication of these findings is that most firings of guns in criminal situations are unplanned. The "plan," to the extent that there was one, was presumably to intimidate the victim and to use the weapon to that end. The actual firing of the weapon was, one senses, a rather unwanted by-product of a situation that "goes sour" for whatever reason: The victim resisted rather than capitulated, the police arrived at the scene, or the offender encountered some difficulty in effectuating his escape. Whatever the reason, however, the finding is reasonably clear: Most of the men who actually fired guns in criminal situations claimed to have had no prior intention of so doing.

On the other hand, 39% of the men in the sample who were armed with a gun during the conviction offense reported firing it during that offense (Table 4.2), so despite the apparent lack of prior intentions, these men clearly had few compunctions about firing when the situation appeared to demand it.

Needless to say, this interpretation of criminal gun use is largely a view from the perspective of the criminal (is based, that is, on what these criminals told us) and may therefore suffer to some extent from the latter's attempt to present his gun use in as sympathetic a fashion as possible. It is, after all, a fine semantic point to claim that carrying a gun "just in case" is not the same as planning for the use of the weapon.

There were, as it happens, 44 men in the sample who were armed with a gun during the conviction crime, who actually fired the gun during the incident, and who said that they had in fact planned to use the gun in the way that they did. Eighteen of these men (41%) were in prison on aggravated assault or "assault with a deadly weapon" charges, 12 of them (27%) were in on a homicide charge, and 21 (48%) were in for armed robbery. (Many were also doing time on a variety of lesser offenses, and, again, several were in on multiple charges, such as robbery with aggravated assault, etc.)

As would be expected, how the gun was in fact used in a crime situation varied rather sharply depending on whether or not it was fired (Table 4.5). By far the most common use in the case of unfired weapons was to intimidate the victim (89%); in contrast, the most common use in the case of fired weapons was "to protect myself" (48%). Injury to the victim was predictably much more common in cases when the gun was fired (26%) than when it was not (9%), as was the victim's death (36 versus 3%).

The consequences for the offender also appear to have varied rather sharply depending on whether the weapon was fired or not. Among those

TABLE 4.5. How Guns Are Used in Crimes, Depending on Whether or Not They Were Fired: Conviction Offenses (in Percentages)[a]

"How did you use the weapon?"	Was gun fired?	
	No	Yes
To scare victim	89	45
(N) =	(218)	(184)
To injure victim	9	26
(N) =	(218)	(184)
To kill victim	3	36
(N) =	(217)	(182)
To get away	26	28
(N) =	(218)	(184)
To protect myself	31	48
(N) =	(217)	(184)

[a]Table is based on those who were armed with a gun at the conviction offense and who used the gun to commit the offense.

armed with a gun during the conviction offense and who used their weapon in some way to commit the offense, the men who actually fired the weapon were much more likely to be doing time on aggravated assault charges than those who did not fire (32 versus 13%); and likewise for homicide (40 versus 3%) and manslaughter (10 versus 1%). In contrast, the men who did not fire were more likely to be in on a robbery charge (66 versus 37% of those who did fire). Interestingly, being in on a weapon's charge was slightly more common among those who did not fire (25%) than among those who did (18%).

PATTERNS OF WEAPONS USE: OTHER OFFENSES

We have already indicated that the conviction crime is, for most of these men, only the most recent in a fairly long series of criminal activities. Not all of the hard-core gun criminals in our sample were, in fact, armed during the conviction offense; indeed, one in five of the two Predator groups was not carrying a weapon at the time he was last arrested (one among many reasons, incidentally, why the conviction offense per se is a rather misleading indicator of the true nature of a person's criminal career).

Many of the questions asked about the conviction offense were also asked about the more general use of weapons in committing crime; results from these "more general" questions are analyzed in the present section. This discussion adds some useful details to the portrait of criminal weapons involvement and also provides an opportunity to replicate and refine some of the patterns that have already emerged. Data are shown in Table 4.6.

These results are based on the series of questions following the initial

TABLE 4.6. Weapons Use in Crimes Other Than the Conviction Offense (in Percentages)

	Gun criminals (N = 871)	Armed— not with a gun— criminals (N = 177)
1. What kinds of gun(s) have you *ever* *used* to commit crimes?		
Handgun	90	—
Sawed-off shotgun	27	—
Regular shotgun	16	—
Sawed-off rifle	7	—
Regular rifle	10	—
Zipgun (homemade)	3	—
All other	4	—
2. What kind of weapons have you *ever* *used* to commit crimes?		
Pocket knife	—	34
Switchblade	—	13
Buck knife	—	38
Hunting knife	—	24
Club	—	34
All other	—	56
3. About how often were you armed . . . when you committed your crimes?		
Only once	26	38
A few times	34	33
Many times	14	6
Most of the time	16	11
All of the time	10	11
(N) =	(819)	(141)
4. What kind of [weapon] have you used *most frequently* in committing crimes?		
Handgun	85	—
Sawed-off shotgun	9	—
Regular shotgun	3	—
All other guns	3	—
Pocket knife	—	23
Buck knife	—	24
Club	—	14
All other non-gun	—	40
(N) =	(797)	(118)
5. When you committed crimes, did you have just a gun or did you usually carry other weapons as well?		
Just a gun	56	—
Other weapons	44	—
(N) =	(794)	—
What other kinds of weapons did you usually carry?		
Pocket knife	37	—
Switchblade	24	—

(continued)

TABLE 4.6. Weapons Use in Crimes Other Than the Conviction Offense (in Percentages) (*continued*)

	Gun criminals (N = 871)	Armed— not with a gun— criminals (N = 177)
Buck knife	45	—
Hunting knife	23	—
Club	18	—
Martial arts	19	—
Butcher knife	10	—
Brass knuckles	10	—
Straight razor	13	—
Chain	11	—
(N) =	(348)	
6. Some men . . . tell us that they [carried a weapon] pretty much all the time. . . . Others tell us they [carried a weapon] only in certain situations. . . . Others *only* [carried a weapon] when they *were* planning to do a crime. Which of these are you most like?		
Carried all the time	30	34
Carried in situations	51	53
Only carried when planning crime	19	13
(N) =	(788)	(131)
[If "only in certain situations"] In what kinds of situations would you tend to carry [a weapon]?		
When doing a drug deal	47	30
Out drinking or raising hell	23	29
Going to strange part of city	50	46
At night	34	41
With others who were carrying	34	23
I thought I might need to protect myself	83	84
All other	—	—
(N [approx]) =	(402)	(70)
7. Did you ever actually use your [weapon] . . . in committing a crime? Circle all that apply.		
To scare victim	70	48
To injure victim	20	22
To kill victim	16	8
To protect myself	50	44
To get away	35	25
All other	2	10
(N [approx]) =	(793)	(145)
8. In all the crimes you have ever committed while armed with a gun, have you ever fired the gun?		
No	43	—
Yes	57	—
(N) =	(796)	

filter questions, which asked whether the felon had ever committed armed crimes and, if "yes," whether he had committed crimes armed with a gun. For present purposes, these questions isolate two groups of interest (call them "Gun Criminals" and "Armed—Not with a Gun—Criminals," respectively) whose weapons behavior is compared throughout this section.

As in the conviction offense data, handguns are by far the preferred weapon among gun criminals. Among the men in the sample who had ever committed a gun crime, 90% had used a handgun for at least one of them; 85% stated that the handgun was the weapon they used most frequently. Next in popularity was the justly infamous sawed-off shotgun, indicated as a crime weapon by 27% of the gun criminals and as the most frequent crime weapon by 9%. Percentages having used other kinds of firearms at least once in committing crime were 16% for unmodified shotguns, 10% for un-modified rifles, and 7% for sawed-off rifles. A variety of "other" firearms were also indicated in the open-ended follow-up, including BB guns, gas-operated pistols, and automatic weapons of various sorts.

Since the sum of the percentages shown in the table totals well over 100% (157%, to be precise), it is obvious that many of the gun criminals had used several types of firearms. (Most of the Shotgun Predators, for example, had also used handguns in one or another of their crimes.)

A small majority of the gun criminals (56%) said that they carried only a gun when they committed their crimes; a large minority (44%) carried other weapons as well, typically, one or another kind of knife. Buck and pocket knives were especially popular back-up weapons among this group, indicated by 45 and 37%, respectively. As might be expected, the carrying of multiple weapons was especially common among the Predators: 56% of the Handgun Predators and 69% of the Shotgun Predators indicated that they had carried multiple weapons versus 34% of the Sporadics and 28% of the One-Time Firearms Users.

Men who had committed armed crime, but not with a gun, used mainly knives and a motley assortment of other weaponry. Among this group (N = 177), 38% had used a buck knife at least once and 24% indicated the buck knife as the weapon used most frequently. Next in popularity were the pocket knives (34% having used one at least once, 23% indicating it as the most frequently used weapon) and clubs (34 and 14%, respectively). "Other" weapons used by these men included switchblades, hunting and butcher knives, brass knuckles, straight razors, mace, pieces of chain, mar-tial arts weapons, baseball bats, etc.

Both groups of armed criminals were asked how often they were armed when they did their crimes. The most substantial difference between the two groups was the percentage responding, "only once." Among the gun criminals, 26% claimed to have been armed only once (these, of course, are the One-Timers in our typology); among the armed—not with a gun—group, the corresponding percentage is 38%. About one-third of both groups

said they were armed "a few times." To have been armed "many times,"
"most of the time," or "all of the time" was characteristic of 40% of the
gun criminals and 28% of the other group.

The next question in the sequence was intended to explore the issue of
habitual carrying of weapons. The question read as follows:

> Some of the men we have talked to tell us they were in the habit of carrying a
> [weapon] with them pretty much all the time, even on days when they were
> not planning to do any crimes. Other men tell us that they were in the habit
> of carrying a [weapon] only in certain situations—for example, when they were
> going out drinking—again, whether they planned to do a crime or not. Still
> others tell us that they carried a [weapon] when they were planning to do a
> crime. Which of these are you most like?

Responses were very similar for both groups. The majority response in
both cases was to have carried weapons "only in certain situations," the
pattern for 51% of the gun criminals and 53% of the others. The next most
frequent response was to have carried a weapon all the time, the pattern
for about one-third of both groups. The least common pattern in both cases
was to have carried a weapon only when planning a crime, indicated by
19% of the gun criminals and 13% of the others. It would appear, therefore, that most of the weapons that are used in crimes, be they firearms or
other weapons, are not carried *specifically* for that purpose; carrying a
weapon specifically for the purpose of using it in crimes was characteristic
of fewer than one fifth of the armed criminals in our sample.

In by far the largest majority of cases, then, weapons were available for
use in crimes either because of a tendency to carry weapons all the time
or through a practice of carrying weapons in particular situations. The follow-up questions concerning these "situations" were quite revealing. The
most common by far was "whenever I thought I might need to protect myself," mentioned by 83–84% of both groups.

As we see in a later chapter, self-protection figures prominently as a
claimed motive in the weapons behavior of these men. Given the lifestyles
involved, this is no doubt a genuine motive in some cases; in other cases,
it is no more than a self-serving rationalization, if for no other reason than
that men like these who carry guns routinely to "defend themselves" against
the endemic violence of their environment contribute to the hostility of the
environment by the very act.

Other situations in which these men would tend to carry weapons include: when doing a drug deal (mentioned by 47% of the relevant gun
criminals and 30% of the others),[7] when going to a strange part of the city

---

[7] This pattern is consistent with related data reported in Chapter Three: Among
the men in the sample who ever dealt drugs ($N = 865$), some 62% said that they
"usually carried a weapon" when dealing.

(mentioned by 50 and 46%, respectively), "at night" (34 and 41%), when they were with others who were carrying weapons (34 and 23%), etc. Most of these "situations" are clearly variations on the self-defense theme.

We further note: A man who tends to carry a weapon whenever he thinks he might need to protect himself, or whenever he is going to a strange part of the city, or whenever it is dark out, etc., clearly tends to carry his weapon(s) on a pretty regular basis, if not quite "all the time." These points in mind, we appear to be dealing, in reality, with only two types of weapons-carrying behavior—habitual carrying for general purposes and premeditated carrying for the specific purpose of committing crimes. And it is the former pattern that predominated, quite heavily, among the armed criminals in our sample.

THE CORRELATES OF "HABITUAL" WEAPONS CARRYING

The above notwithstanding, the tendency to carry a gun more or less all the time is a sufficiently distinctive (and dangerous) pattern of behavior to inquire about its correlates. For this purpose, we focus only on the gun criminals ($N = 786$) simply because it is the routine and habitual carrying of guns that is of greatest interest. To facilitate the analysis, we have also recoded the responses to the "carrying" question so that the men who said they carried "all the time" were assigned a 1 and all others (who answered the question) were assigned a 0. The resulting variable was then correlated with a large number of other variables, with results as follows:

First, the tendency to carry a gun "all the time" was strongly correlated with two additional questions from much later in the survey that also dealt with carrying behavior (r's = .55 and .56). These questions are discussed in more detail later. For now, we merely note that there was considerable internal consistency in the responses.

Aside from the additional items on carrying behavior, the strongest correlates of the tendency to carry a gun "all the time" were whether the felon's family, friends, and associates owned and/or carried firearms. First, the carrying question correlated at .09 with whether the felon's father owned a gun, at .12 with whether his father owned a handgun, and at .17 with whether the father himself carried a handgun with him outside the home. None of these relationships is especially striking, but all are statistically significant. Likewise, the carrying question correlated at −.17 with the felon's age when he first fired a gun (the younger a man was when he first fired a gun, the more likely he was to carry a gun "all the time"). In part, then, the tendency to carry "all the time" is apparently a result of early familial socialization into firearms ownership and use (see also Chapter Five).

More striking, by far, were the effects of gun ownership and carrying among the felon's associates and friends—"the people you hung around with before you came to this prison." One item asked how many of these people themselves owned a gun; responses correlated .20 with the tendency for the felon himself to carry "all the time." Another item asked how many of the felon's associates owned a handgun; responses to this item correlated .24 with the felon's own carrying. Still another item asked, "about how many of them . . . made a habit of carrying a handgun with them outside their home?" This item correlated .32 with the felon's own carrying behavior, and this was the single strongest correlate (other than the two mentioned earlier) revealed in this analysis.

(A parallel three-item series was asked about "the men in your family—your father, brothers, uncles, and so on." These three items correlated with the felon's carrying behavior at .13, .20, and .26, respectively—all statistically significant.)

This analysis clearly suggests that the single most important reason why a felon might decide to carry a gun more or less all the time is that he associates with other men who carry guns routinely. While familial socialization is clearly a factor, peer-group influences appear to be even more important. Such influences might operate in either or both of two ways: First, a felon's peers may influence his weapons-carrying behavior in much the same way that peers often influence one's choice of clothing; peers, that is, may define the "in" things to do. Second, armed peers may constitute a threat to safety; unarmed members of armed groups may be very vulnerable to bullying and coercion. In addition, it should be kept in mind that friends and associates are chosen. The correlation between friends' and felons' carrying behaviors may only imply that these men elected to "hang out" with others who carried guns.

The tendency to carry "all the time" was also correlated with other aspects of weapons behavior. The carrying question, for example, correlated .24 with the number of guns ever owned and .30 with the number of handguns ever owned. Thus, the more guns a felon had owned, the more likely he was to carry one "all the time." Felons who carried "all the time" were also more likely to keep their gun(s) loaded ($r = .22$) than others, and they tended to fire their guns more often ($r = .29$). They were also more likely to have threatened to shoot someone ($r = .25$), and to have actually shot someone ($r = .30$) than those who carried less regularly. Finally, and predictably, the men who carried a gun "all the time" tended to be high-rate criminals; the carrying question correlated at .29 with our Index of Total Criminality.

The tendency to carry a gun "all the time" was especially pronounced among the Predators (Table 4.7). Among gun criminals in general, recall, about 30% said they carried a gun more or less all the time; among the Shotgun Predators, the figure rose to 40%, and among the Handgun Predators, to just over 50%. The Predators, interestingly, were the least likely, by far, to carry only when they were planning to do a crime; this pattern, rather, was more characteristic of those who had committed just one or

TABLE 4.7. Carrying Behavior by Criminal Type (in Percentages)

| | Type | | | |
Carried a gun	One-timer	Sporadic	Handgun predator	Shotgun predator
All the time	13	14	51	40
Only in certain situations	64	57	39	49
Only when planning a crime	22	29	10	11
(N) =	(179)	(235)	(292)	(82)

only a few gun crimes. Thus, as we indicated earlier, the Predators stand out from other groups because of their routine and habitual carrying of fire-arms.

The final items shown in Table 4.6 relate to the actual use of weapons in committing crimes. The general patterns revealed there are quite similar to those discussed in connection with the conviction offense. By far the most common usage of guns in committing crime was intimidation of the victim, mentioned by 70% of the gun criminals. Among those armed—not with a gun, intimidation of the victim was also the most common use, but the proportion was decidedly lower (48%). The percentage difference suggests, reasonably, that felons intent on intimidating their victims preferentially chose firearms as the means.

The second most frequent use in both cases was for "self-protection," mentioned by 50% of the gun criminals and by 44% of the armed—not with a gun—group. "To get away" was third (noted by 35 and 25% of the two groups), followed by "to injure the victim" and "to kill the victim," respectively. One gun criminal in six in this sample said he had used a gun to kill a victim in the course of a crime; the same was true of about one-tenth of the armed—not with a gun—group. Finally, we note that a sizable majority (57%) of the gun criminals reported having fired a gun at least once in the course of a crime.

As was the case in the conviction offense data, how a gun was used in crime depended to some extent on whether or not it was fired. Relevant data are shown in Table 4.8. First, the incidence of the use of guns to intimidate victims was about the same whether the felon ever actually fired the gun (74%) or not (68%). Clearly, the purpose of intimidation is amply served in most cases by the mere presence of a firearm; one normally does not need to fire a round or two to get a potential victim's attention.

In all other cases, however, there were fairly sizable differences in the pattern of use according to whether the gun was (ever) fired. To illustrate, the use of a gun to injure the victim was about 8 times more common if the gun were fired (32%) than if not (4%), and the use of a gun to kill the

victim, about 10 times more common (25 versus 2%). About one gun criminal in four in this sample who said he had actually fired a gun in a crime
situation reported having killed a victim at least once.

Judging from the data on conviction offense, most of these firings—and,
as a consequence, most of the ensuing victim deaths—were probably not
planned in advance but rather resulted from unforeseen circumstances aris-
ing in the event. Consistent with this interpretation, we note further that
men who had fired their gun(s) in a crime situation were much likelier to
report having used their weapon for self-protection (63%) than those who
had never fired (32%) and likewise for the use of the weapon "to get away"
(47 versus 18%).

TABLE 4.8. How Guns Are Used in Crimes, Depending on Whether or
Not They Were Fired: Crimes in General (in Percentages)

	Have you ever fired a gun during a crime?	
How did you use the gun?	No (N = 344)	Yes (N = 452)
To scare victim	74	68
To injure victim	4	32
To kill victim	2	25
To protect myself	32	63
To get away	18	47
All other	2	2
None of the above	9	1

Finally, note that one-tenth of the gun criminals who never fired their
gun also reported never having used the weapon in any of the manners
asked about in the question (versus 1% of those who had fired). These, presumably, were men who carried firearms in the course of their crimes but
never encountered a situation where it was necessary to use them. At the
same time, however, 96% of the gun criminals in the sample (which, by
present definition, means having committed at least one crime armed with
a gun) had actually used a gun to commit a crime in some way. Carrying
a gun but never actually using it to commit a crime was an apparently rare
behavior.

ADDITIONAL DETAILS ON WEAPONS-CARRYING BEHAVIOR

Data presented in the previous section are based entirely on the men in
the sample who have at some time in their careers committed at least one
armed crime. There are some men in the sample, however, who, despite
having owned guns, have never committed a crime with one (and, to be

sure, a few who, despite having never owned a gun, have nonetheless committed gun crimes). The questionnaire included several items on carrying behavior and related matters that were asked of all the gun-owning felons in the sample, whether they had ever committed armed crimes or not; results from these items are discussed in the present section.

Table 4.9 shows, as an entry point to this discussion, the relationship between having owned guns and having committed crimes with them. We have already remarked that about three-quarters of this sample had owned one or more guns at one or another time; the remaining one-quarter had never owned any guns. Table 4.9 confirms that it is not necessary ever to have owned a gun in order to have committed a crime with one; indeed, 18% of the nonowners by their own admission had committed at least one gun crime in their lives. An additional 13% of the nonowners had com-

TABLE 4.9. The Commission of Armed Crime as a Function of Gun Ownership (in Percentages)

	Felon has committed			
	No armed crime	Armed—not with gun	Gun crime	($N = 100\%$)
1. Have you ever owned a gun?				
No	69	13	18	(403)
Yes	32	9	59	(1273)
2. If yes: How many?				
1	47	13	40	(157)
2–3	41	10	49	(302)
4–5	31	11	58	(158)
6–10	24	4	72	(113)
10+	17	4	79	(368)

mitted armed crimes but not with guns, and the strong majority of the nonowners (69%) had never committed any armed crime. Clearly, the rate at which armed crimes were committed was much lower among felons who did not own guns than among the gun owners.

The pattern among felons who had ever owned a gun was, of course, sharply different. Among the gun-owning felons, 59% had committed at least one gun crime. On the other hand, nearly one-third (32%) of the gun owners in this sample had never committed any armed crime at all, whether with a gun or with some other weapon. It is, therefore, clearly not the case that every felon who had ever owned a gun also used his gun to commit crime; about one-third of the group showed at least some restraint in this matter.

The tendency to have committed gun crime increased with the number of guns ever owned. Among those who had owned just one gun, 40% had committed at least one gun crime, a fraction that increased quite regularly up through and including the "10 or more guns" category, where 79% had committed at least one gun crime. Thus, the more guns a felon had owned, the more likely he was to have committed a crime with one of them.

What distinguishes gun-owning felons who use their guns to commit crime from gun-owning felons who do not? As it happens, a key factor implicated in this difference appears to be the gun-carrying tendencies: gun-owning felons who used their guns to commit crimes were, for the most part, those who actually carried their firearms on a more or less regular basis. Relevant data are presented in Table 4.10.

To avoid confusion, data in Table 4.10 are derived from the gun-owning subset of the overall sample, whether the felon ever used a gun to commit a crime or not. Since there are good-sized numbers of gun owners in all categories of our typology, results are shown separately for each type of criminal, as well as for the total sample. Note further: The typology is itself only an expanded version of the three-category variable shown in Table 4.9, the rightmost four categories in Table 4.10 representing, of course, those who had committed at least one gun crime in the course of their criminal careers.

The first two panels of the table show gun-ownership tendencies among the various categories of the typology. Most of the men in all categories had owned at least one gun in their lives, with majorities ranging from 58% of the Unarmed Criminals up to 95% of the Handgun Predators. Large majorities of the gun owners in each category had also owned at least one handgun; here, the majorities ranged from 69% of the Unarmed Criminals to 100% of the Sporadics and Handgun Predators. It is, therefore, of some importance to note that the majority of the men throughout our typology had at some time possessed the instruments necessary to commit gun crimes. Despite this, some of these men, for whatever reason, chose not to do so— a small glimmer of hope, perhaps, in an otherwise generally dismal portrait.

All the handgun owners in the sample were asked if they ever carried their handguns with them outside the home—"for protection or self-defense, or to use in committing crimes." Overall, 19% of the handgun owners said, "Never," and another one-third said that they had done so only "a few times." Thus, a small majority of the handgun owners in this sample (52%) were not in the habit of carrying their handgun(s) on a regular or routine basis. Among the Unarmed and the Armed—Not-with-a-Gun— group of handgun owners, this was true of some 77–84%. Even among the One-Timers and the Sporadics, some 60–70% did not carry their handguns on any regular basis. Only among the Predator groups do we find a strong majority pattern of routine handgun carrying: Among the Handgun Predators, about 90% carried their handgun "many times" or all the time; among

TABLE 4.10. Additional Details on Weapons Carrying, by Type: Gun Owners Only (in Percentages)

					Type			
	Total	Unarmed	Improviser	Knife	One-timer	Sporadic handgun	Handgun predator	Shotgun predator
1. Ever own gun?								
Yes	76	58	64	72	82	93	95	89
(N) =	(1732)	(664)	(73)	(124)	(238)	(243)	(300)	(90)
2. Ever own handgun?								
Yes	87	69	78	70	92	100	100	93
(N) =	(1184)	(330)	(37)	(70)	(189)	(213)	(269)	(76)
3. If Yes: Ever carry handgun outside home?								
Never	19	52	32	45	21	6	1	5
A few times	33	30	52	32	49	54	11	31
Many times	28	12	8	16	20	34	45	32
All the time	19	6	8	7	10	6	44	32
(N) =	(933)	(201)	(25)	(44)	(152)	(192)	(254)	(65)
[If yes to (3)]								
4. Did you carry on your person or somewhere else?								
On person	82	76	75	76	66	82	92	86
Elsewhere	18	24	25	24	34	18	8	14
(N) =	(768)	(106)	(20)	(25)	(121)	(180)	(252)	(64)
5. If on person: Where?								
In pocket	18	15	7	5	26	24	15	5
In belt	46	36	33	42	48	52	47	44
Shoe or boot	2	4	—	10	2	1	2	4
Hip holster	10	14	27	21	8	6	10	4
Leg holster	2	4	—	—	1	1	—	4
Shoulder holster	21	27	33	16	12	16	23	30
All other	1	—	—	5	2	—	—	—
(N) =	(622)	(78)	(15)	(19)	(80)	(146)	(230)	(54)

(continued)

TABLE 4.10. Additional Details on Weapons Carrying, by Type: Gun Owners Only (in Percentages) (*continued*)

				Type				
	Total	Unarmed	Improviser	Knife	One-timer	Sporadic handgun	Handgun predator	Shotgun predator
6. [If yes to (3)]: When not carrying, where did you keep it?								
In gun cabinet	15	24	10	30	13	7	14	9
In drawer	34	30	31	39	33	30	37	46
Bedside table	24	19	17	32	22	20	29	31
Under pillow	17	8	7	14	14	16	28	26
Hidden away	54	51	41	59	48	63	57	47
In garage	4	2	3	4	3	6	4	3
All other	11	8	21	12	12	9	13	8
[N (approx)] =	(961)	(214)	(29)	(44)	(158)	(195)	(257)	(66)
7. All gun owners: How often did you carry a firearm?								
Never	23	46	31	45	23	8	2	11
1–2 times	14	15	29	12	27	17	2	11
From time to time	31	27	26	30	31	51	24	27
Most of the time	20	8	9	6	11	18	44	27
All of the time	12	4	6	6	7	6	29	24
(N) =	(1094)	(302)	(35)	(66)	(176)	(194)	(250)	(71)
8. [If yes to (7)]: Carry on person or in car?								
On person	60	35	46	38	42	68	82	81
In car	40	65	54	62	58	32	18	19
(N) =	(844)	(166)	(24)	(37)	(135)	(180)	(244)	(58)

handgun-owning Shotgun Predators, this was true of 64%. Nearly one-half (44%) of the Handgun Predators carried their handgun "all the time."[8]

Men who reported ever carrying their handgun with them outside the home were asked whether they tended to carry their weapon on their person or somewhere else. To carry on one's person was the strong majority tendency in all groups, with the size of the majority ranging from 75 to 92%. A follow-up for those who carried on their person asked about where and how the weapon was carried. Differences across types were generally minor. Shoved into a belt or waistband was the modal response, given by 46%. A shoulder holster was the next most popular means of carrying, mentioned by 21%, and this was followed by sticking the gun in one's pocket, noted by 18%. Other means of carrying were mentioned by 10% or fewer.

Men who indicated that they carried a handgun with them outside the home were also asked where they kept the weapon when they were not carrying it. Again, differences across types of criminals were generally modest. "Hidden away" was the modal response in the overall sample (54%), followed by "in a drawer" (34%), "in the bedside table" (24%), and "under the pillow" (17%). (Note that the various possibilities given in the question sequence are not mutually exclusive and, thus, that multiple responses were rather common.) In general, keeping the handgun in the bedside table or under one's pillow was more common among the Predators than among any of the other groups. When these men told us that they carried a gun "all the time," we can apparently take the response quite literally. Even while sleeping, many of them kept their handgun within easy reach.

One additional question on carrying behavior was asked of all gun owners in the sample (not just the handgun owners, as in item 3 from the table). Results are shown in Panel 7 and are consistent with all other gun-carrying data so far reviewed. The tendency to carry "most" or "all" of the time characterized a very small fraction of all groups except the Predators (some 12–24% depending on type), whereas among the Predators, it was the clear majority tendency. Note finally (Panel 8) that Predators were much more likely than gun-carrying respondents in other groups to carry on their person as opposed to "in the car," this latter being the majority tendency

[8]Comparable data on carrying practices among handgun owners in general is, at best, thin. One survey (discussed in Wright, Rossi, and Daly, 1983: 142) found that 7% of all U.S. adults, or about 29% of all handgun owners, said "yes" to the question, "Do you ever carry that handgun or pistol outside of the house with you for protection, or not?" Thus, among handgun owners in general, the practice is fairly widespread. On the other hand, only 19% of the handgun owners in the felon sample responded "never" to the handgun-carrying question, so about 80% of them carry their handgun outside the home at least now and again. To the extent that these data are at least crudely comparable, the clear indication is that gun-owning felons carry handguns outside the home much more frequently than handgun owners do in general.

in four of the five non-Predator groups. These men, clearly, were not con-
tent just to have a firearm available in the general vicinity (as were most of
the other gun-carrying men in the sample). Their preference was to have a
gun immediately at hand.

SUMMARY OF PRINCIPAL FINDINGS

The results reported in this chapter sustain the following conclusions
concerning patterns of weapons ownership and use among convicted felons:

1. Felons as a lot tended to own guns frequently and in large numbers.
They also tended in the majority to keep their guns loaded at all times, and
they appeared to fire their guns rather frequently. As in the population at
large, most of these firings were in sport and recreational applications of
one sort or another, but many of the gun-owning felons in our sample had
also fired guns at other people, often (they say) to protect themselves.

2. More than one-half the sample was pharmacologically impaired during the conviction crime; those so impaired were slightly more likely to
have been armed than those who were not, but the difference was slight.

3. The Firearms Predators were, of course, more likely to have been
armed, and armed with a gun, during the conviction crime than were any
of the other categories in our typology, a consequence, as we have seen,
of the habitual carrying of firearms among these men.

4. Among the men armed during their conviction offense, most (72%)
were armed with a firearm, a handgun being by far the most common
weapon. More generally, as is obvious in all other sources of data, the
handgun was by far the preferred crime firearm, indicated as the most frequently used weapon by 85% of the gun criminals in our sample.

5. The carrying of multiple types of weapons was fairly common practice, especially among the more predatory criminals.

6. Despite the obvious preference for handguns among gun criminals,
good-sized fractions have also used other kinds of firearms in committing
crime, including some 27% (of the gun criminals) who have used a sawed-
off shotgun at least once.

7. Most of the men who carried a weapon during their conviction crime
used the weapon in some way in the course of the crime, most frequently
to intimidate the victim. More generally, intimidation of the victim was the
most common use to which criminal weapons were put (whether these are
firearms or other kinds of weapons), followed by self-protection. Nearly all
the men who had ever committed a crime armed with a gun actually used
a gun in the course of a crime; carrying but never using a gun was extremely uncommon.

8. Although nearly two-fifths of the men in our sample who were armed

with a gun during the conviction offense reported that the gun was actually fired during the incident, very few of those who fired their gun planned in advance to do so. Men who carried guns during crimes clearly planned on using them—for intimidation, if nothing else—but very few appear to have planned on actually firing them. In general, it seems obvious that the average criminal would prefer not to fire his gun during a crime, since this could only increase his chances of apprehension and conviction.

9. The consequences to the victim were more serious if a gun were fired in the course of an incident than if the gun were merely present but not fired; and likewise for the offender: Men who were armed with a gun during the conviction offense and who actually fired the gun during the incident were convicted on more serious charges than the men who were armed with a gun but who did not fire it.

10. Among the armed—not with a gun—criminals, knives were the weapons of choice. In general, these men carried their weapons less frequently than gun criminals did.

11. Most (57%) of the gun criminals in our sample said they had actually fired their gun(s) at least once in the course of a crime. Predictably, the use of a gun to injure or kill the victim was much higher if the gun had been fired than if not.

12. Roughly 30% of the armed criminals in the sample (whether armed with a gun or with other weapons) made a habit of carrying a weapon more or less all the time. About 50% carried a weapon only in certain situations—mainly, whenever they felt they might need to protect themselves. Carrying a weapon for the specific purpose of committing crimes with it was fairly uncommon, characteristic of no more than about one-fifth of the sample. Most of the weapons used to commit crimes, in short, were apparently not carried specifically for that purpose.

13. The key distinguishing feature of the men who carried a gun more or less all the time—other than their essentially predatory nature—was that they associated with other men who made a practice of carrying firearms. (Virtually identical results are also reported in Chapter Five.) We think this pattern reflects, in part, peer pressures to "go along" with the predominant practices of one's group, but also, in part, a genuine survival motive: Given the nature of the environment these men inhabited, it would have been rather foolish to have been the only man in the crowd without a gun. In considering the significance of the carrying behavior reported here, we do well to keep in mind that "self-defense" in context means, for the most part, defense against others much like oneself.

14. In general, the gun owners in this sample committed armed crime at a much higher rate than the nonowners. Still, about 40% of the gun owners had never committed a gun crime. The more guns a felon had owned, the more likely he was to have committed at least one gun crime.

15. Most of the handgun owners in this sample did not routinely carry

a handgun with them outside the home; the routine carrying of handguns was strongly concentrated among the Predators and was, indeed, a distinguishing characteristic of the group. Men who carried a handgun typically did so simply by shoving one into their belt; use of a shoulder holster, however, was relatively common.

16. Most predatory criminals were armed with a gun most or all of the time. Even when they slept, they tended to keep their weapons nearby. Judging from the general run of results reported in this chapter, a handgun was their most, and perhaps only, trustworthy companion.

5

FAMILY, FRIENDS, AND FIREARMS: THE EFFECTS OF SOCIALIZATION ON FELONS' WEAPONS BEHAVIOR

It has been widely reported in the literature that the single best predictor of adult firearms ownership in a "normal" (that is, noncriminal) population is whether one's father had owned a gun. (Relevant studies of the topic are reviewed in Wright, Rossi, and Daly, 1983: Ch. 6.) This result is interpreted to mean simply that fathers teach their children—especially male off-spring—about guns, expose them to guns, indoctrinate them, as it were, into what is frequently called "The Gun Culture." Later, as adults, these people acquire and use their own firearms, a predictable result of their early learning and experiences. It is a pertinent and, so far as we know, unre-searched question whether the ownership and use of firearms among fel-ons is similarly influenced by the effects of early socialization, the topic of this chapter.

Recapitulating what was learned in Chapter Four, most (75%) of the men in our sample had owned at least one gun at one time or another, and slightly more than one-half (57%) owned a gun at the time of arrest. Over 90% of the sample had fired a gun at some time; the average age at which they first did so was 13. Likewise, the average man in our sample obtained his own rifle or shotgun at age 15 and his first handgun at age 18. Clearly, most of these men were exposed to firearms at a relatively early age and have owned and used guns throughout their lives, no doubt for a variety of purposes. We stress that in many of these respects, felons are likely little different from many, perhaps most, American adult men.

The survey asked about firearms ownership and carrying practices among four groups of potential "socialization agents": fathers, siblings, "the peo-ple you hung around with before you came to this prison" (hereafter, sim-ply "friends"), and "the men in your family" (fathers, brothers, uncles, cousins). We also asked about seven "socialization experiences" that many men encounter in their youth (here taken to mean prior to age 14). Mar-ginal frequencies for these items are shown in Table 5.1.

As indicated in Chapter Two, about 70% of the fathers of the men in the sample are reported to have owned a rifle or shotgun; more than one-half owned a handgun; a cross-tabulation of the two items shows that 75% had

TABLE 5.1. Measures of Socialization to Firearms Usage (in Percentages)

	Yes	No	(N)		
Fathers					
1. Did father own a rifle or shotgun?	70	30	(1509)		
2. Did father own a handgun?	57	43	(1471)		
3. Did father carry a handgun?	36	64	(1431)		
4. Did father show respondent how to shoot?	48	52	(1575)		
5. Did father give respondent a gun?	46	54	(1460)		
Siblings					
1. Sibs own a rifle or shotgun?	52	48	(1574)		
2. Sibs own a handgun?	44	56	(1541)		
3. Sibs teach respondent how to shoot?	18	82	(1696)		
Associates	None	Some	Most	All	(N)
1. How many friends owned a gun?	12	48	29	12	(1710)
2. How many owned a handgun?	18	51	23	8	(1704)
3. How many carried a handgun?	37	46	13	5	(1712)
Men in family	None	Some	Most	All	(N)
1. How many owned a gun?	20	45	20	16	(1712)
2. How many owned a handgun?	29	48	15	8	(1694)
3. How many carried a handgun?	64	31	4	2	(1693)
Experiences	Yes	No	(N)		
When you were a kid, did you ever:					
1. Go out shooting with father?	48	52	(1647)		
2. Go to camp and shoot?	14	86	(1635)		
3. Go shooting at a range?	19	81	(1630)		
4. Go hunting?	58	42	(1631)		
5. Join Boy Scouts?	38	62	(1615)		
6. Play with toy guns?	78	22	(1633)		
7. Take apart a gun?	36	64	(1625)		

fathers who owned some sort of firearm. Among handgun-owning fathers, about three-fifths carried handguns outside the home. Likewise, about one-half the fathers (48%) showed their son(s) how to shoot guns, and roughly the same proportion (46%) gave their son(s) firearms as gifts.

Unfortunately, comparable questions have not been asked of a sample of legitimate gun-owning adults, and so it is uncertain whether these figures are relatively high, relatively low, or about the same as one would observe in a sample of "normals." To provide at least some comparative data, several of these items were also administered to a large undergraduate class at the University of Massachusetts in the spring of 1984.[1] Among

[1] Survey questionnaires were distributed on the second day of class to 167 students (96 men and 71 women) enrolled in a course on "Guns, Crime, and Violence

the men in the class, 43% reported that their fathers owned a gun (versus 75% of the felons), and 23% reported that their fathers owned a handgun (versus 57% of the felons). Thus, relative to a nonrandom sample of male college students in the northeast, felons are much more likely to have come from gun-owning backgrounds. On the other hand, 48% of the male students reported that their fathers had taught them how to shoot guns, the same percentage as observed among the felons.[2] The rituals of male socialization, it would appear, are much the same for youth everywhere.

Just over one-half of the felons' siblings were reported to have owned shoulder weapons; about 44% were reported to have owned a handgun. In contrast, less than one-quarter of the male college student sample had siblings who owned any kind of gun. About one-fifth of the felons were taught how to shoot a gun by their sibling(s).

Perhaps the most significant data shown in Table 5.1 concern patterns of ownership among the felons' friends. A mere 12% of the sample reported that none of their friends owned a gun; more than two-fifths reported that most or all of them did. Figures for handgun ownership among the felons' friends were similar although somewhat lower. About 20% reported that most or all of their friends carried handguns. (None of these items was included in the college student survey.)

Finally, concerning the "men in your family," some 36% reported that most or all of them owned a gun (compared to about one-tenth of the male college students); 20% reported that none of them owned a gun (versus 24% of the male college students). Fewer than one-third (29%) of the felons reported that none of the men in the family owned a handgun; about one-quarter reported that most or all of them did.

To provide additional details about gun socialization, the survey asked about various experiences the felons might have had when they were younger; all of these items were also asked of the college students. Results for both samples are shown in Table 5.2.

Consistent with the results for the "taught how to shoot" question, just under one-half of the felons (and the male college students) reported that

---

in the American Experience." The "sample" is clearly not "representative" of anything, and the data are cited here for illustrative purposes only. That said, it is worth a note that the reported rate of gun and handgun ownership among the families of these students is respectably close to the known national figures. Initially, this even seems somewhat anomalous since rates of gun ownership are generally lower in New England than in the nation at large. On the other hand, given the subject matter of the course, it is plausible that children from gun-owning backgrounds are proportionally more likely to have enrolled.

[2] It will be noted that the percentage of students who were taught how to shoot guns by their fathers slightly exceeds the percentage with fathers who owned guns. Assuming reliable reports, this suggests that even some fathers who do not own guns feel compelled to make arrangements for their sons' introduction to the shooting sports.

they "went out shooting guns with their father" when they were young (before they were 14 years old). This, interestingly, was the only question of the seven on which results from the felon and student samples converged; in all other cases, the two groups differed, often by a considerable margin. Male college students, for example, were more likely to have played with toy guns (93%) than felons (78%), were more likely to have joined the Boy Scouts than felons (55 versus 38%), were more likely to have gone to a summer camp where guns were used for recreation (32 versus 14%), and were more likely to have gone shooting at a gun club or pistol range (28 versus 19%). In contrast, the felons were more likely than male college students to have gone hunting as children (58 versus 34%) and were also more likely to have taken a gun apart to "see how it works" (36 versus 23%). (One difference between students and felons is that students played with toy guns and felons with real ones!) Note that college students tend to exceed the felons in activities that require funds, reflecting the greater affluence of their families.

TABLE 5.2. "Gun Socialization" Experiences of Felons Compared with a Sample of College Students (in Percentages)

	Felons	Male students (N = 96)	Female students (N = 70)
1. Ever go shooting with father?	48	46	11
2. Shoot at summer camp?	14	32	16
3. Shoot at range or club?	19	28	13
4. Go hunting?	58	34	6
5. Join Boy/Girl Scouts?	38	55	51
6. Play with toy guns?	78	93	60
7. Take apart a gun?	36	23	11

These "socialization" experiences tend to be associated with each other in patterned ways as shown in Table 5.3, where the correlations among pairs of variables are reported. One is struck, first, by the overwhelming predominance of positive coefficients. In addition, all but a handful are statistically significant. Substantively, this pattern of positive and relatively high correlations implies that socialization is patterned and cumulative. Men in the sample who were exposed to any one of the socialization agents and experiences shown in the table were more likely to have been exposed to all the others as well.

Intercorrelations among the variables representing each of the five socialization "domains" (four "agent" domains and one "experience" domain) are indicated by boldface numbers. With the partial exception of the experience domain, correlations (indicated in boldface) are especially strong. To illustrate, the average correlation among the five variables representing

TABLE 5.3. Intercorrelations among the Socialization "Agents" and "Experiences" Variables

	Variable[a]																				
	1	2	3	4	5	6	7	8	9	10	11	12	13	14	15	16	17	18	19	20	21
1 Father own gun																					
2 Father own handgun[b]	**48**[c]																				
3 Father carry HG	35	**62**																			
4 Father teach shoot	51	30	**26**																		
5 Father give gun	31	20	20	**52**																	
6 Sib own gun	31	16	21	31	25																
7 Sib own HG	18	27	28	13	14	**63**															
8 Sib teach shoot	14	10	14	21	13	37	**37**														
9 Friends own gun	22	17	18	21	23	22	21	12													
10 Friends own HG	14	21	23	11	17	14	24	09	**76**												
11 Friends carry HG	11	16	25	08	13	12	22	07	**55**	**66**											
12 Others own gun	39	21	29	42	31	36	30	24	37	27	19										
13 Others own HG	32	45	41	30	23	27	36	20	33	38	31	**70**									
14 Others carry HG	18	30	45	18	19	20	31	16	27	34	44	39	**53**								
15 Go out shooting	39	20	17	59	48	30	13	23	20	09	04	37	25	12							
16 Camp	07	08	08	13	14	07	08	03	09	13	13	08	13	17	**14**						
17 Club or range	16	12	12	25	25	11	06	08	14	10	05	19	17	11	**33**	**34**					
18 Hunting	34	13	10	45	36	29	14	22	19	09	05	31	19	09	**60**	**12**	**27**				
19 Boy Scouts	−01	02	03	07	02	−02	−04	−03	04	05	00	03	02	05	**04**	**17**	**15**	**04**			
20 Toy guns	02	04	03	−02	−03	00	02	−04	03	02	00	01	−01	−01	**06**	**07**	**06**	**05**	**22**		
21 Took apart	21	15	15	26	30	19	18	16	23	21	16	21	18	16	**37**	**23**	**33**	**36**	**06**	**09**	

[a] Decimals omitted.
[b] Hereafter Hg.
[c] Numbers in boldface indicate intercorrelations among variables representing each of the five socializations "domains" (four "agent" domains and one "experience" domain).

115

the fathers was .38; among the sibling variables, .46; among the friends' variables, .66; and among the "men in the family" variables, .54. Concerning the experience variables, the correlations are substantially weaker (averaging only .20) but still modestly high by customary standards.

Substantively, the generally strong positive "intradomain" correlations provide additional evidence for the social nature of firearms ownership and use. Fathers owning shoulder weapons also tended to own handguns ($r = .48$), to carry handguns (.35), to teach their sons how to shoot (.51), and to give guns as gifts to their sons (.31). In degrees, the same coherent tendencies were observed in each of the other agent domains. The behaviors represented by these variables, in short, are not random with respect to one another but rather tend to form a fairly tight "package." Much the same would presumably be true of normal firearms owners as well.

These findings, as well as similar findings based on studies of noncriminal gun owners, are consistent with the idea of an "American Gun Culture," more precisely, a culture composed of persons and families whose ownership and use of firearms are derivative of a shared set of values transmitted through parental socialization. This, of course, is not to say that the average gun-owning criminal in our sample is no different from the average deer hunter, trap shooter, or gun collector. It is to say that the average gun-owning criminal, like the average legitimate gun owner, was raised around guns and introduced early in life to their use. It may well be that there are multiple "gun cultures" [as Lizotte and Bordua (1980) and Lizotte, Bordua, and White (1981) have suggested], some of which strongly disapprove of the illegal (or quasi-legal) uses of guns and some of which do not. In any case, gun ownership in the population at large and among our sample of prisoners displays unmistakable cultural aspects.

The intercorrelations among the variables in each domain are sufficiently strong to justify the construction of scales, each measuring the strength of the relevant sources of gun socialization. Scaling was straightforward: In the cases of measuring the influence of fathers, siblings, and experiences, the scaled variables are simply a count of the number of "yes" answers to the relevant questions. Thus, the Father-Influence Scale ranges from 0 to 5, the Sibling-Influence Scale ranges from 0 to 3, and the Experience Scale ranges from 0 to 7.

Since questions concerning friends and "men in the family" employed four-choice response options, construction of the Peer-Influence Scale and Male-Clan-Influence Scale had to proceed differently. In these cases, the responses to the three relevant questions were again simply summed, so the resulting scaled variables both range from 3 (a "none of them" response to all three questions) to 12 (an "all of them" response to all three questions). Frequencies and intercorrelations for the resulting variables are shown in Table 5.4.

We note first that the missing data rates for the scaled variables are rel-

TABLE 5.4. Frequencies and Intercorrelations for Influence Scales ($N = 1874$)

	Scale value	Relative frequency	Adjusted frequency
Father-Influence Scale	0	12	19
	1	7	11
	2	9	14
	3	13	21
	4	11	18
	5	12	18
	Missing	36	—
Sibling-Influence Scale	0	34	43
	1	14	17
	2	21	26
	3	12	15
	Missing	20	—
Peer-Influence Scale	3	10	11
	4	5	5
	5	14	16
	6	26	28
	7	9	10
	8	11	12
	9	9	10
	10	3	4
	11	1	2
	12	3	3
	Missing	9	—
Male-Clan-Influence Scale	3	16	18
	4	9	10
	5	20	22

	Scale value	Relative frequency	Adjusted frequency
Male-Clan Influence Scale (continued)	6	18	22
	7	10	20
	8	7	10
	9	5	8
	10	3	6
	11	1	4
	12	2	1
	Missing	10	—
Experiences Scale	0	4	5
	1	17	20
	2	18	22
	3	15	17
	4	14	17
	5	9	10
	6	5	6
	7	2	3
	Missing	15	—

Intercorrelations[a]

	Father	Sibling	Peer	Male Clan
Sibling	.36	—		
Peer	.27	.24	—	
Male clan	.54	.39	.42	—
Experiences	.46	.25	.20	.30

[a]Missing data deleted pairwise. Ns for each cell vary from 1040 to 1662. All coefficients are significant at .001 or beyond.

atively high, ranging from 9% missing on the "friends" variable to 36% missing on the "fathers" variable. The high rate for fathers, of course, only reflects a point noted in Chapter Two, that many of these men grew up in fatherless environments. Also, some of them had no brothers or sisters, which accounts for part of the 20% missing data for siblings. Finally, the seven experience questions appeared toward the end of a very long questionnaire; most of the missing data on this variable results from men simply not answering these questions.

Perhaps the most important substantive point to make about the frequency distributions concerns the relatively low percentages found in the low-end categories of each scale. More than 80% of the men who answered all the fathers' questions, for example, reported that their fathers either owned a gun, carried a gun, taught their sons how to shoot, or gave their sons firearms as gifts; thus, some four-fifths of the men with fathers appear to have received at least some firearms exposure from that source. Likewise, some 95% of the sample (who answered all the pertinent questions) had at least one (or more) of the seven firearms experiences.

Results for the "Peer-Influence Scale" bear a special note. Recall that these questions referred to "the men you hung around with before you came to this prison." About 90% of the sample reported that at least some of these men either owned or carried firearms. As we see later, the firearms practices of a felon's associates were particularly relevant in accounting for his own criminal firearms use.

It is an interesting question just how many of the men in the sample were exposed to none of the agents or experiences recorded in the table; or in other words, how many men fell at the de facto zero point on all five scales. As it happens, this is true of only 7 of the men in the sample. Ignoring the "experience" domain, the number of men at the de facto zero point on all four agents' variables is 28. In short, virtually all of these men had at least some exposure to firearms early in their lives.

Intercorrelations among the five scaled variables are all moderate to high (ranging from .20 to .54), positive in sign, and statistically significant, as, indeed, one would expect given the results in Table 5.3. We thus emphasize again: Men exposed to firearms in any of these contexts are likely to have been exposed in them all.

The scaled variables provide convenient and efficient ways to assess the effects of early socialization on the sample's own firearms behavior. For this purpose, we have selected 16 items of possible interest, grouped loosely into four topical areas, as follows:

Age: How old the felon was when he (1) first fired a gun, (2) first obtained his own shoulder weapon, (3) first obtained his own handgun, (4) committed his first armed crime, and (5) committed his first handgun crime.
Gun Ownership in General: Has the felon ever owned a gun, ever owned a

TABLE 5.5. Correlations between Felon's Firearms Behavior and Influence Scales[a]

Firearms behaviors	Influence scales				
	Father	Sibling	Peers	Male clan	Experiences
Age[b]:					
At first firing	−.36	−.23	−.19	−.26	−.39
At first gun	−.38	−.14	−.20	−.23	−.31
At first handgun	−.18	−.06	−.25	−.11	−.08
At first armed crime	−.01	−.01	−.14	−.01	.02
At first handgun crime	−.07	−.00	−.15	−.04	−.00
Gun ownership[c]					
Ever own gun?	.35	.30	.30	.27	.28
If yes: How many?	.25	.24	.36	.26	.22
If yes: Own handgun?	.02	.09	.25	.12	−.03
How many?	.18	.22	.39	.20	.16
How often fire?	.14	.11	.21	.15	.12
Criminal gun use					
Armed at conviction	.08	.07	.22	.12	.06
How often armed with gun?[d]	.20	.18	.33	.17	.14
Trouble to get one?	.11	.11	.20	.11	.16
Predator[e]	.18	.18	.34	.17	.12
Unarmed	−.11	−.14	−.28	−.14	−.11
Carrying practices					
Carry handguns?	.11	.06	.28	.14	.03
Carry firearms?	.15	.15	.40	.19	.04

[a] Missing data deleted pairwise.
[b] "Never" is treated as missing data for this analysis.
[c] "Ever own" was asked of everyone. Remaining questions were asked only of those who had ever owned.
[d] Asked of gun criminals only.
[e] Type is represented here by two dummy variables, one for Predators and one for Unarmed Criminals.

handgun? How many guns and handguns has he ever owned? How often did he fire his guns before he came to prison?

Criminal Gun Use: Was the felon armed at the conviction offense? How often was he armed with a gun when he committed crimes? How much trouble will it be for him to obtain a handgun upon release? Is he a Predator or not?

Carrying Practices: Two questions on how often the felon carried a firearm with him outside the home.

Zero-order correlations among the variables just discussed and the five scaled socialization variables are shown in Table 5.5. With only a few exceptions, the patterns are much as one would expect: The higher the felon's prior exposure to the agents and experiences of firearms socialization, the more pronounced his own firearms behavior tends to be. (Since any coefficient greater than approximately .05 is statistically significant for this sample size, we will adopt a more rigorous standard than customary and only consider coefficients whose absolute magnitude is at least .10.)

Considering first the "how old were you when . . ." questions, we note that the correlation coefficients are predominantly negative, as would be expected. In general, the higher the degree of exposure, the younger a felon was when he first "got into" guns. The age at which he first fired a gun is correlated -.36 with the Father's-Influence Scale, -.39 with the Experiences-Influence Scale, and somewhat more weakly (but still negatively) with the other three scales. The age at which the felon acquired his first firearm follows a very similar pattern. In short, fathers and the experiences sons share with their fathers seem to be the predominant influences on firing and acquiring a gun for the first time.

In the remaining three cases, however, the pattern shifts somewhat; the age at which a felon acquired his first handgun, committed his first armed crime, and committed his first handgun crime were all more strongly correlated with the Peer-Influence Scale than with any of the other four, a pattern that recurs elsewhere in the table.

All five influence scales were moderately to strongly correlated (.27 to .35) with whether the felon had ever owned a gun; among those who had ever owned at least one, all five variables were likewise moderately to strongly correlated (.22 to .36) with the total number of guns the felon had owned. Among those ever owning a gun, however, the tendency to have owned a handgun was strongly correlated only with the Peer-Influence Scale ($r = .25$) and was essentially uncorrelated with the other four variables. Friends also appeared to exert a greater influence on the number of handguns ever owned and on the rate at which a felon fired his guns than any of the other socialization agents. Considering the number of handguns owned, for example, the effect of the Peer-Influence Scale was about twice that of any other.

In regard to criminal gun use and carrying practices, the general drift of the findings can be quickly summarized: Firearms ownership and carrying among the felon's friends were by far the most important factors. For example, the tendency to have been armed at the conviction offense is correlated at .22 with the Peer-Influence Scale and essentially uncorrelated with all other scales. Among those who have committed at least one gun crime, the frequency with which they were armed with a gun during their crimes was correlated .33 with the Peer-Influence Scale, by far the strongest effect of the five. Likewise, the effects of the Peer-Influence Scale on the felon's carrying practices were more than twice as great as the effects of any other variable. We note finally: Whether the felon is categorized as a Predator is correlated at .34 with the Peer-Influence Scale but much more weakly correlated with all other variables; the correlation of the Peer-Influence Scale with the Unarmed category is -.28, again the strongest effect of the five.

Since all five socialization variables are rather strongly intercorrelated

TABLE 5.6. Multiple Regression of Selected Firearms Behavior on the Five Influence Scales

Dependent variables		Influence scales					
		Father	Sibling	Peers	Male clan	Experiences	R^2
Age[a]							
Age at first firing	$b=$	−.46	−.27	−.12	−.06	−.67	.20
	$SE=$	.09	.12	.06	.07	.08	—
Age at first armed	$b=$	−.09	.04	−.56	.19	.17	.03
crime	$SE=$	.19	.26	.13	.16	.17	—
Ownership							
Ever own a gun?	$b=$	.05	.06	.04	.00	.03	.21
	$SE=$	.01	.01	.01	.01	.01	—
Number owned	$b=$	.08	.19	.23	.03	.10	.17
	$SE=$	.04	.05	.03	.03	.04	—
Own a handgun?	$b=$	−.01	.02	.04	.01	−.02	.07
	$SE=$	.01	.01	.01	.01	.01	—
Crime							
Armed at	$b=$	.00	.01	.05	.01	.00	.05
conviction?	$SE=$	.01	.02	.01	.01	.01	—
How often armed?	$b=$	.08	.09	.18	−.03	.02	.13
	$SE=$	.04	.05	.03	.03	.03	—
Carrying							
How often	$b=$	.05	.07	−.01	−.01	−.06	.17
carry?	$SE=$	.03	.05	.03	.03	.03	—

[a]b, Unstandardized partial regression coefficient; SE, standard error of the estimate.

(Table 5.4), the zero-order analyses just reported may be potentially misleading. Selected results for a multivariate analysis of these same variables are shown in Table 5.6.

Table 5.6 reports regression coefficients and standard errors for 8 separate regression equations. Dependent variables are a representative selection of the 16 firearms behaviors discussed above; independent variables are the five influence scales.

These analyses tend to confirm the conclusions advanced on the basis of the zero-order results. Legitimate aspects of firearms behavior tended to be related to all the influence scales (Male Clan being the consistent exception) and especially to the Father Influence and Experiences Scales. Clearly illicit aspects of a felon's firearms behavior tended to be related only to the Peer-Influence Scale.

The pattern can be illustrated with two examples. The tendency ever to have owned a gun was significantly related to every socialization variable except the Male-Clan-Influence Scale. Fathers and siblings apparently exerted the strongest effects. The tendency to have been armed at the conviction offense was significantly related to none of the influence scales except the Peer-Influence Scale. The results for the carrying variable were, in essence, identical.

In short, we witness in these data a rather intriguing pattern. When considering the more normal or legitimate aspects of firearms behavior (whether the felon ever owned a gun, how many he has owned, how old he was when he first fired or acquired one, etc.), fathers appeared to be the predominant influence (reinforced, to be sure, by all the other agents of socialization as well). When considering the seamier or clearly criminal aspects of firearms behavior, however, the influence of fathers (and other family agents) paled considerably, and the effects of one's peer group came to dominate. (A very similar run of results was also reported in some of the analyses of Chapter Four.)

We infer from this pattern that much of the material presented in this chapter, while of interest, is not especially relevant to the clearly criminal acquisition and use of firearms. It is of some interest to learn, for example, that one-half the felons in this sample were taken out by their fathers and taught how to shoot guns, and that, on the average, they were about 13 years old at the time. We suspect, however, that similar questions asked of a national sample of legitimate firearms owners would produce nearly identical results. What we witness in these data is probably not unique in any sense to the early childhood experiences of felons but rather are fairly common experiences for young males generally in our society. Although hazardous, the comparisons with data from a sampling of male college students are generally consistent with this impression.

Judging from the data reported in this chapter, especially that shown in Tables 5.5 and 5.6, the critical variable affecting criminal uses and abuses of firearms is the prevalence of guns among the felon's peer group—the number of his friends and associates who owned or carried firearms. The "friends" variable was correlated consistently, and at times quite strongly, with all the criminal gun use questions; without exception, it was the strongest correlate (of those examined in this analysis).

The key turning point in the lives of most of these men, we suggest, was not the occasion in their early adolescence when their fathers took them out to teach them how to fire guns. Rather, it was the day they realized that many of the people they hung around with were carrying guns themselves. Some adolescent males, of course, would respond to this information by finding new people to hang around with. This, for example, could well describe some (perhaps many) of the college students we surveyed. Others would respond by obtaining a gun themselves, and these, it appears, were often the ones who ended up in prison.

In the best of circumstances, adolescence can be a much-troubled period in a young man's life; and the men in our sample clearly did not grow up "in the best of circumstances." Most of the men in this sample, as we noted in an earlier chapter, had gotten drunk, tried drugs, and committed at least one fairly serious crime before their sixteenth birthday. Nearly two-thirds reported having been expelled from school; more than one-quarter reported having been beaten by their fathers. Although our study contains no direct questions on such matters, it is easy enough to imagine that the respect and friendship of others in their social environments was, at best, a sometime thing.

Under the circumstances, it is understandable that they might turn to peers for companionship (delinquent gangs are rarely choosy about whom they admit, so long as geography and race are in order) and to firearms for a measure of power and respect. One can also easily imagine an addiction to the ensuing sense of control every bit as intoxicating in its way as heroin or alcohol are in theirs. Student athletes wear their "letter sweaters" to signify their accomplishments and win the admiration and respect of others. Not insignificantly, the same sweaters signify victory in aggressive, even if ritualized, encounters with other young men. In fundamental symbolic respects, this strikes us as not entirely different from the possession and routine carrying of guns among the "tough kids"—the drop-outs or expellees who, at age 16, are already out of school, on their own, prowling the streets.

6

MOTIVATIONS TO GO ARMED

Why do felons acquire and carry weapons? The answer to this question may appear to be obvious, but it is not. For the commission of some crimes, to be sure, a weapon is a great convenience, if not an absolute necessity: Armed robbery is one example and willful, premeditated homicide another. And yet, as we have seen, many of the men in the sample carried weapons during burglaries and thefts, where the need for a weapon is much less obvious; further, many were in the habit of carrying even on days when they were not planning to do any crimes (Chapter Four).

Furthermore, weapons carrying is not without some potential costs; in many jurisdictions, the involvement of a weapon in a crime would eventuate in a stiffer sentence (e.g., Cook and Nagin, 1979), either through mandatory sentence enhancement laws or through the normal sentencing practices of the courts, so there is at least some inducement not to carry. Finally, carrying a weapon in the course of one's daily affairs, especially a firearm, is at least a modest inconvenience, if not a considerable encumbrance.[1] Since the prevalence of weapons carrying among felons is clearly greater than one would expect on the basis of their instrumental use in crime alone, the question why felons bother to carry weapons is not at all a trivial one.

THE "RATIONALITY" OF FIREARMS USE IN CRIME

Some previous discussions of why criminals carry guns have tended to depict the behavior mainly as the carrying of the "tools of the trade," in short, a view of the felon as a rational economic actor. Cook's (1976) "strategic choice analysis" of robbery, for example, suggests that robbers carry guns (versus other weapons or no weapons) because it allows them to rob more lucrative targets and thus to maximize their take. Others suggest that it is more a matter of convenience: A gun is a very intimidating weapon,

---

[1] One reader of a previous draft pointed out that once a person becomes accustomed to it, a small handgun in the pocket is no more an encumbrance than a thick wallet or full key chain; indeed, after carrying a gun for many years (to be sure, in a holster), some policemen apparently feel uncomfortable without it.

and it is just easier to commit crimes (less resistance from the victim, for example) if one is armed with a gun than if not.

On the other hand, some of the analyses so far presented point as much to habit as to rational calculation as an important, if not predominant, motive. In Chapter Four, for example, we found that about 30% of the weapons users in the sample carried weapons almost all of the time, whether planning a crime or not; weapons also enhanced some felons' sense of security, these being the additional 50% who carried weapons in "certain situations," mainly, whenever they felt the need for self-protection. Only about one armed felon in five said that he had carried only when he had been planning to do a crime. From these findings alone, one can safely infer that the crime-facilitative aspects of a weapon did not represent the only, or (perhaps) even the major, motive for carrying one, that habit or fear were of at least equivalent importance.

Of course, a "habit" is not necessarily nonrational or irrational behavior. In everyday life, many of our "habits" consist of patterns of behavior that are the product of long-standing decisions that have proved so useful we no longer subject them to close scrutiny. For example, many Americans habitually wear watches, putting them on in the morning without giving a thought to whether or not wearing a watch on the day in question "makes sense." Through experience, we know that whatever our scheduled activities may be, there are likely to be many occasions when knowing the time would be desirable. Similarly, the habitual carrying of weapons may also make sense in the pursuit of a criminal career in hostile and threatening surroundings. Opportunities to commit crimes may occur, and other predators may attempt to make one a victim.

We reported in Chapter Four that only about 30% of the gun owners in the sample had ever acquired a firearm specifically for use in crime; thus, the large majority (70%) had not. The firearms actually used by these men to commit crimes must have been originally acquired, therefore, for other reasons, possibly a mixture of reasons in which criminal use did not explicitly dominate. What these "other reasons" might have been is in part the topic of this chapter.

It would, of course, be mistaken to formulate the issue as one of "rational calculation" or "crime facilitation" versus habit, fear, or "self-defense," since in important ways these are false oppositions. A felon who carried a gun mainly because of possible encounters with armed victims (and many did, as we see later) could be said to carry out of fear, out of a sensed need for self-defense, or as a means of more efficiently robbing potentially armed victims. In the abstract, these seem like entirely separate classes of motives, but in reality they are not.

The last point requires some emphasis. In discussing the weapons motivations of "the criminal class," it is misleading to look at strictly criminal behaviors as divorced from the broader day-to-day style of life that characterizes the criminal population. As we have stressed earlier, many of the men in our sample were not calculating, "rational" criminals but rather strict opportunists whose "strategic choice," when they made one, was to commit some crime that was suddenly there for them to commit. It is not as though they get out of bed on certain days, decide that this is a day on which they will commit crimes, and arm themselves accordingly. They get out of bed knowing that theirs is a violent and uncertain existence, that today *may* be a day when they are assaulted in a bar, hassled by others on the street, confronted by an armed victim or by the police, or presented with an opportunity to commit a crime. Our point is that a firearm is a useful hedge against *all* the above contingencies. When we say that crime-facilitation, self-protection, fear, and habit are interrelated motives for the firearms behavior of the felons in our sample, what we mean to imply is that all of these are ever-present realities in the day-to-day existence of these men and thus that the decision to arm oneself must derive from some "mix" of what otherwise appear to be distinctive and clearly separable motivations.

MEASURING WEAPONS-CARRYING MOTIVES

Most of the information we have on the motivations to acquire and carry weapons was obtained by directing questions to respondents according to their special circumstances. Men who indicated early in the questionnaire that they had never committed an armed crime were skipped to a set of questions asking, in essence, Why not? Men who had committed crimes with guns were likewise skipped to a sequence asking about their motives for carrying firearms; men who had committed armed crimes, but not with guns, were asked two sequences: why they carried the weapons they carried, and why they chose not to carry a gun. Marginal frequencies for all four of these question sequences are shown in Table 6.1.

It must be stressed in advance that all the data reported here should be treated with some skepticism, in that people are not always the best witnesses about their own motives. As we saw in Chapter Five, for example, having grown up around guns is no doubt an important part of the explanation of the firearms behavior of the felons in the sample, and yet it is likely that socialization factors would rarely be mentioned if people were asked, point blank, "Why do you own a gun?" People, in short, are not always aware of all the relevant reasons for their behavior and need not always be honest in reporting them even when they are aware.

Then too, as we hasten to add, certain "response-set" tendencies may also be at work. On the one hand, it might be easier to say, for example, that "I needed a gun to protect myself" than to say, "I wanted the gun to threaten my friends, if they should try to push me around." Alternatively, some readers of earlier versions of this material suggested that the more

TABLE 6.1. Motivations to Go Armed: Marginal Results (in Percentages)

	Very	Somewhat	A little	Not at all	$\overline{X}$	(N)
			Importance			
Gun criminals: Why did you carry a gun?						
1. Don't have to hurt victim	57	15	7	21	3.1	(721)
2. Chance victim would be armed	50	12	13	25	2.9	(712)
3. Prepared for anything	48	20	11	20	3.0	(698)
4. Ready to defend myself	44	14	13	29	2.7	(709)
5. Easier to do crime	42	17	12	29	2.7	(696)
6. Might need gun to escape	40	15	12	33	2.6	(695)
7. Need gun to do crime	39	13	12	37	2.5	(698)
8. Felt better with gun	34	20	17	29	2.6	(706)
9. People don't mess with you	30	21	14	36	2.4	(686)
10. Easy to hurt someone	27	13	13	47	2.2	(686)
11. Gun is "tool of trade"	25	16	16	43	2.2	(690)
12. Police have guns	20	10	12	58	1.9	(688)
13. Friends carried guns	13	11	14	61	1.8	(702)
14. Made me feel like a man	4	4	12	80	1.3	(674)
Armed-not-with-a-gun: Why did you carry a weapon?						
1. Don't have to hurt victim	39	8	13	39	2.5	(133)
2. Feel better with a weapon	33	12	9	46	2.3	(133)
3. Ready to defend myself	30	13	13	45	2.3	(135)
4. Easier to do crime	29	12	10	48	2.2	(133)
5. Chance victim would be armed	27	12	8	53	2.1	(135)
6. Prepared for anything	24	14	12	50	2.1	(132)
7. Easy to hurt someone	24	6	10	60	1.9	(135)
8. People don't mess with you	20	11	17	52	2.0	(133)
9. Might need weapon to escape	18	11	10	61	1.9	(133)
10. Friends carried weapon	17	11	12	59	1.9	(138)
11. Weapon's "tool of trade"	16	8	9	68	1.7	(133)
12. Need weapon to do crime	11	8	10	71	1.6	(132)
13. Police have weapons	10	5	13	72	1.5	(135)
14. Made me feel like a man	5	6	7	82	1.4	(130)
Armed-not-with-a-gun: Why not carry a gun?						
1. Just asking for trouble	56	13	6	25	3.0	(143)
2. Get a stiffer sentence	54	15	6	25	3.0	(138)
3. Never needed gun for my crimes	54	13	9	24	3.0	(138)
4. Somebody would get hurt	49	9	7	35	2.7	(140)
5. Wouldn't feel right	42	7	13	37	2.5	(137)
6. Never thought about it	38	6	16	40	2.4	(139)
7. Wouldn't trust myself	36	7	7	50	2.3	(135)
8. Never owned a gun	35	7	12	46	2.3	(137)
9. Don't like guns	30	8	11	50	2.2	(135)
10. Against the law for me to own gun	25	7	13	56	2.0	(137)
11. Too much trouble to get one	16	5	7	72	1.6	(134)

(continued)

	Importance					
	Very	Somewhat	A little	Not at all	X̄	(N)
12. Costs too much	11	6	11	72	1.6	(138)
13. Wouldn't know how to use one	11	4	8	76	1.5	(132)
The unarmed: Why not carry a weapon?						
1. Just asking for trouble	69	12	5	14	3.3	(553)
2. Get a stiffer sentence	67	12	6	15	3.3	(535)
3. Never needed gun for my crimes	61	7	6	26	3.0	(523)
4. Somebody would get hurt	60	11	7	22	3.1	(531)
5. Wouldn't feel right	53	9	7	31	2.8	(528)
6. Never thought about it	52	9	10	28	2.9	(537)
7. Against the law	51	8	6	36	2.7	(513)
8. Don't like weapons	46	11	8	34	2.7	(517)
9. Never owned a weapon	38	6	7	48	2.3	(506)
10. Wouldn't trust myself	34	8	9	50	2.3	(502)
11. Wouldn't know how to use one	14	8	7	70	1.7	(495)
12. Wouldn't know how to get one	14	6	7	73	1.6	(499)
13. Too expensive	12	7	8	73	1.6	(516)

likely effect would be in the opposite direction, the hypothesis being that felons would stress (or fabricate) tougher, more aggressive reasons so as to project an image of self as fundamentally "bad." Our hope, of course, is that these represent offsetting tendencies. In any case, it is clear that the reasons felons themselves gave for why they owned and carried weapons constitute interesting and useful information but do not provide the final word on the matter.

The lead-in to the "motivations" questions read as follows: 'There are many different reasons why a person might decide to carry a [GUN or WEAPON] while doing a crime. Following is a list of some of these reasons." For each reason listed, the respondent was asked to state how important that reason was in his own decision to carry a gun (or weapon). Response options were "very," "somewhat," "a little," or "not at all important." Frequencies reported in Table 6.1 are arranged in rank order (most to least important reason), based in all cases on the percentage that cited each reason as "very important."

We focus first on the responses of the Gun Criminals (men who have committed at least one gun crime). As these men told it, the single most important reason why they decided to carry a gun while doing crime was, "if you carry a gun your victim doesn't put up a fight, and that way you don't have to hurt them" ("very important" to 57% and the most commonly mentioned motive of the 14 listed, by a fairly substantial margin).[2]

[2] This result is consistent with a suggestion once made by Phil Cook that many robbers carry guns as a means of avoiding, not perpetrating, violence. It is not con-

Per se, this is not a particularly surprising result: We saw in Chapter Four that intimidation of the victim was, by far, the most common use to which crime weapons were put; we now learn that it was also the single most important motive for carrying a gun during crime. Confronted by a gun-wielding felon, the typical victim is, one presumes, less likely to resist, no doubt a highly desirable outcome from the felon's point of view. One predominant motive to go armed was clearly to minimize the "hassles" from victims that a felon might otherwise encounter and, hence, to maximize the chances that the crime would be successfully completed.

In much the same vein, the second most important reason cited for the decision to carry a gun was, "There's always a chance my victim would be armed" ("very important" to 50%). It is of considerable interest that both the first and second most important motives relate to victims; one-half the men who had committed gun crimes said that one "very important" reason to carry a gun during crime was the prospect that the intended victim would be armed. The role that actual or potential encounters with armed victims played in the firearms behavior of this sample is of sufficient interest that we have devoted the next chapter exclusively to this topic. It bears notice in this context that felons are not above preying upon their fellow criminals as victims in their crimes; hence, the probabilities that victims might be armed are not trivial.

Intimidation of the victim and defense against an armed victim are the only motives of the 14 that were said to be very important by one-half or more of the sample. Other motives of nearly equal weight included, "when you have a gun, you are prepared for anything that might happen" ("very important" to 48%), and "a guy like me has to be ready to defend himself" (44%). Self-preservation was clearly the common theme in both these responses: Carrying a gun was seen, apparently, as a useful hedge against the uncertainties that accompany a life of crime.

That "it is easier to do crime if you are armed with a gun" was the fifth (but only the fifth) most commonly cited motive and was rated as "very important" by 42%. This plus the first-place result make it clear that the increased ease with which crime can be committed if armed with a gun was one important motive for carrying one; the other results also suggest, however, that self-preservation was a motive of equivalent or greater importance. Of course, the line between self-preservation and efficiency in accomplishing crimes is blurred, especially if one considers that success in a crime most likely includes coming away from the incident without physical harm or apprehension.

---

sistent, however, with the argument just reviewed in the text, that these felons would exercise every opportunity to let the researchers know just how "bad" they were. "And that way you don't have to hurt them . . ." strikes us as an almost sissified response, hardly the sort of thing that a Richard Pryor-like "we bad" felon would be inclined to confess to. Among the Gun Criminals, however, it was the most frequently given response.

The twin motifs of self-preservation and efficiency recur throughout the results. "I felt I might need a gun to escape" was very important to 40%; "you need a gun to do the kind of crime I did," to 39%. Some men "just felt better when I had a gun with me" (34% "very important"). That "people just don't mess with you if you are carrying a gun" was very important to 30%. Motives of apparently minimal importance included "a lot of the people I hung around with carried guns" (but see the previous chapter), and "carrying a gun made me feel more like a man."

Data on the motivations of the gun criminals in the sample therefore support the conclusion that they carried guns both to facilitate the commission of crimes and for their own self-protection. We emphasize again that these are not entirely different motives. A resistant victim not only complicates the commission of the crime but also might imperil the well-being of the offender; being able to effectuate one's escape could be scored as either an "efficiency" motive or a "self-preservation" motive; and so on through the list. The important point to be made from these results is not that one or the other of these was the single most important motive for a felon to carry a gun, but rather that guns were important because they allowed for the commission of crimes with minimum trouble from victims and maximum security for the felon. Whether or not this mixture of motives amounts to some postulated syndrome of "economic rationality" is more a semantic problem than an empirical one. To be sure, many of the factors mentioned as important by these men went well beyond the rational calculations of a profit-maximizing "businessman," relating, instead, to survival in an uncertain and inherently dangerous lifestyle. At the same time, a man who has decided to maximize his chances of survival has obviously made a quite rational decision.

THE MOTIVATIONS OF NONGUN USERS

Results for the Armed-Not-with-a-Gun Criminals were similar in some respects but quite different in others. We note first that all the possible motives for carrying were generally less important to the men who carry weapons other than firearms than to the gun criminals. To illustrate, the mean response for the first-place finisher among the Armed-Not-with-a-Gun group was 2.5 (39% "very important"). Among the Gun Criminals, there were six motives with higher mean scores. From this pattern (which is quite general throughout the table) one can safely infer that the reasons why gun criminals carried guns were generally more strongly held than were the reasons why the men who carried other weapons carried the weapons they did. The motives for carrying guns, in other words, were more sharply crystallized—more fervently held, as it were—than the motives for carrying other weapons.

As among the Gun Criminals, the most important reason for carrying a weapon among the Armed-Not-with-a-Gun group was so that the victim would not put up a fight. Indeed, the two groups were agreed on four of the top five motives. Men who carried weapons other than guns, that is, appeared to do so for pretty much the same reasons that gun-carrying felons carried firearms—a combination of efficiency and protection. The difference was mainly that these reasons were less strongly held among the nongun group than among the gun group. One possible interpretation of this difference is that guns are simply better devices both for efficiency in the commission of crime and for general protection against victims and a hostile environment; men to whom these factors were very important might have preferentially chosen to carry guns. Another possible reason may have to do with the types of crimes committed by nongun criminals, crimes in which firearms may not provide an important edge or advantage (e.g., rape).

The Armed-Not-with-a-Gun criminals were also asked why they had opted not to carry firearms; the Unarmed Criminals were asked why they had opted not to carry any weapons. Remarkably, there was virtually perfect agreement between the two groups through the first six reasons on the list. In both cases, the most important reason for not carrying was that "the guy who carries [a gun or a weapon] is just asking for trouble" (very important to 56% of the Armed-Not-with-a-Gun and to 69% of the Unarmed), followed by "you get a stiffer sentence if you get caught with a [gun or a weapon]" (very important to 54 and 67%, respectively). The other four top finishers in both groups were: "I never needed a [gun or a weapon] for the kinds of crime I did" (54 and 61% "very important"); "if you carry a [gun or a weapon], somebody is going to get hurt" (49 and 60% very important, respectively); "I just wouldn't feel right carrying [a gun or weapon]" (42 and 53%); and "I just never thought about carrying a [gun or weapon]" (38 and 52%).

Despite the high rank-order agreement on the reasons not to carry, we note again that all the cited reasons were less important, on the average, to the Armed-Not-with-a-Gun Criminals than to the Unarmed Criminals. The highest mean score among the former group was 3.0 and among the latter 3.3; and again, this pattern was quite general throughout all relevant comparisons. Interestingly, then, it appears that the Armed-Not-with-a-Gun criminals carried weapons for much the same reasons that the Gun Criminals carried guns, but they chose not to carry guns for much the same reasons that the Unarmed opted not to carry anything. Their motives, in short, were apparently mixed: Like the Gun Criminals, they sensed the need to be armed; like the Unarmed, they agreed that carrying a gun was "just asking for trouble." As a compromise among competing motives, they carried other weapons instead.

Some of the item-specific results warrant more extended comment. First, the strong showing of "you get a stiffer sentence if . . ." should be acknowledged. As noted in the opening of this chapter, a weapons involvement would have eventuated in a stiffer sentence in many jurisdictions; the perception of the sample on this point is probably accurate. It is impossible to say for sure just how many of the Unarmed or the Armed-Not-with-a-Gun criminals would have been Gun Criminals were it not for this fact; but presumably some, perhaps many, would have been. The sentencing provisions for weapons involvement, in short, do not represent a perfect deterrent since many Gun Criminals appear in our sample (and therefore have clearly not been deterred); but they do appear to represent at least some deterrent to some men who might have otherwise carried guns.

On the other hand, that it was "against the law" for most of these men to own a firearm appears to have been a minimal deterrent, especially for the Armed-Not-with-a-Gun group, among whom this finished tenth as a reason not to carry guns. This suggests (as an admittedly remote but interesting inference) that more might be gained in this area through sentencing practices than through legislative action: The provisions of new firearms legislation are things these men would find easy enough to ignore; sentencing practices in which stiffer penalties are given to those who use guns in crime, in contrast, clearly are not.

Finally, it is of some relevance to note that the decision not to carry a weapon had little, if anything, to do with availability, knowledge, or price. The least important of all factors asked about was, "A good [gun or weapon] just costs too much money"; this factor was said to be not at all important by about three-quarters of both relevant groups. "It is too much trouble to get a [gun or weapon]" and "I wouldn't know how to use [a gun or weapon] if I had one" were also not at all important to the large majority. As noted previously, a substantial majority of the Unarmed Criminals in the sample, in fact, had owned guns. That these men did not use guns to commit crimes is not, therefore, the result of inadequate knowledge about or exposure to them.

Interestingly, there were some apparent commonalities in the reasoning of men who carried weapons and those who did not. The major reason cited by noncarriers for the decision not to carry was that to carry a weapon (be it a gun or some other weapon) was to "ask for trouble." The major reason cited by carriers for the decision to carry was that if you had a weapon, the victim did not put up a fight. In both cases, avoiding unwanted trouble was clearly a principal motive. Where the two groups differed was in what kind of trouble they wanted to avoid—hassles from uncooperative victims, on the one hand, trouble with the law (or longer sentences), on the other.

COHERENCE IN MOTIVES

Table 6.2 shows the intercorrelations among the 14 "motivations" questions for the Gun Criminals portion of the sample. Remarkably, all the coefficients are positive; all are statistically significant; most are respect-

TABLE 6.2. Intercorrelations among the Motives to Go Armed

	Gun criminals only													
	1	2	3	4	5	6	7	8	9	10	11	12	13	14
1. Friends carried	—													
2. Victim could be armed	18[a]	—												
3. Defend myself	31	39	—											
4. No victim hassles	10	41	21	—										
5. Felt better	28	25	41	23	—									
6. Easier to do crime	13	41	21	46	37	—								
7. Felt like a man	26	11	18	09	27	17	—							
8. Police have guns	26	28	36	17	22	27	23	—						
9. Need to escape	16	45	36	35	29	37	15	33	—					
10. Easy to hurt	22	26	24	15	27	33	16	29	31	—				
11. Tool of trade	23	30	38	25	32	35	16	40	29	35	—			
12. Need to do crime	08	33	21	28	22	40	09	22	30	30	39	—		
13. Prepared for anything	19	39	37	28	33	35	11	26	41	40	46	44	—	
14. People don't mess	19	21	22	30	32	33	19	18	21	20	25	35	38	—

[a] Missing data deleted pairwise; decimal points omitted.

able in magnitude; and quite a few are substantial (.30 or higher). What this implies, of course, is that men who found any of these factors important tended to see each of the others as important as well, which might have been a major reason why they were Gun Criminals in the first place. Stated in somewhat different terms, most men who were able to cite any reason to carry a gun would often be able to cite numerous reasons. Presumably, the more reasons a man has for carrying a firearm, the more difficult it would be to persuade him to stop it, and in this sense, the uniformly positive coefficients reported in the table are not encouraging.

Little need be said about the coefficients themselves. As noted previously, the single most important reason given for carrying a gun was that the victim would be less likely to resist. This factor was strongly correlated with "there's always a chance the victim would be armed" $(r = .41)$, "it is easier to do crime when you are armed with a gun" $(r = .46)$, and "I felt I might need a gun to escape" $(r = .35)$. These correlations nicely illustrate the similarity between the efficiency and self-preservation motives; phrased otherwise, self-preservation is, itself, part of the meaning of efficiency and vice versa.

The single largest coefficient reported in the table $(r = .46)$ was between "when you have a gun, you are prepared for anything that might happen" and "for a guy like me, a gun is just a 'tool of the trade.'" We note this result simply because it too illustrates the relationship between the efficiency and survival motives. All else equal, the "tool of the trade" response would suggest a very pragmatic orientation, to wit, that the gun is just a piece of equipment necessary to get the work done. And yet, this response was strongly correlated with all the "survival" responses. From this one infers that to these men, the gun was a "tool of the trade" not just in the sense that it facilitated getting the work done but also in the important sense that a truly useful "tool" is one that prepares its users for any eventuality they could reasonably expect to encounter as they went about their daily affairs.

THE IMPORTANCE OF GUN CARRYING

The uniformly positive coefficients reported in Table 6.2 suggest that a useful measure of the "seriousness" of gun carrying among the men in the sample can be constructed simply by summing the number of "very important" responses over the 14 offered options. This, in essence, is a count of the number of "good reasons" a felon gave for why he carried a gun. Table 6.3 reports the means on this measure by type, as well as the mean responses on each of the 14 motivation items.

Over the total gun criminals sample, the average number of "very important" reasons was 3.6; in other words, the average gun criminal had 3 or 4 very important reasons why he carried a gun. This average varied sharply across the categories of the typology, from 1.6 "very important" reasons among the One-Timers to 5.2 "very important" reasons among the Handgun Predators. In general, as the frequency of gun use in crime increased, the number of important reasons for carrying a gun also increased. The higher rate criminals in our sample evidenced a much greater seriousness of purpose in their gun-carrying behaviors than the others.

TABLE 6.3. The Motivation to Go Armed, by Type

	One-timers	Sporadics	Handgun predators	Shotgun predators
1. Friends carried	1.4	1.6	2.0	2.1
2. Victim could be armed	2.1	2.8	3.3	3.1
3. Defend myself	2.1	2.5	3.2	2.9
4. No victim hassles	2.5	3.2	3.3	3.1
5. Felt better	1.9	2.6	3.0	2.5
6. Easier to do crime	1.9	2.7	3.1	3.0
7. Felt like man	1.2	1.3	1.4	1.3
8. Police have guns	1.5	1.7	2.3	2.4
9. Need to escape	1.9	2.4	3.1	2.9
10. Easy to hurt	1.7	2.0	2.5	2.5
11. Tool of trade	1.5	1.9	2.8	2.7
12. Need to do crime	2.1	2.4	2.9	2.5
13. Prepared for anything	2.3	2.8	3.4	3.2
14. People don't mess	2.1	2.4	2.6	2.7
$\overline{X}$ "Very important"[a]	1.6	3.2	5.2	4.0

[a] Average number of reasons rated as "very important." See text for details.

The item-by-item results showed a remarkably consistent pattern: Every reason for carrying a gun was more important to the Predators than to either the One-Timers or the Sporadics. The data reveal no exceptions to this pattern.

Among the Predators (both types), the single most important reason for carrying a gun was, "When you have a gun, you are prepared for anything that might happen." Among the Handgun Predators, this was followed by the two "victims" responses and then by self-defense. Other items with mean scores (among Handgun Predators) of 3.0 or higher included the need to escape, that it was easier to do crime when armed with a gun, and that "I just felt better. . . ." In general, the patterns for the Shotgun Predators were very similar. Relative to responses in the total gun criminals sample, then, these results suggest that the crime facilitative (or "efficiency") factors were somewhat less important and the survival factors somewhat more important to the Predators than to the other groups. This, of course, is an inference from the rank order of responses; in absolute terms, to emphasize, every reason for carrying was more important to the Predators than to the other groups.

REASONS FOR THE "MOST RECENT" FIREARMS ACQUISITIONS

Additional evidence on motivations was obtained from all the gun owners in the sample (not just the Gun Criminals) in connection with questions about the reasons why they acquired their most recent firearm(s). These data are shown in Table 6.4.

Concerning the most recent handgun acquisitions, the predominant motive by far was self-protection: 58% of the handgun owners in the sample cited this as a "very important" reason why the most recent handgun was obtained. No other reason even comes close: The next highest "very important" percentage was for "target shooting" (31%). Thus, most felons who acquired a handgun did so, they said, for their own self-defense.

Remarkably, "to use in my crimes" was cited as a "very important" reason by only 28% of the sample; the proportion citing self-protection was more than twice as large. As suggested earlier, acquiring a handgun *specifically* for its use in crime was relatively uncommon among the felons in this sample.

Given that the themes of efficiency and self-protection are clearly related, one infers that most of the handguns that were actually used in crime were acquired for "self-protection" (as seen by the felons) but that the protection involved was "defense" against the risks stemming from a life of crime. Apparently, felons view weapons as general tools that serve a variety of purposes, in which "self-protection" serves as an important symbolic rubric.

Sport and recreational applications (hunting, target shooting, gun collec-

TABLE 6.4. Reasons Why Felons' Most Recent Firearms Were Obtained (in Percentages)

	Not important	Somewhat important	Very important	(N)
Most recent handgun				
Hunting	54	20	26	(736)
Target shooting	38	31	31	(746)
Gun collection	56	19	25	(718)
Protection	16	26	58	(819)
Just wanted one	38	36	26	(772)
To use in crimes	52	20	28	(737)
Stole to sell	65	18	17	(715)
Needed to get someone	80	10	10	(688)
Most recent shoulder weapon				
Hunting	23	14	64	(844)
Target shooting	30	30	40	(778)
Gun collection	56	19	26	(741)
Protection	44	25	31	(779)
Just wanted one	43	33	23	(765)
To use in crimes	70	13	17	(736)
Stole to sell	73	13	14	(726)
Needed to get someone	87	6	7	(694)

tions) were mentioned as important reasons by roughly one-quarter of the handgun owners in the sample; specific criminal applications (stole a handgun to sell; needed a handgun to get somebody) were cited less frequently (10–20%), except, of course, general use in crime, which was noted by 28%. Judging from these data, a felon was as likely to acquire a handgun for some sport or recreational purpose as he was to acquire one for a specific criminal use. Many, no doubt, had both purposes in mind, just as a salesman might buy a car for both pleasure and business applications.

Concerning the most recent rifle or shotgun acquisition, sport and recreational uses dominated the results. Hunting was cited as very important by 64%, and target shooting by 40%. Following in third place was self-protection, very important to 31%. Specific criminal applications were less commonly cited: Still, 17%—nearly one in five—mentioned "to use in my crimes" as a very important reason for their most recent acquisition.[3]

---

[3] The careful reader will notice that "I stole it to sell . . ." was cited about equally often in connection with both the most recent handgun and shoulder-weapon acquisition. Chapter 10 discusses the matter of gun theft in some detail; gun theft, like other theft, is mainly an opportunity crime. What the result in Table 6.4 means, we suspect, is that felons in general stole guns whenever they came across them. Since shoulder weapons are more common than handguns in the private arsenal of the U.S. population, one would expect felons to come across shoulder weapons rather more frequently. Still, a shoulder weapon would be more difficult to steal than a

TABLE 6.5. Reasons Why Felons' Most Recent Handguns Were Obtained, by Type

	Type[a]						
Reason	Unarmed	Improviser	Knife	One-timer	Sporadic	Handgun predator	Shotgun predator
Hunting	2.0	1.8	1.9	1.8	1.5	1.5	1.7
Target shooting	2.2	2.4	2.2	2.0	1.8	1.7	1.8
Collecting	1.8	1.8	2.0	1.7	1.5	1.7	1.8
Self-protection	2.2	2.1	2.3	2.4	2.5	2.6	2.3
Just wanted one	1.9	1.8	1.6	1.8	1.9	2.0	2.0
Use in crimes	1.1	1.1	1.4	1.4	1.9	2.3	2.2
Stole to sell	1.4	1.3	1.5	1.4	1.7	1.6	1.6
Get someone	1.1	1.2	1.3	1.2	1.2	1.5	1.6
(N)[b]	(167)	(21)	(37)	(134)	(172)	(231)	(57)

[a]Responses are very important (=3), somewhat important (=2), and not important (=1).
[b]Missing data deleted item by item. Ns shown are the largest Ns in the table.

Felons who owned handguns but did not use them to commit crimes tended predominantly to have been sport and recreational owners (Table 6.5). Among the Unarmed Criminals, for example, "target shooting" was, on the average, as important as self-protection as a reason for acquiring the most recent handgun, and the same was more or less equally true of Improvisors and Knife Criminals as well. In all three cases, to be sure, self-protection was as important as (or, in one case, slightly more important than) any of the sport and recreational reasons. On the other hand, it was only among the nongun criminals where sport and recreational motives competed favorably with the other reasons listed.

Self-protection was a relatively important motive in all seven groups; means varied from 2.1 to 2.6 (out of a possible maximum of 3). Among the four groups of Gun Criminals, self-protection was the single most important motive in every case. Even among Handgun Predators, self-protection was more important than any of the specific criminal use applications; the mean response among Handgun Predators on "self-protection" was 2.6 versus 2.3 on "to use in my crimes." In short, even the more predatory criminals acquired handguns primarily, as they saw it, for their own self-protection and only secondarily to use in crime. (At the same time, use in crime was clearly more important to the Predators than to any of the other groups.)

The overall pattern revealed in this and previous analyses is, therefore,

_____

handgun, and the black market demand for firearms is, one presumes, predominantly a demand for handguns. If felons made a practice of stealing every (or nearly every) handgun they came across in the course of their burglaries but only the occasional (say, every third or fourth) shoulder weapon, it would largely account for the pattern being discussed.

both intriguing and somewhat counterintuitive. Relatively few men in this sample said they had ever acquired a gun specifically to use in crime; relatively few cited such uses as a primary reason why their handguns had been obtained. Likewise, relatively few men were in the habit of carrying just when they were planning to do crime, and again, the crime-facilitative aspects of firearms, while unquestionably important, certainly did not dominate the reasons given for why they carried guns. The real or potential criminal applications of firearms, in most analyses, seem not to have been the dominant factor in the firearms behavior of these men. Of course, the key to the meaning of this finding is that self-protection has at least two referents: (1) protection against other predators in a hostile environment; and (2) protection against the risks involved in the commission of crimes.

Self-protection was clearly an important motive in both the acquisition and carrying of guns. "When you have a gun, you are prepared for anything that might happen." Men in the sample who carried guns with them outside the home did so either all the time or whenever they felt the need to protect themselves; survival factors figured quite prominently in the motivations analyzed in this chapter; self-protection as an acknowledged motive appeared to be about twice as important as use in crime as a reason for their most recent handgun acquisitions, although self-protection also clearly includes protection in the context of the commission of crimes. All the evidence we have assembled, therefore, points to the same conclusion, namely, that gun criminals carried guns at least as much to protect themselves against the uncertainties of their environment as to prey upon the larger population.

That these men inhabit a violent and generally hostile world is easy to demonstrate. Over 70% of them had been involved in assaults; over 50% had gotten into bar fights; about 40% had been stabbed with a knife; 52% reported having been shot at with a gun; 34% said they had been "scared off, shot at, wounded or captured" by a victim who was armed with a gun (see the following chapter). That they felt some need to protect themselves is hardly surprising. Violence, clearly, was very much an integral part of the daily lives of these men—and this was as true on days when they were not committing crimes as on the days when they were. In this framework for existence, such as it is, a gun was perceived, no doubt, as a very useful hedge against an uncertain and fearful future, an "equalizer" that these men came to possess and carry as much to aid in surviving life on the streets as to use in committing crime.

7

CONFRONTING THE ARMED VICTIM

Many private citizens claim to own guns for protection against crime, a finding that has been confirmed in a number of national surveys (see Wright, Rossi, and Daly, 1983: Ch. 7, for a review of relevant studies). Whether the people who own guns for such reasons are in fact any safer from crime is a matter of considerable and often rancorous dispute. Some believe that guns represent a potent and efficacious defense against crime; others believe that the "typical" American gun owner is less likely to capture a criminal in the act than to shoot himself in the foot (or perhaps, to shoot a loved one in a moment of rage).

Which of these is the correct view cannot be resolved, of course, through a survey of prisoners, and our point in this chapter, therefore, is not to come to some conclusions about whether people "should" or "should not" own guns to protect themselves from crime. What our data can tell us, however, is how often these prisoners had encountered armed victims and how they reacted to those encounters. About one-half of the prisoners claimed that defense against an armed victim was an important reason for acquiring and using guns (Chapter Six). Apparently, felons believe that armed victims are of sufficient concern to justify owning and using firearms. In addition, we asked the felons a number of direct questions about encountering an armed victim, findings from which are reported in this chapter. We cover two main topics: First, we consider evidence from the survey on whether an encounter with an armed victim is something about which felons worried in the course of committing crimes; and second, how frequently armed victims were encountered during the felons' criminal careers.

One piece of information that we do not provide (not having thought at the time to ask the appropriate questions) is just who the armed victims were that these men reported confronting. One potent and oft-exploited image of the armed victim is that of the hard-bitten, law-abiding home owner valiantly defending self and family from the incursions of the predatory criminal class. This, for example, is the image one obtains from "The Armed Citizen" column in the NRA's *American Rifleman*, where news accounts of these kinds of incidents are collected and printed. Such incidents doubtlessly occur, perhaps with considerable frequency. National survey data suggest that some 2–6% of all U.S. adults have at some time actually fired a gun in their own self-defense (Wright, Rossi, and Daly, 1983: Ch 7); a 1981 survey by Peter Hart found that 9% of all handgun-owning households had used the handgun for defense in the previous five years.

On the other hand, one must also keep in mind in reviewing the materials presented in this chapter that felons often prey on others much like themselves, and that in many of these encounters, the issue of who is victim and who is perpetrator is decidedly ambiguous. An illustration: We report later that about one-third of our sample obtained its most recent handgun through direct theft by the felon himself. About 31% of these thefts were reported to have been thefts from the felons' own friends and family members, and another 30% were thefts from fences, drug dealers, and other black-market sources. Only about 29% of them involved thefts from the cars, homes, and apartments of total strangers.

That the predatory felons in this sample hung around with others who owned and carried guns has already been reported; that they tend to have preyed on the people they associated with (or others in their immediate environment) is suggested by the gun theft data just reviewed and is confirmed in detail by the many criminal victimization surveys (e.g., Hindelang, Gottfredson, and Garofab, 1978). Given these points, one has to expect that the rate at which these men confronted armed victims would be rather high, which, indeed, it is. To emphasize, many of the confrontations reported by these men (precise percentage unknown) would have involved their own friends and associates, that is, others of like background, circumstance, and (perhaps) felonious inclinations.[1]

ARMED VICTIMS AS RISKS TO CRIMINALS

Generally speaking, a criminal poised at the edge of a decision to commit a crime faces a range of possible risks and benefits. The benefits consist

[1] The point, that criminals tend to prey upon others much like themselves, is illustrated by some of the commonplace findings in criminological research. For example, it has been widely reported that most homicides and homicidal assaults involve persons who are known to one another prior to the event—family members, friends, acquaintances, and so on (see, e.g., Curtis, 1974; Zimring, 1968). Less than one-half of all household burglaries (where characteristics of the offender are known) are committed by strangers (Bureau of Justice Statistics, 1985); about one-half are committed by relatives and acquaintances of the victim. Concerning the crime of robbery, "most robbers . . . typically operate close to home," that is, in their own or adjacent neighborhoods (Cook, 1983: 19). A related finding pertinent to this discussion is that "there is a tendency for robbers to choose victims who are similar to themselves in terms of demographic characteristics" (Cook, 1982: 30). In most of the major categories of crime, in short, the odds are good that the victim is a relative, acquaintance, or reasonably nearby neighbor of the offender. The rate at which offenders would expect to encounter armed victims is therefore a function of the rate of gun owning and carrying among felons' relatives, acquaintances, and neighbors, which, as we have already noted, is apparently rather high.

of the potential economic or other gains, however conceived, from the contemplated crime; the costs include the possibility of being caught and imprisoned, of being shot at in the course of the crime, either by the police or by the victim, the likelihood of social disapproval, etc. Each cost (and each benefit) can be described in two parameters: (1) the value (positive or negative) of the anticipated outcome and (2) the probability that the outcome will be achieved. The expected benefit (or cost) of the behavior is the value of the outcome times its probability. In standard utility theory, one commits the act in question if and only if the expected benefits exceed the expected costs.

In principle, a crime-control measure based on utility theory operates on the decisions faced by potential criminals by changing the value of the expected costs of crime—either through affecting the probabilities of a cost being incurred by a criminal (e.g., by increasing the chances that one will be caught), or through changing the values associated with the outcome (e.g., by increasing the sentence meted out to those who are caught), or, of course, both. In theory, either of these should have equivalent effects, since a cost is to be reckoned as a simple multiplicative function of its associated probabilities and values.

Empirically, it has been shown (Anderson, Harris, and Miller, 1983) that a normal, noncriminal population is, in fact, more responsive to changes in the probabilities than to changes in the values, or in other words, that normal people are more sensitive to the certainty of punishment than to the severity of punishment. Whether this is also true of the "deterrence calculus" of a felon population has not been thoroughly studied.

Whether "The Armed Citizen" functions to deter, prevent, or thwart crime therefore appears to turn on two questions: First, what is the probability that a felon will encounter an armed victim in the course of his criminal affairs? Second, what are the potential costs of these encounters?

The probability of encountering a victim who possesses a firearm is by no means trivial, as it happens. National surveys conducted periodically since 1959 have routinely found that one-half the households in the United States possess at least one firearm (Wright, Rossi, and Daly, 1983: Ch. 5). All else equal, then, a burglar would expect to find at least one gun in every second home. This, of course, is not to say that one-half of all households are fully prepared to thwart a crime with a gun: The weapons may be inaccessible, no ammunition may be present, there may be no one home to use the gun, etc. Still, with one-half of all households possessing at least one gun, the prospect of encountering an armed victim who is at the time prepared to use his or her weapon is clearly greater than zero. We also emphasize again that criminals often prey upon each other: Those who would venture, say, to rob their own drug dealers can expect that the dealers would be armed and have their weapons ready to hand.

There are no firm estimates of the proportion of the American population who routinely carry handguns or the proportion of businesses whose managers and proprietors keep guns handy on the premises. All evidence suggests that these proportions are small, but nonzero, and in some environments may actually be quite large. In any event, it is not just the burglar who faces the possibility of encountering an armed would-be victim but also those who commit other crimes as well.

The potential costs of encountering an armed victim vary all the way from being forced to abandon the intended crime and running away through being captured and turned over to the criminal justice system to being shot and physically harmed or killed. It is conceivable that would-be victims might be even more likely to fire their weapons than the police would be (when discovering a crime in progress), and if so, then the potential cost of encountering an armed victim may exceed the potential cost of, say, running into the police.

The possibility of greater damage from armed victims is offset by the possibility that victims might not have their guns handy, might not want to use their guns if they had them at hand, or for some other reason might not want to risk escalating an encounter into a full-scale shootout.

Whatever the true probabilities and costs, the prospects of an armed-victim encounter no doubt contribute to the general uncertainty of a life of crime. In the usual run of things, a criminal would seldom know for sure whether the intended victim were armed or what kinds of behaviors to expect even if the victim were armed. All he would know for sure is that there is some possibility the victim is carrying (or possesses) a gun and some possibility that the gun will be used against him. How large these probabilities are is unknown, but they are clearly larger than zero, and in the case of some classes of would-be victims, especially other criminals, store owners, banks, currency exchanges, etc., are likely to be quite high.

There is, in short, good reason to expect that felons would be made nervous by the possibility of running into an armed victim: Since there are so many armed potential victims "out there," the probability of such an encounter is relatively high and the possible consequences, potentially dreadful. On this basis, one may assume that criminals are no more anxious to encounter armed victims than victims are to encounter armed criminals.

ATTITUDINAL RESULTS

Fear of imprisonment is not a significant barrier to participation in crime because many felons do not expect to get caught in any case.[2] Our sample

---

[2] More correctly, hard-core predatory felons committed to a career in crime are rarely dissuaded from their commitment by the fear of imprisonment. Many do not expect to be caught; others are not bothered by the thought of prison even if they are caught. These points aside, it is also obvious that the fear of imprisonment is

was asked, in reference to their conviction offense, "At the time you committed that crime, were you worried about getting caught?" Over three-quarters (76%) were not. Results shown later suggest that our sample was not entirely indifferent to the prospect of apprehension and imprisonment, but these outcomes were so clearly unlikely to occur as the result of any one crime that they were not a cause for worry. Given the customary clearance and incarceration rates for crimes known to the police in most jurisdictions, it is also clear that the felons were not making unrealistic judgments. Objectively, the odds are very good that a felon will not be charged with any one crime that he has committed and even less that he would be sent to prison for that crime. This is a useful finding for our present discussion only because it sets a comparative context: It gives an initial idea of how worried our felons were about the prospect of getting caught, something that we can compare later with their anxieties about encountering armed victims.

We asked the sample a series of agree–disagree questions, each concerning the matter of armed victims in one or another way. Results from these items are shown in Table 7.1. There is a very consistent pattern to the results; in all cases, the majority opinion was that felons are made nervous by the prospect of an encounter with an armed victim.

The first item in the sequence asked men to agree or disagree that "a criminal is not going to mess around with a victim he knows is armed with a gun." About three-fifths of the sample (56%) agreed. Another item read, "A smart criminal always tries to find out if his potential victim is armed." More than four-fifths (81%) agreed with that. Yet another item read, "Most criminals are more worried about meeting an armed victim than they are about running into the police." About three-fifths (57%) also agreed with that. There were also two direct questions on whether guns thwart crimes: One reads, "One reason burglars avoid houses when people are at home is that they fear being shot during the crime." Three-quarters of the sample (74%) agreed. (Of course, there are other reasons for avoiding occupied homes, such as fear of being reported to the police, about which we did not ask.) The other reads, "A store owner who is known to keep a gun on the premises is not going to get robbed very often." About three-fifths (58%) again agreed. The possibility that one's intended victim is armed was evidently a concern to most of these men: The strong majority agreed that it is wise to find out in advance if one's potential victims are armed and to avoid them if they are.

How easy it is for felons to find out whether a potential victim is armed is not revealed in these answers. Some would-be victims are almost certainly armed (e.g., banks, currency exchanges, other criminals such as drug

one factor that prevents millions and millions of people from committing crimes—these being ordinary, law-abiding citizens.

TABLE 7.1. Attitudes toward Encountering Armed Victims: Total Sample
(in Percentages)

	Strongly agree	Agree	Disagree	Strongly disagree	(N)
1. A criminal is not going to mess around with a victim he knows is armed with a gun.	25	31	35	9	(1646)
2. One reason burglars avoid houses when people are at home is that they fear being shot.	35	39	20	7	(1628)
3. Most criminals are more worried about meeting an armed victim than they are about running into the police.	21	36	32	10	(1615)
4. A smart criminal always tries to find out if his potential victim is armed.	30	51	15	4	(1608)
5. A store owner who is known to keep a gun on the premises is not going to get robbed very often.	18	40	32	9	(1645)
6. Committing crime against an armed victim is an exciting challenge.	10	14	34	42	(1604)

dealers). Other would-be victims, while not certain to be armed, may nonetheless have a high probability (e.g., residents of neighborhoods that have reputations for high levels of gun ownership or associates and friends who the felon knows to carry guns on a regular basis). Still others would have very low probabilities of being armed (e.g., elderly women going shopping, children). In each of these cases, whatever prior expectations may be, there is undoubtedly an element of uncertainty that increases with lack of knowledge about the specific would-be victim.

One final question in the sequence was designed to explore the "other side" of this issue, namely, the possibility that "committing crime against an armed victim is an exciting challenge." For about three-quarters of the men in this sample, it was not.

A few of these findings warrant additional comment. For example, it has long been noted that most burglaries occur when the homes in question are unoccupied. (Estimates of the proportion unoccupied during burglary vary from about 75% to more than 90%.) This fact has been used (by Yaeger, Alviani, and Loving, 1976) to argue against the advisability of keeping a firearm "for protection" in one's home; in most burglary cases, at least, the odds are excellent that no one will be home to use it. We now learn that the possibility of being shot during the crime is one of the reasons burglars avoid occupied residences in the first place. (This, in any case, is the predominant view of three-quarters of our sample.)

The result reported in Table 7.1 is for the total sample, not all of whom had ever done burglaries. We thought it possible that the burglars in the sample might have had a different opinion, but agreement with the item ran to about 75% among almost all groups, whether they had ever done a burglary or not. (Only in the highest-rate group, those who had done "hundreds" of burglaries, did the level of agreement fall off, in this case to 57%.) Burglars and nonburglars alike, therefore, agreed that one reason burglars avoid occupied residences is the fear of being shot. There was also a fair-sized majority agreement that one would normally avoid stores that are known to keep a gun on the premises, too. Finally, more than one-half the sample also agreed that criminals are more fearful of being shot by their victims than by the police, and later results show that these men were themselves about equally fearful of these two prospects.

In sum, the prospect of being shot by the victim is clearly something the men in this sample worried about. This concern, it appears, is not unrealistic; one study has reported that in any given year, more criminals are shot to death in "justifiable homicides" by ordinary civilians than are killed by the police (Kleck, 1983).

We also call attention to the overwhelming majority who agreed that "a smart criminal always tries to find out if his victim is armed." Apparently, many of the felons in our sample took this advice to heart. Data reported later show that about two-fifths of these men (39%) had at some time in their lives decided not to do a crime because they "knew or believed that the victim was carrying a gun." Nearly one-tenth of the sample (8%) had had this experience "many times." Clearly, the fact or prospect of an armed victim encounter prevented at least some of the crimes these men would otherwise have committed.

Finally, it is worth emphasizing that while three-quarters of our felons did not agree that "committing crime against an armed victim is an exciting challenge," the remaining one-quarter did, about one-tenth of them "strongly." Some, in short, were apparently not at all nervous about the prospect of an armed victim; to the contrary, the prospect seemed to excite them. Who, then, are they? The answer, at least in part, is that they are the more predatory felons. Among the nonpredatory categories of our typology, agreement to the statement ran to about 20%, and among the Predators, to about 40%. For a substantial minority of the Predators, in other words, the thrill of confrontation with an armed victim appears to be part of the positive motivation to commit crime.

All the preceding items deal with criminals in general; we also asked each man about the kinds of things he personally thought about "when you were getting ready to do a crime" (Table 7.2). The three things most often on a felon's mind when getting ready to commit crime were, it ap-

TABLE 7.2. What Felons Worry about When Contemplating Criminal Activity: Total Sample (in Percentages)

	Regularly	Often	Seldom	Never	(N)
Might get caught	34	20	28	18	(1584)
Might get shot at by police	20	14	25	40	(1534)
Might get shot at by victim	19	15	27	39	(1521)
Might have to go to prison	30	20	24	25	(1555)
Your friends might look down on you	14	11	19	56	(1535)
Family might look down on you	30	18	17	35	(1557)
Might hurt or kill someone	20	12	18	51	(1554)

pears, the possibility of getting caught (cited as something one thought about "regularly" or "often" by 54%), the possibility of going to prison (50%), and the possibility that "your family might look down on you" (48%). Just over one-third thought regularly or often about the possibility of getting shot by the police; an identical percentage thought regularly or often about getting shot by one's victim. The possibility of hurting or killing someone was also thought about regularly or often by roughly one-third. That one's friends "might look down on you" was a concern to only about one-quarter.

Initially, there would appear to be some inconsistency between these responses and a result reported earlier, namely, that only about one-quarter of the sample was worried about getting caught during its conviction offense. On the other hand, to think about something, even regularly, is not the same thing as being worried about it. The possibility of being caught during a crime is, one presumes, ever present; it was, accordingly, "on the minds" one-half the sample more or less regularly. Whether this is something to worry about, however, depends on how much one disvalues getting caught (or if caught, going to prison). Our sample, recall, averaged some 10 prior arrests and 3 prior imprisonments; this notwithstanding, they still led active criminal lives. Clearly, these men might well have thought about the consequences of their actions, but they do not appear to have been especially worried about them.[3]

---

[3] For the record, there is a clear correlation between being worried about getting caught during the conviction offense and thinking about getting caught in general. Among those who said they were worried about getting caught during their conviction offense (N = 354), 47% thought "regularly" and 22% "often" about getting caught when they did crime; only 7% "never" thought about it. Among those who were not worried (N = 1028), only 29% said they thought about getting caught "regularly." Another 19% thought about it "often"; 22% never thought about it.

Percentaging the table in the other direction: There are 460 men in the sample who "regularly" thought about getting caught when they were doing crimes. Of these, just over one-third (36%) were worried about getting caught during the con-

As already noted, just over one-third thought regularly or often about being shot by the police; an identical percentage thought regularly or often about being shot by the victim. Utter indifference to these possibilities ("never" thinking about them) was indicated by about two-fifths in each case. The overall judgment of the sample reported earlier—that most criminals are more worried about being shot by their victims than by the police (with which 57% agreed)—therefore may be an example of a familiar pattern of imputing to groups certain motives that one is less likely to admit about oneself. Judging from these results, it appears that most of our sample was at least as worried about the one as they were about the other, still a noteworthy result.

It is of some interest to ask, Which felons thought most about being shot by their victim in the course of a crime? A major factor appears to be having had the experience of encountering an armed victim at some prior time. We asked the sample in a later question series whether they, personally, had ever "run into a victim who was armed with a gun." Results from this and several closely related questions are discussed more fully later. Among those who had never had the experience ($N = 919$), 48% said they "never" thought about being shot by their victim; among those who had ($N = 553$), only 23% "never" thought about it. Likewise, 45% of those who had at some time confronted an armed victim thought about being shot by their victim regularly or often; among the remainder, the comparable figure was 28%. Here as in many other instances, experience appears to be a capable teacher.

The survey contains some additional information on the relative importance of armed victims and the police in the minds of felons, namely, the questions on the "motivation to go armed" that were discussed in the previous chapter. Findings from that chapter relevant to the present discussion are shown in Table 7.3, which compares the relative importance of "there's always a chance my victim would be armed" with "the police have guns [or weapons], so criminals have to carry them too." These, to be sure, are not precisely parallel questions, and so the comparison of responses is somewhat hazardous. Still, in both cases, the armed victim appears to have been a much stronger motivating factor than the armed policeman.[4]

---

viction offense. This is consistent with the point made in the text, namely, that thinking about and worrying about getting caught are two different phenomena.

As it happens, those who were worried about getting caught during the conviction offense were also more likely to think regularly about being shot at by the police (24 versus 19% of the remainder), about going to prison (38 versus 27%), about the possibility that friends (19 versus 11%) and family (40 versus 26%) might "look down on you," etc.

[4] Of course, police do not automatically shoot anyone who is either a suspect or is seen in the process of committing a felony. The main menace of police to felons may be the latter's starting the criminal justice processing by making a felony arrest.

TABLE 7.3. Armed Victims and Police as Motivations to Carry Weapons (in Percentages)

	Importance				
	Very	Somewhat	A little	None	(N)
Gun criminals					
There's always a chance my victim would be armed.	50	12	13	25	(712)
The police have guns, so criminals have to carry them too.	20	10	12	58	(688)
Armed, not-with-a-gun criminals					
There's always a chance my victim would be armed.	27	12	8	53	(135)
The police have weapons, so criminals have to carry them too.	10	5	13	72	(135)

Among the Gun Criminals, as we emphasized earlier, 50% indicated that the possibility of an armed victim was "very important" to them; only one-quarter stated that this was not important at all. The comparable figures for the item concerning police were 20 and 58%, respectively. Among criminals who were armed but not with a gun, 27% said that the possibility of an armed victim was "very important" to them, and 53% said that it was not important at all; here, the comparable figures for the item on police were 10 and 72%, respectively. In both cases, then, the possibility of confronting an armed victim appears to have been a more important motivator in the felon's decision to carry a weapon than the fact that the police have guns. The general picture that emerges from Table 7.3 is, therefore, much the same as has emerged in the other data so far presented. Beyond all doubt, criminals clearly worry about confronting an armed victim.

In order to get a better sense of who seemed to worry about "The Armed Citizen" and who did not, we created a simple summated index from five of the six items shown in Table 7.1.[5] The average scores on the index var-

---

[5] Correlational analysis revealed that the item concerning "an exciting challenge" was not related to any of the other five items in the table; accordingly, it was omitted from the index. The other five items were all moderately and positively correlated with one another, the correlation coefficients ranging from about .17 to about .38. To create the index, responses were scored as follows: strongly agree = 4; agree = 3; do not know and no answer = 2; disagree = 1; strongly disagree = 0. Summing over the five items, the possible scores thus range from 0 (strongly disagree with all five items, the lowest possible degree of concern) to 20 (strongly agree with all five items, the highest possible degree of concern). Empirically, only 7 "0" scores were observed; there were 60 observations in the top category of the index. The overall mean = 12.1 (standard deviation = 3.8), or two scale points above the midpoint. This is only a restatement of results that are obvious in Table

ied significantly across the 10 states included in the study. The high value (most concern about armed victims) was registered in Georgia, followed by Maryland and Arizona; the low value was registered in Massachusetts, then Minnesota. The state means are positively correlated ($r = .51$, $p = .07$, $N = 10$ states) with a measure of the density of gun ownership within the state derived from Cook (1979). On the average, in other words, the highest concern about confronting an armed victim was registered by felons from states with the greatest relative number of privately owned firearms.

The effects of personal-level characteristics on the index of "concern about an armed victim" are shown in the multiple regression analysis reported in Table 7.4. With only a few exceptions, none of the observed effects is particularly striking, and the overall R^2 ($= .07$) is, at best, modest. Still, some of the patterns revealed here are intriguing.

None of the social background variables is strongly related to the tendency to have worried about armed victims. There is a weak tendency for concern to increase with the number of dependents and a somewhat stronger tendency for concern to increase with age. Also, veterans appear to be less concerned than nonveterans. Finally, there is a slight tendency for concern to decline with increasing weight; bigger men, in short, worry less about armed victims than smaller men. We emphasize, however, that none of these effects achieves customary levels of statistical significance; only one, the effect for age, even comes close.

Criminal background variables show somewhat stronger effects. Our "Index of Total Criminality" (see Chapter Three) has a statistically significant and negative effect on concern about an armed victim; so, too, does the number of prior arrests. Thus, more experienced (or higher rate) criminals worry less about armed victims than the less-experienced (or lower rate) felons. Of course, the direction of influence here is ambiguous: More experienced felons might have believed that they had the skills to cope with armed victims, but it may also have been the case that the more foolhardy (or courageous?) were more likely to engage in a great deal of crime.

The categories of the Armed Criminals typology were entered into the regression as a set of dummy variables, with the Unarmed serving as the omitted category. None of the coefficients is significant, although there is a clear tendency for all of them to be negative. In general, in other words, the Unarmed tended to worry most about encountering armed victims (but only slightly).

The survey contained one question about doing crime with partners versus doing crimes alone and another question about the tendency of felons to plan crimes in advance. We expected that felons who spent the most time planning their crimes would worry less about armed victims, and that

---

7.1, namely, that a majority of the sample was concerned over the prospect of encountering an armed victim.

TABLE 7.4. Regression of "Concern about an Armed Victim" on Selected
        Felon Characteristics[a]

Independent variables	b	SE	p
Education of respondent	−.03	.08	NS[b]
Number of dependents	.08	.06	.16
Race (1 = white)	−.12	.23	NS
Marital Status (1 = married)	.13	.28	NS
In service (1 = yes)	−.34	.25	.18
Age (in years)	.03	.02	.09
Weight at arrest (divided by 10)	−.05	.04	.20
Total criminality (divided by 10)	−.02	.01	.01
Improvisers	.14	.53	NS
Knife criminals	−.15	.42	NS
One-timers	−.38	.33	NS
Sporadics	−.12	.35	NS
Predators	−.05	.36	NS
Number of prior arrests (divided by 10)	−.02	.01	.01
Do crime with partners[c]	−.03	.11	NS
Plan crimes[c]	.08	.15	NS
Substance abuse index[c]	.08	.05	.12
Age at first felony	.01	.02	NS
Ever own gun?	−.27	.27	NS
Ever shot at?	−.21	.23	NS
Current crime: Worried about getting caught?	.42	.24	.08
Think about getting shot by victim?	.39	.09	.00
Ever scared off by armed victim?	.10	.27	NS
Friends scared off by armed victim?	.41	.11	.00
Ever run into armed victim?	−.73	.28	.01
Gun-knowledge test[c]	.13	.08	.10
Word-knowledge test[c]	−.18	.05	.00
Intercept	11.4	.83	.00
F = 3.39			
p = .000			
R^2 = .07			

[a] Dependent variable is "Index of concern about armed victims."
[b] NS, Not significant.
[c] See text for details on how these variables were measured.

felons who worked with others would also worry less. Contrary to these
expectations, neither of these variables is significantly related to the index
of concern. Likewise, the felon's age at the point of his first serious crime
also has no significant effect.

Another composite variable included in this analysis is an index of substance abuse—a simple count of the number of drugs (including alcohol)
that the felon said he took "many times" or "most of the time." (See Chapter Two for marginals on the relevant questions.) This index has a modest

positive effect on the index of concern: Heavy drug users, in other words, tended to be more concerned about armed-victim encounters than the lighter users.

Two of the other "attitudinal" questions discussed earlier in this chapter show significant effects on the index of concern. Persons who were worried about getting caught during their conviction offense were also more likely to worry about confronting an armed victim. Likewise, the more often a felon thought about "being shot at by your victim" during his crimes, the more concern he evidenced over the possibility. Unsurprisingly, this latter is the strongest effect shown in the table.

There is no significant effect of having ever owned a gun on the index of concern; likewise, felons who had ever been shot at with a gun were no more concerned than those who had not. On the other hand, our "Gun Knowledge" Index (a seven-item true-false test concerning guns; see Chapter 8) shows a moderately strong positive effect on concern about armed victims. The more knowledgeable a felon was about guns, the more concerned he was about encountering a victim who had one.

The regression contains three "experiential" variables that measure the felon's prior experiences in encountering armed victims. All three are analyzed later. One asks, "Did you personally ever run into a victim who was armed with a gun?" Those who had were significantly less concerned about armed victims than those who had not; this, too, is among the strongest effects revealed in this analysis. Another question asks, "Have you ever been scared off, shot at, wounded, or captured by an armed victim?" The effect of this experience is positive on the index of concern, but it is not statistically significant. Finally, we asked, "Have any of the criminals you have known personally every been scared off, shot at, wounded, captured, or killed by an armed victim?" Response options were none, only one, a few, and many; the effect of this variable on concern is positive and statistically significant.

The general pattern revealed here is thus quite interesting. Felons who had themselves experienced a confrontation with an armed victim were significantly less concerned about the possibility, perhaps because they knew from their own experience that one can survive such an experience. Felons whose friends had had the experience, on the other hand, were significantly more concerned.

The final variable included in this analysis is the felon's score on a 10-word vocabulary test, which is negatively and significantly related to the index of concern: As the word-knowledge score increases, concern about armed victims declines. It is unclear to us why this should be the case.

In summary, most felons appear to have experienced some anxieties in thinking about encounters with armed victims; on most relevant questions, the majorities were quite substantial; a consistent pattern is that most criminals were at least as worried about confronting an armed victim as they were about confronting the police. Generally speaking, felons from states with proportionally more gun owners worried proportionally more about "armed victim" encounters than did felons in other states. Felons who worried most about such things tended to be older and with more dependents, less criminally active, more likely to be substance abusers, more knowledgeable about guns, less verbally sophisticated, more likely to have known other criminals who had encountered an armed victim, but less likely to have had the experience themselves. We close with the emphasis that most of the individual-level effects summarized above are quite weak—they represent modest patterns, not sharp lines of differentiation.

ARMED VICTIM CONFRONTATIONS: EXPERIENTIAL RESULTS

To worry about confronting an armed victim is one thing; to actually have had the experience is something else again. In the previous section, we examined briefly the role of experience in creating these concerns; here, we analyze the experiences directly. Our measures of encountering an armed victim are contained in a four-item sequence; questions and marginal results are shown in Table 7.5.

Most of these results have been noted earlier and therefore require only a passing comment. Just under two-fifths of the sample (37%) had at some time in their careers run into a victim who was armed with a gun. A slightly smaller percentage (34%) said they had been "scared off, shot at, wounded, or captured by an armed victim," and about two-thirds (69%) had at least one acquaintance who had had this experience. (One-tenth knew "many" criminals who had been thwarted by an armed victim.) As noted earlier, about two-fifths of the sample (40%) had at some time decided not to do a crime because they knew or believed that their intended victim was armed.

A cross-tabulation of the first two items shown reveals that encountering an armed victim is not the same thing as being thwarted by one. About 37% of the sample had run into an armed victim, but a slightly smaller percentage, 34%, said they had been scared off, shot at, or otherwise opposed forcefully by one. The correlation between these two experiences is strong ($r = .52$) but short of perfect. As it happens, there were 1049 men in the sample who said they had never "run into a victim who was armed with a gun," and of these, some 15% said they had been scared off, shot at, etc. This appears to be an inconsistency but may in fact not be. "Run into" might be interpreted to imply a direct face-to-face encounter, and clearly, one could be "scared off," or even "shot at," by a gun-wielding victim and never confront that victim face-to-face.

There were, likewise, 609 men in the sample who had encountered an armed victim. Of these, just two-thirds said they had also been scared off, shot at, etc.; the remaining one-third had not been. This implies, first, that not all encounters with an armed victim eventuate in a thwarted crime;

TABLE 7.5. Confronting the Armed Victim: Experiential Results

---

1. Thinking now about all the crimes you ever committed, . . . did you personally ever run into a victim who was armed with a gun?

No	63
Yes	37
	100%

   (N) = (1667)

2. Have you ever been scared off, shot at, wounded, or captured by an armed victim?

No	66
Yes	34
	100%

   (N) = (1673)

3. Was there ever a time in your life when you decided not to do a crime because you knew or believed that the victim was carrying a gun?

No, never	61
Yes, just once	10
Yes, a few times	22
Yes, many times	8
	101%

   (N) = (1627)

4. Think now about other criminals you have known in your life, . . . have any of the criminals you have known personally ever been scared off, shot at, wounded, captured, or killed by an armed victim?

No, none	31
Yes, but only one	10
Yes, a few	48
Yes, many	11
	100%

   (N) = (1627)

---

one-third of the men who had ever encountered an armed victim said they had never been deterred by one. But it also implies, second, that at least some of these encounters do result in a thwarted crime. Two-thirds of the men who had ever encountered an armed victim said they had also been deterred or thwarted by an armed victim at least once. This is, to be sure, very imperfect evidence on the efficacy of private firearms as a defense against crime, but it is at least some evidence that armed citizens abort or prevent at least some crime. That 40% of the sample had at some time decided not to do a crime because the intended victim was carrying a gun is additional evidence favoring the same point.

We can only speculate about the circumstances under which a felon might find out that a potential victim had a weapon. Except in the few states where open gun toting is legal and customary, it would normally be rather difficult to determine whether a potential victim was armed, unless the victim was a policeman or an armed guard, or was carrying his or her weapon in some outrageously obvious way. It would, in short, be quite difficult to know whether the victims of ordinary street crimes, muggings, robberies, etc., were armed or not. So also with burglaries of strange homes in strange neighborhoods. It may also be difficult to make such judgments about stores and gas stations, although specific store and gas station owners may develop appropriate reputations.

Thus, knowledge about a victim's armament is probably highest and most accurate when the victims are one's friends and neighbors or persons with whom one has frequent dealings. Hence, a felon might well decide not to rob his drug dealer when he knows that his drug dealer carries a weapon all the time, might decide not to hijack the loot from a fellow thief when the thief is an associate known to be armed, etc. Indeed, it could be argued that the process that results in these men saying they have been thwarted in at least one crime by an armed victim is, in fact, the opposite side of the self-protection theme about which the prisoners made much as a motive for their own acquisition and carrying of guns.

Our point here is simply that it is not at all clear what these men were saying when they told us that they had decided at least once not to do a crime because they knew or suspected that the intended victim was armed. This might involve a street robbery that was not committed because of a suspicious bulge under the victim's jacket, or it might involve a burglary thwarted in progress because the home owner opened fire, or it might involve nothing more than a general tendency to avoid victimizing other thugs in the immediate environment whom these felons knew to be armed. In all probability, it involves all of these possibilities and more, but the relative proportions are undetermined in these data.

The four items in Table 7.5 are fairly strongly correlated one with the other; the correlation coefficients range from .27 to .52. Substantively, this implies that those who had run into an armed victim were also likely to have been deterred or thwarted by one and to have had friends and acquaintances who had had similar experiences. The correlations among the items are strong enough to justify combining them into a simple summated index of armed victim encounters, consisting of a count of experiences such that the index varies from 0 (for respondents who had none of the four experiences described) to four (those who had all four). The mean on the "Encounter Index" = 1.8 (standard deviation = 1.4). Of the sample, 21% answered "no" to all four questions, which means that about 80% of the sample had had at least some experience with an armed victim—either directly or vicariously, through the experiences of friends and acquaintances.

Table 7.6 shows means on the "Encounter Index" separately for each of the categories of our Armed Criminals typology. The table makes an important point, namely, that the more crime one has committed, the higher the odds on encountering an armed victim. The least likely ever to have had such an encounter were the Unarmed Criminals (mean = 1.18); the most likely, by far, were the Predators, especially the Handgun Predators, among whom the average = 2.73. The probability of an encounter with an armed victim, in other words, appears to be directly proportional to the rate at which crimes were committed. Consistent with this latter point, the correlation between the Encounter Index and our Index of Total Criminality is .31.

TABLE 7.6. The "Encounter Index" by
Criminal Type

	$\overline{X}$	SD
Unarmed	1.18	1.2
Improvisers	1.61	1.3
Knife criminals	1.58	1.3
One-timers	1.63	1.2
Sporadics	2.24	1.3
Handgun predators	2.73	1.1
Shotgun predators	2.53	1.2
$F = 63.4$		
$p = \quad .000$		

Table 7.7 shows the regression of the "Encounter Index" on selected background characteristics. These results are clearly dominated by the criminal history variables; the more crime one had committed, the higher the probability of having encountered armed victims. Neither Improvisers nor Knife Criminals were significantly more likely (than the Unarmed, the omitted category) to have had such encounters, but the coefficients for the other three types are all positive, correctly ordered, and statistically significant.

Holding constant the number of assaults, burglaries, drug deals, and robberies the felon had ever committed, the coefficient for the "Total Criminality" Index turns negative; but the coefficients for each of the crime-type variables are positive and statistically significant: The more crimes (of each type) ever committed, the higher the probability of an armed victim encounter. In the same vein, the coefficient for age is positive and significant (older felons were more likely to have had these encounters); the coefficient for age at first felony is negative and significant (the older one was when starting in one's criminal career, the less likely one is to have encountered armed victims). Whites were significantly less likely than non-whites to have had these encounters. Finally, armed-victim encounters were more common among the serious drug abusers than others.

The multiple R^2 for the equation = .30; experience with armed victims is clearly more structured than concern about it. As is obvious in the above results, the structure in question is driven by an apparently simple probability process. Each crime a felon commits exposes him to some risk of en-

TABLE 7.7. Regression of the "Encounter Index" on Selected
Background Variables [a]

Independent variables	b	SE	p
Improviser	.11	.16	NS
Knife criminal	−.02	.13	NS
One-time gun user	.27	.10	.01
Sporadic gun user	.46	.11	.00
Predators	.70	.11	.00
Total criminality (divided by 10)	−.01	.00	.00
N assaults	.17	.03	.00
N drug deals	.05	.03	.05
N burglaries	.14	.03	.00
N robberies	.13	.03	.00
N arrests (divided by 100)	.03	.03	NS
Age	.02	.00	.00
Age at first felony	−.03	.01	.00
Race (white = 1)	−.26	.07	.00
Word-knowledge test	−.01	.01	NS
Drug-abuse index	.03	.02	.05
Intercept	1.16	.16	.00

F = 37.2
p = .00
R^2 = .30

[a] Dependent variable is "index of encounters with armed victims."

countering an armed victim; the greater the number of "exposures," the
higher the probability of having come across a victim who is armed with a
gun.

SUMMARY

The principal conclusions to be derived from the analyses reported in
this chapter are as follows:

1. The felons in this survey were clearly concerned about encounters
   with armed victims. Most felons agreed that "a smart criminal always
   tries to find out if his victim is armed" and with a series of other items
   expressing the same general sentiment.
2. In general, encounters with armed victims seemed to be about as
   worrisome to these men as encounters with the police.
3. Most felons apparently thought about, but did not worry about, the
   prospect of being caught during their crimes.
4. Felons who had no prior encounters with armed victims, but who
   knew of other felons who had had these encounters, expressed more
   concern about such encounters than felons who had not; felons in

states with higher rates of private gun ownership also expressed more concern; the more predatory felons expressed less concern.

5. Confrontations with armed victims were a fairly frequent occurrence for these men. About two-fifths had run into an armed victim at least once; about one-third had been scared off, shot at, wounded, or captured by one; about two-fifths had decided at least once in their lives not to commit a crime because they knew or suspected that the victim was armed; about 80% had had at least some experience with an armed victim, either directly or vicariously, through the experiences of their associates.

6. The more crimes a felon had ever committed, the greater were his chances of encountering an armed victim. Perforce, then, predatory felons had had more of these encounters than any of the other felon groups.

7. The principal ambiguity in these results is that we do not know who the armed victims were. Some would have been law-abiding citizens successfully defending themselves against crime; others would have been friends and associates of the felons who, in different circumstances, as easily could have been the perpetrator as the victim. Nothing in our data speaks to the relative frequencies in this regard.

8

THE CRIMINAL AS A FIREARMS CONSUMER

We have presented an abundance of evidence that, when out of prison, felons were relatively heavy consumers of firearms. Three-quarters of the sample had owned at least 1 gun, and among those who had owned at least 1, the average number ever owned was on the order of 6, with a sizable fraction claiming to have owned more than 10. As heavy consumers, one might expect felons to have relatively sophisticated demands; on the other hand, their heavy consumption may only mean that they were wasteful consumers, destroying firearms through misuse, losing them through carelessness, trading guns frequently among their associates, perhaps heedless in general of the specific characteristics of weapons and interested only in a few attributes of particular concern to them.

This chapter addresses itself to the quality of criminal firearms consumption: what felons look for in their firearms, what characteristics are important to them, whether they qualify as reasonably sophisticated firearms consumers, etc.

It is often assumed that criminals prefer small, cheap handguns, the so-called Saturday Night Special (SNS), or, the currently more fashionable phrase, the "snubbies," the light-weight, short-barreled, typically smaller caliber weapons that are easily and cheaply obtained, readily concealable, and serve the purpose of intimidation as well as any other. Whether the characteristics just enumerated are among the traits felons look for in their handguns is therefore a primary concern of the ensuing analysis.

That criminals prefer concealable equipment above all else has been inferred from the high fraction of crime guns that are handguns, from the predominance of relatively small handguns among crime handguns, and from the fact that shoulder weapons involved in crimes are often modified to make them more concealable (see Wright, Rossi, and Daly, 1983: Ch. 9, for a review of the pertinent literature). Most of these findings are based on analyses of weapons confiscated by the police in the course of criminal investigations (e.g., Bureau of Alcohol, Tobacco, and Firearms, 1976a, 1976b; Brill, 1977; National Bureau of Standards, 1977).

On the other hand, a concealable handgun, per se, need not be cheap or, for that matter, particularly small. The handgun market contains some quite elegant and quite expensive equipment no larger than a man's hand;

and likewise, under the right circumstances, even the largest of handguns can be readily concealed on one's person (e.g., in a shoulder holster beneath a sports coat).

As just noted, the assumed criminal preference for small, cheap handguns has largely been inferred from studies of confiscated weapons. In the well-known Bureau of Alcohol, Tobacco, and Firearms (BATF) Project Identification study (1976a), to illustrate, one-half the handguns in the sample were judged to be worth less than $50, 70% had barrel lengths of 3 inches or less, and 60% were .32 caliber or less; all told, 45% were deemed to be "Saturday Night Specials." Brill's (1977) analysis suggested a somewhat, but not dramatically, lower fraction of SNSs among the handguns used in crime. Of course, Project Identification's handgun prices were obtained in the early 1970s, and since that time inflation has raised the prices of all goods by as much as 125%; thus a handgun that sold for $50 then would now sell for over $100.

In all these studies, the question, "Compared to what?" is relevant and largely unanswered. Since no credible study has ever been done of the characteristics of handguns owned by legitimate handgun owners, we have no way of knowing whether the preference for small, cheap handguns among criminals is any more (or less) pronounced than the preferences that exist among the gun-owning population at large. This, of course, is equally problematic in the analyses reported in this chapter.

WHAT FELONS LOOK FOR IN A HANDGUN

To assess the traits that felons look for in a handgun, every man in the sample (whether a gun owner or not) was given a list of handgun characteristics (e.g., "that it is cheap," "that it is big caliber") and was asked to state how important each characteristic "would be to you in looking for a suitable handgun." In all, 13 handgun traits were used for this analysis; each man was also asked to pick from the list of 13 the single most important factor he would look for in a handgun.

Initially, we deal with responses for the total sample; later, we consider handgun owners only, and still later, we consider the men who have used their handguns to commit crimes. Marginal frequencies for the 13 "how important" questions are shown in Table 8.1.

Judging first from the fraction rating each trait as "very important," the three most desirable handgun characteristics were accuracy (62% rating this as very important), untraceability (60%), and the quality of the construction (that it was a well-made gun, 58%). That it was "easy to shoot" was very important to 54%, that it was "easily concealed" was very important to 50%. "Easy to get" and "has a lot of firepower" were also relatively important (48 and 42%, respectively).

In contrast, the characteristics usually associated with criminal hand-

TABLE 8.1. What Felons Look For in a Handgun

Trait	Very important	Somewhat important	A little important	Unimpor- tant	(N)	Percentage "single most important" (N = 894)
Cheap	21	21	20	37	(1429)	6
Concealable	50	25	12	13	(1434)	13
Firepower	42	25	14	18	(1444)	22
Small caliber	11	20	22	47	(1382)	3
Large caliber	30	23	15	31	(1382)	4
Accurate	62	21	8	9	(1413)	9
Easy to shoot	54	24	10	12	(1427)	2
Scary-looking	21	18	16	44	(1421)	5
Well made	58	20	9	13	(1431)	17
Untraceable	60	12	9	19	(1434)	13
Easy to get	48	23	12	17	(1423)	4
Ammunition cheap	19	19	19	43	(1394)	—
Ammunition easy to get	45	26	11	18	(1436)	2

guns were not particularly important to these men: "That it is cheap" was very important to only 21%; "that it is small caliber," to only 11%. These data clearly do not suggest a strong preference for SNS-style handguns among these felons.

Results for the "single most important" question were generally similar: Based on these results, the ideal handgun from the felon's viewpoint was one that had a lot of firepower (22%), was well-made (17%), could not be traced (13%), and was easily concealed (13%). Price, in contrast, was the single most important factor to only 6%; small caliber, to only 3%. In both cases, the importance of concealability was apparent, but beyond that, the traits characteristic of heavier duty handguns seemed far more important to these men than did the traits of snubbies or the SNSs.

The 13 handgun traits asked about in the sequence can be grouped roughly into four categories. First are the traits that, for our purposes, define the SNS: cheapness and small caliber. Second are the traits that, for want of a better term, we will refer to as the "serious handgun" traits: accuracy, firepower, big caliber, well-made gun. Third are a set of three traits that would normally matter only to a felon who intended to use the handgun for criminal or illicit purposes—that it is concealable, intimidating, and cannot be traced—to which we will refer as the "criminal-use" traits.[1] Finally, there are four "convenience traits—easy to shoot, easy to get, ammunition is cheap, ammunition is easy to get—which might be of some

[1] To nonfelons, of course, some of these "criminal-use" traits, especially concealability, may be of value for reasons other than the use of the gun in crime. Police officers who are required to be armed even when off-duty, for example, would value concealability even though their purposes are noncriminal.

TABLE 8.2. Intercorrelations among Desirable Handgun Characteristics

	1	2	3	4	5	6	7	8	9	10	11	12	13
SNS traits													
1. Cheap	—												
2. Small caliber	.34	—											
Serious-handgun traits													
3. Accurate	.09	.08	—										
4. High firepower	.11	.07	.50	—									
5. Large caliber	.07	−.01	.31	.58	—								
6. Well made	.03	.11	.59	.57	.45	—							
Criminal-use traits													
7. Concealable	.37	.22	.31	.25	.13	.16	—						
8. Scary	.27	.21	.04	.24	.26	.07	.25	—					
9. Untraceable	.17	.17	.28	.29	.20	.27	.46	.24	—				
Convenience traits													
10. Easy to shoot	.22	.17	.59	.45	.28	.46	.40	.19	.32	—			
11. Easy to get	.31	.17	.29	.31	.22	.28	.45	.28	.49	.39	—		
12. Cheap ammunition	.49	.38	.14	.17	.13	.12	.28	.29	.26	.28	.38	—	
13. Easy ammunition	.27	.20	.37	.31	.24	.33	.36	.18	.38	.41	.53	.48	—

importance to a handgun consumer regardless of the intended use. Intercorrelations among the 13 items, grouped as indicated, are shown in Table 8.2.

One is struck, first, by the predominance of positive correlations; indeed, there is but one negative (and, as it happens, insignificant) correlation in the table, between big and small caliber.[2] The implication, of course, is that felons who looked for any one of these traits in a handgun tended to look for each of the others as well, which, per se, is not an implausible result: The "ideal" crime handgun may well be one that is cheap and easy to obtain, accurate, well-made, easy to shoot, and on through the list of *desiderata*.

In general, the correlations among the variables within each of the four groupings were especially strong; all were positive, statistically significant, and varied in magnitude from .24 (scary and untraceable) to .59 (accurate and well-made). The two SNS traits (cheap and small caliber) correlated .34; both these traits also correlated rather strongly with concealability (.37 and .22, respectively) and with the two questions concerning ammunition.

---

[2] One would expect, of course, that big and small caliber would be strongly and negatively related; that is, felons who preferred large-caliber guns would be inclined not to favor small-caliber guns, and vice versa. The lack of a significant negative relationship may imply, therefore, that felons are not particularly knowledgeable about firearm characteristics, as other data presented later also show. It might also mean that felons are largely indifferent about caliber and therefore accord the same importance to both large and small calibers.

In general, the correlations of cheap and small caliber with all three of the criminal-use traits make it plain that at least some criminals did look for SNS-style handguns to use in crime; later, we use these items in an attempt to determine just who the criminal consumers of small, cheap handguns were.

The four "serious-handgun" characteristics were particularly strongly correlated with one another; the average correlation among the four was .50. All four traits were very weakly correlated with the SNS traits, as would be expected. On the other hand, the correlations of these four with the criminal use traits were unexpectedly strong, averaging .21. This finding also makes it plain that some criminals looked for heavy-duty equipment to use in their crimes; who these people were is, of course, also the object of a later analysis.

The three criminal use traits were correlated at .32, on the average, with one another, and tended to be positively (and rather strongly) correlated with all other traits reflected in the table. Much the same was also true of the four convenience traits, about which nothing further need be said.

Given these intercorrelations, it is possible to reduce the 13 traits to the four more general variables we have just discussed. Scaling consisted simply of summing responses to the component variables. To reduce all four variables to a common metric, the resulting sum was divided by the number of component items; each scaled variable therefore ranged from 1 (all component traits said to be "not at all important") to 4 (all component traits said to be "very important"). Distributions, means, standard deviations, and intercorrelations for the resulting variables are reported in Table 8.3.

The distributions on these variables suggest rather strongly that the "serious-handgun" traits taken as a whole were the most important factors fel-

TABLE 8.3. Distributions, Means, Standard Deviations, and Intercorrelations among the Four Handgun Characteristic Variables (in Percentage)

Scale value	SNS traits	"Serious"	Criminal use	Convenience
1–1.9	40	13	14	15
2–2.9	37	25	27	32
3–3.9	17	42	47	40
4	6	20	12	13
$\bar{X} =$	2.1	3.0	2.8	2.8
SD =	.91	.88	.85	.83
(N) =	(1356)	(1317)	(1374)	(1346)

	Correlations			
	SNS	Serious	Criminal use	Convenience
SNS	—			
Serious	.09	—		
Criminal use	.39	.35	—	
Convenience	.47	.48	.58	—

ons looked for in a handgun. The mean on the "serious-handgun" factor was 3.0, clearly the highest of the four means; 62% of the sample scored 3 or higher on the "serious handgun" variable (somewhat or very important); relatively few men (about 13%) considered the "serious-handgun" traits to be generally unimportant.

Next in importance were the criminal-use and convenience traits, with means of 2.8 in both cases. By far the least important were the SNS traits: The mean for this variable was 2.1, and only 23% of the sample regarded these traits as very or somewhat important to look for in a handgun.

The substantive conclusion is reasonably obvious: The characteristics of SNSs were not high on the list of things felons looked for in their handguns; the serious-handgun traits were. With one exception, the intercorrelations among these four variables were positive and strong. The exception was, of course, a substantively trivial correlation of .09 between the SNS and serious handgun traits. The criminal-use and convenience traits were both correlated at about the same level with the SNS and serious-handgun traits; or in other words, the convenience and criminal-use traits were about equally important to men who preferred SNS-style handguns and to those who preferred the heavier duty equipment. We note finally that the strongest correlate of the criminal-use traits was the convenience traits ($r = .58$): men who valued a handgun for its suitability for use in crime also tended strongly to value guns that were easy to obtain and fire and for which ammunition was cheap and readily obtained.

There is, of course, no guarantee that felons, in fact, can translate their expressed preferences into actual ownership. Just as all consumers have some ideas about the the kinds of goods they would like ideally to possess, but only limited ability to indulge those preferences, so, too, criminals may not always be able to obtain the kinds of weapons they desire. Later in this chapter, we inquire about the relationship between what the sample preferred and what they actually owned.

Table 8.4 shows the relationship between the "handgun-traits" preferences and the gun-ownership variables (ever own a gun? ever own a handgun?) The relationship to the armed criminals typology is also shown. Concerning the gun ownership variables, only three of the eight mean comparisons were statistically significant: Men who had never owned a gun tended to value the SNS traits more highly than men who had, and, likewise, the nonowners tended to value the serious-handgun traits less highly than the gun owners did. Finally, men who had owned a handgun valued the criminal-use traits more highly than gun owners who had not owned handguns.

Substantively, perhaps the most interesting result reported here is that the preference of felons for SNS-style handguns was concentrated disproportionately among felons who had never even owned a gun; among gun-

TABLE 8.4. Handgun-Characteristics Preference by Gun Ownership and Type

	SNS	Serious	Criminal use	Convenience
Ever Owned a Gun?[a]				
No	2.3[a]	2.7[a]	2.8	2.8
Yes	2.0	3.1	2.8	2.8
If yes: Own Handgun?				
No	2.1	2.9	2.6[a]	2.8
Yes	2.0	3.1	2.8	2.8
Type				
Unarmed	2.2	2.9	2.7	2.8
Improviser	2.1	3.1	2.7	2.7
Knife	2.2	3.0	2.8	3.0
One-timer	2.0	2.9	2.7	2.8
Sporadic	2.1	2.9	3.0	2.9
Handgun predator	1.9	3.3	2.9	2.9
Shotgun predator	1.9	3.2	2.9	2.8
$F =$	4.54	7.32	5.03	1.79
$p =$	.000	.000	.000	.097

[a]The difference between owners and nonowners is statistically significant.

owning felons, the importance of the SNS traits was even less than suggested in earlier analyses.

The relationship of the trait variables to the criminal typology proves instructive. The preference for SNS characteristics was generally highest among the nongun-using criminals, especially among the Unarmed and Knife Criminals, and lowest among the Predator categories. Likewise, preference for the serious-handgun traits was lowest among the nonusers and highest among the Predators, as was the preference for the criminal-use traits. (The relationship of the convenience factor to type was not statistically significant.)

We can now provide at least part of the answer to a question posed earlier, namely: What kinds of felons preferred small, cheap handguns? The preference for these handguns was highest among felons who had never owned a gun and never committed a crime with one. The obverse of this relationship can also be noted: Serious criminals preferred serious equipment.

We noted earlier that the men in this sample acquired their most recent handguns for a variety of reasons, among which self-protection and use in crime were clearly of considerable importance. Correlations between the various reasons for their most recent handgun acquisition and the four handgun characteristics variables are shown in Table 8.5. With only a few exceptions, these correlations were small and substantively insignificant. The implication is that felons looked for largely the same traits in a handgun

TABLE 8.5. Correlations of Handgun Characteristic Preferences with Motives for Acquiring Their Most Recent Handgun and with "Gun-Socialization" Variables

| | Handgun traits | | | |
	SNS	Serious	Criminal use	Convenience
Motive for handgun acquisition				
Hunting	.02	.06	−.08	−.04
Target shooting	.01	.10	−.08	−.03
Collection	−.03	.16	−.08	−.02
Protection	.00	.19	.10	.10
Just wanted one	.07	.11	.11	.14
Use in crime	.02	.12	.26	.17
Stole to sell	.17	.04	.15	.12
Needed to get someone	.11	.12	.06	.08
Socialization variables				
Fathers	−.11	.13	−.08	−.05
Siblings	−.03	.10	.00	.03
Friends	−.07	.19	.06	.03
Male clan	−.06	.14	−.03	−.00
Experiences	−.13	.13	−.08	−.04

whatever the intended use. Exceptions of some possible interest were as follows:

Men who had stolen their most recent handgun to sell for money showed a slight preference for SNS traits ($r = .17$). Perhaps, in their view, the smaller handguns were more readily portable, easier to get out of a house, and possibly, easier to sell. Men whose motive was that they needed a gun "to get someone" also showed a slight preference for SNS traits ($r = .11$). These were the only two motives that correlated with the SNS preference.

"Serious-handgun" characteristics were relatively more important to men whose intended application was target shooting ($r = .10$), a gun collection ($r = .16$), self-protection ($r = .19$), and use in crime ($r = .12$). Clearly, none of these relationships was very strong; all were statistically significant.

As might be expected, the only strong correlate of the criminal-use traits was the criminal-use motive ($r = .26$): Men who had acquired their most recent handgun specifically to use in crime tended to value things such as intimidation value, concealability, and untraceability more than other felons valued them. The criminal-use trait was also weakly correlated with "stole to sell" ($r = .15$). It is also worth a note that the convenience traits were also more strongly correlated with the criminal-use motive than with any of the other motives ($r = .17$).

A final point to emphasize is that the criminal-use motive was not significantly correlated with the SNS traits ($r = .02$). There were, it appears, a few felons who did prefer SNS-style handguns, but not those who intended to use their handgun for criminal purposes.

Table 8.5 also shows the correlations of the handgun-trait preferences with the "gun-socialization" variables that were analyzed in Chapter Five. All these correlations are weak. The only pattern of possible significance revealed in these data was that all five socialization variables were negatively correlated with the SNS traits and positively correlated with the serious-handgun traits: The greater a felon's early exposure to firearms, the less he valued SNS handguns and the more he valued the more serious equipment.

The final question in the "preference" sequence asked respondents how much they would be willing to pay "to get a handgun that was suitable in all other respects." Our intention in asking the question was to estimate the handgun price elasticity for the felon population. Unfortunately, the responses appear useless for the purpose. There is, first, a small group who volunteered that they would be willing to pay nothing, many adding the note that they would simply steal the gun they wanted. Among the remainder, the modal response was $100, and 70% indicated they would be willing to pay $150 or less. As it happens, the going street price for handguns is about $100 per copy (as best as we have been able to determine[3]), and it can be assumed that even imprisoned felons were aware of this fact. We infer from this that the responses to the "how much would you pay?" question meant only that felons were willing to pay the going rate; hence, no further analysis of this variable has been undertaken.

WHAT FELONS ACTUALLY CARRY

The preceding describes the characteristics of the "ideal handgun" from the criminal viewpoint. It is a useful question whether the traits they preferred in a handgun were to be found among the handguns they actually owned. It is certainly possible that many felons, for whatever reason, found it difficult to lay hands on the preferred equipment and as a consequence owned something else instead. On the other hand, we have already seen

---

[3] Determining the going street price of black-market handguns is a chancy business at best. We asked graduate students whom we knew to be familiar with the sleazier side of life to ask around among their associates (small-time drug dealers, mainly) about the availability and price of stolen handguns. We also asked two of our policemen friends, one a city policeman, the other a state policeman, to confirm whether the reports we obtained were at least reasonable so far as they knew. The report: Stolen handguns can be had more or less anywhere in Massachusetts in any reasonable quantity at the rate of roughly $100 per handgun, findings that neither of our police friends disputed. High-quality handguns cannot be obtained at this rate but can be obtained at higher rates, if one is willing to spend the money. "Any reasonable quantity" apparently means in lots of 25 or less. These inquiries also found that anyone who deals in drugs, even small quantities of marijuana for a predominantly college market, also either deals in stolen guns or at least knows someone who does.

that these men had owned handguns in fairly large numbers; we see in the following two chapters that many were also heavily involved in firearms thefts. The implication is that over any reasonable span of time, most of these men would have sooner or later come into possession of a handgun that was ideally suited to their preferences, which suggests that the correlation between preferred and actual handgun traits ought to be reasonably strong.

Each handgun owner in the sample was asked a series of questions about the most recent handgun he had owned: approximate retail value, manufacturer, caliber, and barrel length. Marginal frequencies for these four items are shown in Table 8.6. For one (but only one) of these four variables, namely, caliber, comparable U.S. national data exist and these data are also shown.

The apparent preference for serious equipment suggested in the first section of this chapter is amply evident in the handguns these men actually owned. On the whole, these were relatively expensive handguns: Only about 11% were judged to be worth $50 or less, and just under one-third (31%) were judged to be worth $100 or less.[4] Most of these handguns (37%) fell into the $100–200 range; about one-third (32%) were worth more than $200. Consistent with the price data, about three-fifths of these handguns (57%) were manufactured by Smith and Wesson, Colt, or Ruger Arms, all three manufacturers of quality handguns.[5] (To be sure, a sizable fraction of the respondents, 30%, did not know the manufacturer of their most recent handgun.)

It would, of course, be mistaken to think that the prices noted above were what these men actually had paid for their handguns. The question asked for their opinion on what these guns would have been worth on the retail market, not what they actually had paid. Many of the high-priced handguns reported here would no doubt have been stolen, if not by the respondent then by the source from whom the respondent obtained the gun.

---

[4] Rather than take these "retail worth" estimates at face value, we compared brand-for-brand the prices these men stated with the prices listed in *Gun Digest* in every case where the felon gave us enough information about the handgun to make the comparison. In general, the convergence between their estimates and the *Gun Digest* prices was striking. These men had an exceptionally good idea of what their equipment was worth, no matter how they obtained it.

[5] As Brill (1977) has pointed out, it is very difficult to obtain manufacturing data from the U.S. small-arms industry, and so we have not attempted a brand-for-brand comparison with total production figures. It is well-known, however, that Smith and Wesson and Colt are the two leading handgun manufacturers (the General Motors and Ford of the industry, as it were), and these are, as we have just pointed out, also the two manufacturers whose products show up most frequently among the handguns owned by our sample. This provides at least one fragment of evidence suggesting that the criminal-handgun arsenal is probably not much different from the arsenal of the handgun-owning public in general.

TABLE 8.6. Characteristics of the Felons' Most Recent Handguns

	Percentage in felon sample
Approximate retail value	
$50 or less	11
51–100	20
101–150	19
151–200	18
201–300	17
301 +	15
(N) =	(922)
Manufacturer	
Smith and Wesson	36
Colt	16
Ruger	5
All other brands	13
"Don't know" brand	30
(N) =	(900)
Barrel length	
Short (3 inches or less)	30
Medium (4–6 inches)	53
Long (7 inches or more)	17
(N) =	(914)

	Felons (%)	U.S. handguns[a]
Caliber		
.22	16	34
.25	5	13
.32	9	6
.357	20	13
.38	29	27
.41	1	—
.44	6	2
.45	8	3
9 mm	7	2
(N) =	(940)	—

[a] Source: Wright, Rossi, and Daly (1983: 43).

Many others would have been obtained at substantial discounts off the retail price through various gray- or black-market sources (fences, pawn shops, drug dealers, etc.) It should also be noted that these prices may or may not have been adjusted for the heavy inflationary trends of the past decade, and hence, if anything, may well underestimate the current prices of the equipment involved. As an indication of the approximate quality of the felon's equipment, however, these price (and manufacturers') data are probably not too misleading; to emphasize, they do not suggest much interest among the felon population in cheap, low-quality handguns.

Data on caliber and barrel length sustain the same conclusion. Fewer than one-third (30%) of the sample's most recent handguns had barrel lengths of 3 inches or less; most (53%) were standard-sized handguns of the sort normally carried, say, by policemen (4–6-inch barrels); a considerable number (17%) were large handguns of the "Dirty Harry" type (7-inch or longer barrels).

The data on caliber are especially informative, because roughly comparable data for nonfelon handguns exist. We stress that this comparison is not precise. Data shown in the table for "U.S. Handguns" represent the calibers of all handguns manufactured in the United States in 1973–1974. Imported handguns, therefore, are not included. Still, relative to admittedly imprecise data on the calibers of handguns in general, the handguns carried by felons were disproportionately large, not small, caliber.

The differences are fairly substantial. More than one-third (34%) of all handguns manufactured in the United States in 1973–1974 were of the .22 caliber variety. In contrast, only about one-sixth of the felons' most recent handguns were .22s. All told, just over one-half (53%) of all handguns qualify as small caliber weapons (.32 caliber or less); fewer than one-third of the felons (30%) owned handguns of these calibers. Relative to the totals shown, felons were considerably more likely to carry .357s (20 versus 13% in the total), .44s (6 versus 2%), .45s (8 versus 3%), and 9 mm firearms (7 versus 2%).[6] As in all other analyses reported in this chapter, the felon's preference for serious equipment is again obvious.

Neither barrel length nor caliber per se is sufficient to isolate the true SNSs in this sample of handguns. Some short-barrel weapons are chambered in large calibers; some small caliber weapons are not short-barreled. The cross-tabulation of caliber by barrel length is shown in Table 8.7. In general, the relationship is as one would anticipate: The longer the barrel, the larger the caliber. Still, it is worth a note that over one-half of the short-barreled handguns were chambered in large calibers. If, following Project Identification, we define an SNS as being both short-barreled and small caliber, then 125 of the most recent handguns owned by these men were SNSs, which amounts to 14%. This, moreover, is certainly an overestimate of the true percentage, since at least some of the short, small-caliber weapons would not have been especially cheap.

There is, in short, a serious disparity between what these men told us

---

[6]The prevalence of 9 mm handguns in these data is worth a special note. We have remarked elsewhere on the apparent growing popularity of the 9 mm semiautomatic among the police (Wright, Rossi, and Daly, 1983: Ch. 4); judging from the data discussed in the text, this weapon is also enjoying an increase in popularity among felons as well. (In any case, very few 9 mm weapons are reported in Brill's [1977] analysis.) Judging from other characteristics of these weapons, we infer that most of them are manufactured by Browning, and that they are the 13-round autoloader that has been referred to as "the handweapon of choice among terrorists world-wide."

about their most recent handguns and what has been inferred about criminals' handguns from the confiscation data. In the Project Identification study noted earlier, to illustrate, one-half the handguns in the sample were judged to be worth less than $50; two-thirds of the handguns in our sample were said to be worth $100 or more, a disparity that can be easily accounted for by the intervening inflationary process. However, other characteristics showed very large disparities: Some 70% of the Project Identification handguns had 3-inch or smaller barrels versus 30% of the handguns in our sample; 60% of the Project Identification handguns were small caliber versus 30% in our data. More generally, our data show a much heavier predominance of serious equipment among the handguns of felons than has been suggested in any of the confiscation studies, including Brill's (1977). How can this disparity be explained?

TABLE 8.7. Barrel Length by Caliber of Criminal Handguns

Caliber	Barrel length		
	Short	Medium	Long
.32 or less	47	22	18
.357 or higher	53	78	82
(N) =	(264)	(475)	(148)

One possibility, of course, is that our data are misleading and the confiscation data are correct. It is conceivable, for example, that the felons in our sample exaggerated the size, caliber, and worth of their handguns, perhaps to impart a "macho" image to the field team. It is also possible that the states available to us for study have biassed our results; for example, 7 of the 10 states in the study are either clearly or at least arguably southern or western states, and perhaps felons in these states carried bigger handguns than felons in other areas of the country.

Then too, all our data relate to the most recent handguns these felons had acquired; assuming multiple handguns in their arsenals, they actually might not have carried, day to day, these "most recent" handguns but rather other, smaller handguns that had been acquired at some earlier time. (It does seems likely that a felon who owned several handguns would tend to carry the smaller of them, all else equal.)

Finally, our sample of imprisoned felons cannot pretend to be a probability sample of all criminals, being biased toward persons with longer and more violent careers in crime. If one-time, less violent, and/or juvenile offenders used smaller and different armaments from our more "serious" criminals, which also does not seem unlikely, then the Project Identification findings may well be accurate as a depiction of the "typical" crime handgun.

It is also possible that our data are correct and that the confiscation data are biased toward small, cheap, low-caliber weapons. There are, we think, at least a few possible reasons why this might be the case.

First, as Brill (1977) has pointed out, the confiscation studies are typically based on all the handguns that come into the possession of the police. This includes not only handguns actually used in crime, but also handguns that police find and ones that they confiscate on simple carrying charges. Indeed, according to Brill, as many as 40% of the handguns in the Project Identification study were confiscated on illegal possession or carrying charges. The prevalence of light, inexpensive handguns in the confiscation samples may tell us, therefore, as much about the arsenal of the gun-carrying American public at large as about the equipment preferences of felons.

Of course, the felons in our sample are also not necessarily representative of all felons, tending, as we have pointed out earlier, to have long records of previous offenses and incarcerations. Experienced criminals such as these may have different preferences in handguns from amateurs, and the confiscation samples may reflect more the arsenals of the latter. Indeed, the relative preference of Unarmed and Knife Criminals for SNS-type guns tends to support this interpretation.

Another possibility exists. Many of the handguns that appear in the confiscation samples are handguns found by the police at the scene of a crime. We think it conceivable that the tendency for a criminal to simply drop his handgun at the scene (as he makes his escape) might vary as a function of the quality of the weapon. To illustrate, a burglar carrying a handgun worth, say, $50 might not want to run the risk of being apprehended with the weapon in his possession, since this might result in a more serious charge. In contrast, a burglar carrying a handgun worth several hundreds of dollars might well be loathe to leave it behind, regardless of the increased risk. In short, we think felons might be more inclined to drop a cheap gun than to drop a quality sidearm. If so, this would also tend to bias the confiscation samples toward smaller and lower quality handguns.

Clearly, we have no way to judge the relative credibility of the various possibilities outlined above. Realistically, all the possibilities mentioned are probably operating to some unknown degree—both those that bias our data and those that bias the confiscation data. Lacking better information than presently in hand, we have no choice but to stick to the obvious substantive conclusion suggested by our results: The men we interviewed in these 10 prisons tended both to prefer and to own higher quality handguns than previous studies of criminal handguns led us to expect.

The zero-order correlations between the characteristics these men said they preferred in a handgun and the characteristics of the most recent handguns they actually owned were in the right direction but were not very strong. The SNS traits preference was negatively correlated with the approximate retail value of the felon's most recent handgun ($r = -.16$), with caliber (recoded so that .22s, .25s, and .32s are small caliber and everything else is large, $r = -.09$), and with barrel length ($r = -.07$); and in contrast, the "serious handgun" preference was positively correlated with value ($r = .23$), with caliber ($r = .22$), and with barrel length ($r = .17$).

One reason why these correlations are not higher, of course, is that many of these "most recent" handguns had been stolen by the felon. As we see in Chapter Ten, felons stole handguns because they were there to steal, not because they were looking specifically for a firearm; for any given stolen handgun, then, one would expect no more than a random "fit" between *desiderata* and actual characteristics. If one omits handguns stolen by the felon himself from the analysis, then the correlations between preferred and actual handgun characteristics go up: absent the stolen handguns, the SNS traits preference was negatively correlated with retail value ($-.22$), caliber ($-.11$), and barrel length ($-.13$); and likewise, the "serious-handgun" preference was positively correlated with value (.27), caliber (.24), and barrel length (.21). Although these correlations are still rather modest, the general tendency is clear enough: The criminals in our sample tended actually to own what they preferred to own, which for the most part meant fairly heavy-duty handguns.

How the handguns carried by our felons compare with the total handgun arsenal of the American gun-owning population is largely unknown; except for the limited data on caliber, the appropriate information to make the comparison simply does not exist (so far as we know). We suspect, however, that the criminal arsenal and the total arsenal differ rather little, if only because the criminal arsenal consists, in major part, of handguns stolen from legitimate (or quasi-legitimate) gun owners (see Chapter Ten).

Judging from various fragmentary sources of data (cf. Wright, Rossi, and Daly, 1983), the most commonly owned handgun in the United States today is a Smith and Wesson .38 revolver equipped with a 4-inch barrel; this, as it happens, is also the sidearm of issue in roughly 90% of all U.S. police departments, and it was also the most frequent handgun reported by the men in our sample. One possible implication is that the equipment data reviewed in this section tell us as much about the handgun arsenal in general as they do about the handguns used specifically in criminal applications.

CONSUMER SOPHISTICATION

How knowledgeable were our felons about firearms? About firearms laws? Were they relatively ignorant consumers who knew only that they liked guns and liked to own and carry them? Or did they qualify as reasonably sophisticated firearms consumers?

To get some sense of their consumer sophistication, the survey protocol included a 7-item true–false "gun-knowledge" test and an 8-item true–false test dealing with federal firearms laws. The results for these 15 items are shown in Table 8.8. In order to provide some comparative data, the same 15 items were also included in a survey administered to an undergraduate class at the University of Massachusetts in spring, 1984; results for the male respondents in this survey are also shown in the table. In both cases, "don't know" was treated as an incorrect response. In the felon sample, men who simply skipped the entire sequence were omitted from the analysis.

Concerning first the felons' knowledge of guns, the only fair conclusion is that they appear well-informed on some things but seriously uninformed about others; the same was true of the male college students as well.

Male college students, but not felons, recognized the distinction between a pistol and a revolver (all revolvers are also pistols, but not all pistols are revolvers): 69% of the students, but only 26% of the felons, correctly answered this question. In contrast, felons were slightly more likely (85%) than male college students (75%) to know that one difference between a magnum and a regular handgun is that the magnum will fire a more powerful cartridge.

In the remaining five cases, the differences between the two samples were effectively trivial. Both felons and male college students knew, for example, that a long-barreled handgun is more accurate, all else equal, than a short-barreled one; likewise, both groups knew that most U.S. policeman carry .38 caliber revolvers.

Things that most people in both groups did not seem to understand are that (1) a double-action revolver does not have to be cocked to be fired; (2) handgun cartridges do not contain 300 grains of powder (the *lead* in a standard police .38 cartridge only weighs 158 grains; the powder load would weigh from 20 to 30 grains; a 300-grain powder load would cause most handguns to explode on firing); and (3) the price of a new Colt Python is about $600, not about $150.

Whether these results represent a high or a low degree of consumer sophistication, we cannot say. All that can be said with confidence is that the average felon in our sample appeared to know about as much (or as little) about guns as the average male student in our class. Clearly, the comparison is complicated in any case by the much lower educational attainment of the felons.

Concerning knowledge of federal firearms laws, much the same conclusion holds. Felons were much more likely (82%) than male college students (54%) to know that it is illegal for a convicted felon to buy a gun; college students, in contrast, were more likely than felons to know that federal laws do not prohibit handgun ownership among all except the police (94 versus 77%). Clear majorities in both groups also knew that one does not have to 25 years old to legally purchase a handgun (the stipulated age in the federal Gun Control Act of 1968 is 21: 63% of the felons and 72% of the students correctly answered this question); and that gun dealers are

TABLE 8.8. Knowledge of Guns and Gun Laws

	Percentage correct	
Knowledge	Felons (N = 1732)	Male students (N = 96)
Guns		
1. A pistol and a revolver are two words for the same thing (False)	26	69
2. A magnum [handgun] will fire a more powerful bullet (True)	85	75
3. Most handgun cartridges contain about 300 grains of powder (False)	22	17
4. A double-action revolver has to be cocked before you can fire it (False)	28	26
5. A long barrel is more accurate than a short barrel (True)	67	79
6. Police carry .38 revolvers (True)	69	74
7. The price of a new Colt Python is about $150 (False)	22	21
	(N = 1657)	(N = 96)
Gun-law		
1. It is illegal for a felon to buy a gun (True)	82	54
2. Federal laws ban [handgun] ownership except by police (False)	77	94
3. An alcoholic or addict can buy a gun if he has no record (False)	13	3
4. You have to be 25 to legally buy a handgun (False)	63	72
5. It is illegal to mail handguns across state lines (True)	50	45
6. It is illegal to trade for a handgun unless it is reported to the police (False)	18	16
7. Gun dealers are required to get a Federal license (True)	82	81
8. The major agency that enforces Federal gun laws is the FBI (False)	25	21
Gun-knowledge scores		
$\bar{X}=$	3.2	3.6
SD =	1.5	1.6
Percentage of 5 or more correct =	20	28
(N) =	(1732)	(96)
Gun-law scores		
$\bar{X}=$	4.1	3.9
SD =	1.5	1.4
Percentage of 5 or more correct =	43	33
(N) =	(1657)	(96)

required to get a federal license (82 and 81% correct, respectively). Just about one-half of both groups (50 and 45%, respectively) knew that it is illegal to mail handguns across state lines.

Points on which both groups were about equally misinformed included: First the major agency that enforces federal firearms laws is, of course, the Bureau of Alcohol, Tobacco, and Firearms, not the FBI. Second, federal law does not make it illegal for people to trade guns among themselves, whether the trade is reported to the police or not. (To be sure, some local jurisdictions do have restrictions of this general sort.) Third, alcoholics and drug addicts are prohibited from firearms purchases, according to the Gun Control Act of 1968.

Overall scores (number correct) for both groups on both "tests" are reported at the bottom of the table. Concerning knowledgeability about guns, the mean score for the felons was 3.2 (out of a possible 7) and for male college students, 3.6; concerning gun laws, the means were 4.1 and 3.9, respectively (out of a possible 8). Male college students, it appears, were slightly better informed than felons about guns per se; felons, in contrast, were slightly better informed than students about firearms laws. These differences were, of course, relatively modest; the scores on both "tests" for both groups were not much better than one would expect on chance alone.

For both felons and college students, of course, there was substantial variability around the mean scores, and it is interesting to ask just who the more knowledgeable felons were. Pertinent data are shown in Table 8.9.

We can note first that the two "test" scores were, themselves, positively correlated at .40; men who were knowledgeable about guns tended also to be knowledgeable about gun laws. Given this and the fact that the patterns shown elsewhere in the table were quite similar for both variables, we can speak of "knowledgeability" in general and not discuss the two sets of results separately.

By and large, the patterns shown here were much as one would expect. Felons who had owned guns were substantially more knowledgeable than felons who had not; gun-owning felons who had owned handguns were the most knowledgeable of all. Knowledgeability also increased with the number of guns and the number of handguns ever owned. In the same vein, both measures of knowledgeability were positively (and, at times, rather strongly) correlated with all the socialization variables discussed in Chapter Five; both measures were negatively correlated with the age at which the felon first fired a gun and first obtained a gun of his own. The general pattern, therefore, was straightforward: The younger a felon was when first exposed to guns, the more exposure to guns he has received, and the more guns he has ever owned,—the greater his knowledge of guns and gun laws. Experience, again, proves to be a capable teacher.

The breakdown according to categories of the armed criminals typology also shows that men who had used guns to commit crimes were generally more knowledgeable than men who had not. Interestingly, the Handgun

TABLE 8.9. Relationship of Gun and Gun-Law Knowledgeability to Other Variables of Interest

	Gun knowledge			Law knowledge		
	X̄	SD	(N)	X̄	SD	(N)
By gun ownership						
Ever own gun?						
No	2.3	1.4	(409)	3.5	1.6	(383)
Yes	3.5	1.4	(1277)	4.3	1.4	(1234)
Ever own handgun?						
No	3.1	1.4	(151)	4.1	1.3	(150)
Yes	3.6	1.4	(1010)	4.3	1.5	(1009)
By type						
Unarmed	2.8	1.5	(667)	3.9	1.5	(627)
Improviser	2.9	1.6	(76)	4.2	1.5	(71)
Knife user	3.1	1.5	(122)	4.1	1.5	(123)
One-timer	3.1	1.5	(241)	4.1	1.6	(231)
Sporadic	3.4	1.4	(239)	4.4	1.4	(231)
Handgun predator	3.9	1.4	(297)	4.3	1.5	(287)
Shotgun predator	3.5	1.7	(90)	4.2	1.4	(87)

	Correlation coefficients	
	Gun knowledge	*Law knowledge*
Gun knowledge	—	.40
Traits preferences		
SNS	−.20	−.08
Serious handgun	.25	.19
Criminal use	.00	.06
Convenience	−.03	.05
Gun-ownership variables		
N guns owned	.29	.17
N handguns owned	.27	.10
Socialization variables		
Father	.29	.19
Siblings	.18	.15
Friends	.20	.09
Male clan	.21	.12
Experiences	.31	.24
Age when first fired	−.26	−.17
Age when first obtained	−.19	−.11

Predators knew more about guns (but not about gun laws) than any other single group. In the same vein, the Unarmed Criminals were less knowledgeable on both scores than any other group. Relative to their peers, the Predators, therefore, turned out to be the most sophisticated firearms consumers of the lot.

Concerning the correlations between knowledge and the '"trait-preference" variables discussed earlier in this chapter, the pattern is quite simple: As knowledgeability increased, the preference for "serious-handgun" traits increased, and the preference for SNS-style traits declined. The more a criminal knew about guns (and gun laws), the more he preferred serious firearms equipment. In contrast, the preference for small, cheap handguns was concentrated among men who knew relatively little about guns.

SUMMARY

The principal conclusions of the analyses reported in this chapter can be summarized as follows:

1. In contrast to much speculation and the general run of results from studies of confiscated weapons, the felons in our sample neither preferred to own, nor did they actually own, small, cheap, low-quality handguns. The strong preference, rather, was for large, well-made guns.
2. The preference for large, well-made handguns was especially strong among felons who had owned guns and who had used guns to commit crimes; the preference for small, cheap handguns was concentrated among felons who neither owned guns nor used them in crime. Serious criminals preferred serious equipment.
3. Not more than about 15% of the most recent handguns possessed by this sample qualified as SNSs, even with an inclusive definition of the term.
4. As best as can be judged with the limited data available, the handgun arsenal of our sample was little different from the total arsenal of handguns possessed by the gun-owning public at large, with the possible exception that large-caliber handguns were overrepresented among the sample.
5. Felons, in general, were not highly informed about either guns or gun laws; rather, they appeared to be about as knowledgeable on both topics as a nonrandom sample of male college students in the northeast. Overall, felons who had owned guns and who used guns to commit crimes were more knowledgeable than their opposite numbers.

   Since most college students do not own guns, and most felons do, one would perhaps expect felons to be notably better informed about firearms than male college students, which, as we have seen, is not the case. None of the material reviewed here suggests that the average felon is an especially knowledgeable firearms consumer. One might therefore inquire as to the source of their apparent preference for the larger, better made, higher quality handguns. One plausible (indeed, rather likely) interpretation of all the material presented in this chapter is that the average felon wishes to be at least as well-armed as the average policeman, their most likely adversaries in a genuine shootout. Judging from the characteristics of their most recent handguns, it would also appear that most gun-using felons, especially the more predatory among them, have succeeded in this goal.

9

PATTERNS OF ACQUISITION:
WHERE AND HOW FELONS OBTAIN GUNS

Where and how felons obtain their firearms have obvious implications for the design of sensible firearms-control regulations. Many existing regulations, including some of those embodied in the Gun Control Act of 1968 and in the laws of many states, attempt to interdict the criminal acquisition of guns primarily at the point of retail sale. Under the provisions of the Gun Control Act, federally licensed gun dealers are forbidden to sell firearms to persons with a felony record.[1] In some jurisdictions, this only means that the prospective purchaser must sign a statement saying that he does not have a criminal record; in other jurisdictions, applications are forwarded to the local police for a criminal-records check.

State and local jurisdictions can, and frequently do, impose additional restrictions, for example, bans on sales to certain groups, required "waiting periods," required reporting of all firearms transfers, whether they involve a retail sale or not, registration of guns, permits to purchase, own, or carry guns. These many Federal, state, and local regulations, however, only will have an impact on the subset of criminal-firearms transfers that involve sources likely to be concerned about the legality of the transaction. The fraction of firearms transfers to felons that do involve such sources is, therefore, a relevant (and largely unresearched) issue.

Relatively little is known about the mechanisms through which firearms circulate in either the licit or illicit markets. It has long been suspected that many felons obtain their guns through theft, a suspicion that is confirmed in this chapter and analyzed in detail in the next. It is also commonly as-

[1] The Omnibus Crime Control and Safe Streets Act prohibits all firearms possession by persons with a felony record, so any transfer of a firearm to a felon is an illegal act, whether it involves a normal retail outlet or not. Many states have additional laws to the same effect. We focus in this chapter on acquisitions through retail channels not because these acquisitions are somehow "more illegal" or more reprehensible than acquisitions through other sources but because governments at least have a passing chance to enforce regulations that impinge at the point of retail sale. Enforcing regulations that attempt to govern informal transfers between private parties is a much more difficult task although, given the data reported in this chapter, no less an essential one.

sumed, but has never been thoroughly researched, that many felons exploit informal, black market, and other relatively hard-to-regulate sources of supply. This too is confirmed in the analyses reported below.

Burr's (1977) study of Florida felons represents, so far as we know, the only previous attempt to explore patterns of criminal gun acquisition by direct questioning of a felon sample. Data were gathered on the sources from which 176 criminal handguns were obtained. Just over one-third were acquired through private party transactions (purchases or swaps between private individuals), and about one-quarter were obtained through theft. Another one-quarter were obtained through a retail dealer; a few were obtained as gifts (5%), through pawn shops (2%), or simply had been borrowed (4%). Taking "retail dealer" and "pawn shop" as customary retail transactions where there might be some concern with legality and the remainder as informal, off-the-record transactions, the latter predominate in these data by about three to one (74 to 26%).

Burr also surveyed a sample of nonfelon gun owners and asked where they obtained their handguns. Their responses differed in degree, but not in kind, from the felons' responses. Of the 433 legitimate handguns in this analysis, 43% were purchased from a retail dealer and 6% were bought from a pawn shop; thus, only about one-half of the *legitimate* handguns were acquired through customary retail channels. Another 16% were bought from a private party, 15% were received as gifts, and 7% were acquired through informal swaps and trades, the remainder having been acquired in a variety of oddlot ways. Nationally representative results from a 1978 survey of gun owners show largely identical patterns (see Wright, Rossi, and Daly, 1983: 118–119). Thus, it appears that informal mechanisms of circulation are quite important in both the licit and illicit firearms markets, but especially in the latter.

Our questionnaire obtained fairly comprehensive information as to where and how our felons had acquired their guns. Since our respondents tended to have owned guns in fairly large numbers, it was impractical to ask where and how they had procured every gun they had ever owned. Thus, all our questions refer specifically to their *most recent* firearms acquisitions; a separate series of questions asked about the most recent handgun and about the most recent shoulder weapon. Marginal frequencies for all the variables employed in this analysis are shown in Table 9.1. Absent any reason or evidence to suggest otherwise, we assume that patterns of acquisition for these "most recent" guns were typical of all the firearms transactions these men undertook.

HOW AND WHERE DO FELONS OBTAIN HANDGUNS?

Each man in the study was asked whether he had ever owned a handgun; 1032 said "yes." This amounts to 55% of the total sample and to 79% of those who had ever owned any kind of gun. Each of these handgun owners

TABLE 9.1. Where and How Felons Obtain Guns: Marginal Frequencies (in Percentages)

Handguns

1. How did you get your most recent handgun?

Stole	32
Rent/borrow	9
Trade	7
Cash purchase	43
Gift	8
(N) =	(970)

2. Where did you get it?

Friend	40
Gun shop	11
Pawnshop	6
Family	4
Fence	5
Street	14
Drug dealer	4
Black market	3
Hardware/department store	4
All other	9
(N) =	(943)

3. Was it new or used?

Used	62
New	33
Don't know	5
(N) =	(980)

4. Did you get it in or out of state?

In state	77
Out-of-state	23
(N) =	(968)

5. Once you decided to get it, how long did it take?

Few hours	60
Day	12
Few weeks	18
Week	4
Few weeks	3
Month or more	3
(N) =	(934)

Shoulder weapons

1. How did you get most recent rifle or shotgun?

Stole	23
Rent/borrow	6
Trade	7
Cash purchase	42
Gift	22
(N) =	(951)

2. Where did you get it?

Friend	33
Gun shop	17
Pawnshop	4

(continued)

TABLE 9.1. Where and How Felons Obtain Guns: Marginal Frequencies (in Percentages) *(continued)*

Family	22
Fence	3
Street	5
Drug dealer	2
Black market	2
Hardware/department Store	11
All other	2
(N) =	(718)

were asked where and how his most recent handgun had been procured.

Concerning "how," outright cash purchase was the most common means of acquiring a handgun, indicated by about 43%. The only other fairly common means of acquisition was theft, indicated by 32%. Small but roughly equal proportions obtained their most recent handgun as gifts (8%), by borrowing (8%), or through trades (7%).

The most surprising of these results is the relatively high fraction of handguns procured via theft, which appears to be a much more important source of supply for criminal firearms than has been suggested in previous studies. Indeed, previous studies based on traces of firearms confiscated by police routinely have suggested that about one-fifth of the firearms used in crime are stolen weapons; as indicated earlier, Burr's results suggested that about one-quarter of them were. Here we learn, in contrast, that one-third of our sample had obtained their most recent handgun through theft. Moreover, this proportion is only a lower boundary to the fraction of stolen guns among the firearms used by this sample, since many of the weapons obtained through purchase, trade, etc., were likely also stolen (if not by the felon, then by the person from whom he acquired the weapon). The entire matter of stolen guns is sufficiently important that the next chapter is devoted exclusively to it; as such, no more need be said on the topic here.

Concerning where felons obtained handguns, the most important source was clearly friends, mentioned by 40%. "Off-the-street" was a distant second, mentioned by 14%, followed by gun shops, which were mentioned by 11%. Others sources of at least some importance included pawnshops (6%), fences (5%), and family members and drug dealers (4% each). Combining categories in obvious ways, we find that friends and family were by far the most common source for the felons' most recent handguns (44%), followed by various informal gray- and black-market sources (fences, drug dealers, off-the-street, etc., with 26%), followed finally by customary retail outlets (gun shops, pawn shops, hardware and department stores, with 21%).[2] The remaining 10% were acquired from a variety of other sources.

The cross-tabulation of the "where" and "how" questions is shown in

[2]The term, "gray- and black-market sources," is used in a very loose way. It includes fences, drug dealers, and "off the street," as well as the response, "black

Table 9.2. We note first that friends and family were the predominant source of supply whatever the means of acquisition, including theft. Indeed, among those who had obtained their most recent handgun by stealing ($N = 297$), 31% reported stealing from friends or family members. Another 30% reported stealing from a gray- or black-market source (fence, drug dealer, etc.). About one-tenth of the thefts were directly from retail outlets, and the remaining 29% were from "other sources" (in this case, overwhelmingly, from homes and apartments). Much additional detail on the theft of firearms is reported in the following chapter.

Concerning outright cash purchases, family and friends were again the predominant source of supply (38%), followed by customary retail outlets (35%). The black market also received a sizable share of the cash purchase market, in this case 26%.

TABLE 9.2. Means by Sources of Handgun Acquisitions (in Percentages)

Sources	Means[c]				
	Purchase	Theft	Rent/borrow	Trade	Gift
Family/friends	38	31	85	54	79
Gray/black market[a]	26	30	10	41	15
Retail outlet[b]	35	10	2	3	5
All other	1	29	3	2	1
(N) =	(415)	(297)	(82)	(70)	(75)

[a] Fence, off-the-street, drug dealer, or black market.
[b] Gun shop, pawnshop, hardware or department store.
[c] Each column totals 100%.

Table 9.2 thus contains an answer to the question posed at the onset of this chapter, namely, what fraction of felons' handgun acquisitions involved a straightforward transaction (cash purchase) with a conventional retail outlet? As it happens, this describes 147 of the 939 men represented in the table, or 16%. One out of six of the men in this sample acquired his most recent handgun through means and sources likely to be concerned about the legality of the transaction; five out of six did not. Clearly, regulations imposed at the point of retail sale miss the overwhelming majority of all criminal handgun transactions.

The remainder of Table 9.2 can be summarized very quickly: Borrowing a handgun or receiving one as a gift almost always involved family and friends; swaps and trades were about equally likely to involve family and friends (54%) and black-market sources (41%). Other sources of supply in these cases were generally unimportant.

_____
market." We do not wish to imply that these "gray- and black-market sources" amount to organized enterprises, much less that they are organized enterprises specializing in firearms transactions.

TABLE 9.3. Means and Sources of Handgun Acquisition, by Type (in Percentages)

				Type[a]			
	Unarmed	Improviser	Knife	One-timer	Sporadic	Handgun predator	Shotgun predator
How obtained							
Theft	18	42	18	22	40	42	48
Rent/borrow	3	8	4	15	13	8	6
Trade	11	—	11	6	6	8	4
Purchase	58	46	48	50	34	36	33
Gift	10	4	18	8	7	6	9
(N) =	(207)	(26)	(44)	(163)	(199)	(262)	(69)
Where obtained							
Family/friends	38	42	50	53	41	48	33
Black market	23	12	20	17	36	26	37
Normal retail	32	31	20	23	13	12	21
All other	7	15	10	7	11	13	9
(N) =	(200)	(26)	(44)	(160)	(160)	(255)	(67)
Percentage purchasing most recent handgun from normal retail outlet	30	23	18	21	7	7	10

[a] All columns total 100%.

As one might anticipate, there were fairly sizable differences in the means and sources of handgun acquisitions across the categories of our typology; these data are shown in Table 9.3. In the less predatory categories, cash purchase was clearly the most common means of acquisition, and in the more predatory categories, it was theft. One-timers and Sporadics were noticeably more likely to have borrowed (or rented) their most recent handguns than were the other types; knife criminals were noticeably more likely to have received their handguns as gifts.

Concerning sources: Family and friends were the major suppliers in all cases but one; among Shotgun Predators, black-market sources were slightly more common. Normal retail outlets were exploited by about one-third of the Unarmed Criminals and the Improvisers, and by about one-fifth or fewer of everyone else. Fractions who obtained their most recent handgun through cash purchase from a normal retail outlet varied from 30% of the Unarmed Criminals to 7% of the Handgun predators. Thus, felons in general avoided usual retail outlets, and the more predatory felons were especially likely to do so.

CRIMINAL HANDGUNS VERSUS CRIME HANDGUNS

The obvious presence of sizable numbers of handgun owners in all categories of the typology presents a convenient occasion in which to stress once again that not all of the handguns acquired by these men were, in fact, crime guns; what we have said so far pertains to the acquisition of guns by criminals in general, and not specifically the acquisition of guns to use in crime. We can provide, however, at least some data on this latter topic as well.

Men who indicated that they owned a handgun were asked about the reasons why they had acquired it. One of the options was, "to use in my crimes." (These data were analyzed, of course, in detail in an earlier chapter.) As it happens, just over one-half the men who answered this question sequence said that use in crime was not at all important; 20% indicated that it was "somewhat important," and 29% said that it was very important. The cross-tabulation of this item with the questions on where and how handguns were obtained is shown in Table 9.4.

For fairly obvious reasons, the patterns in Table 9.4 are very similar to those observed in Table 9.3. Handguns acquired by felons for reasons other than use in crime tended to be outright cash purchases (50%), typically from family and friends (45%); handguns acquired specifically to use in crime tended instead to be stolen. All told, about 20% of the "noncriminal" acquisitions involved cash purchase from a usual retail outlet versus about 7% of the acquisitions where use in crime was somewhat or very important. Thus, our essential point remains: More predatory criminals, acquiring a handgun specifically for use in crime, heavily exploited informal, off-the-record means and sources and rarely went through customary retail channels.

TABLE 9.4. Means and Sources of Handgun Acquisition by Motives for Obtaining a Handgun (in Percentages)

	"To use in crime"[a]		
	Very important	Somewhat important	Not important
How obtained			
Theft	43	49	24
Rent/borrow	14	9	6
Trade	6	6	9
Purchase	32	29	50
Gift	5	8	11
(N) =	(208)	(146)	(374)
Where obtained			
Family/friends	43	49	45
Black market	32	27	22
Normal retail	12	12	24
All other	13	13	9
(N) =	(204)	(142)	(359)
Percentage purchasing from normal retail outlet	7	7	20

[a]Each column totals 100%.

One plausible reading of these data is that the GCA of 1968 and related state and local regulations have been quite successful in preventing routine, over-the-counter firearms acquisitions by felons, since, quite apparently, few of the felons in our sample acquired their most recent handgun in this way. It would be pertinent to know in this connection whether the patterns observed here were also typical modes of gun acquisition by felons before 1968, but no earlier study of sufficient detail exists.

On the other hand, it is possible that the modes of acquisition just described long predate the 1968 legislation, and moreover, that they are characteristic of many of the consumer transactions that felons undertake, not just their firearms acquisitions. It would be pertinent to know in this connection how the felons' most recent automobiles or television sets had been obtained, that is, how many were stolen, how many acquired used from friends and family, and so on. Unfortunately, these questions were not included in the survey.

It is also of some interest to inquire about the criminal records of the (relatively) small ($N = 147$) subset of the sample who did acquire their most recent handgun through a normal retail transaction. As it happens, these men averaged seven prior arrests, three prior convictions, and two prior imprisonments. All of these averages were less than the corresponding values for men whose most recent handgun was obtained in other ways, but they amount to fairly lengthy criminal records nonetheless. (We cannot determine from our data how many of these previous convictions were for felonies.) It therefore appears that at least some men with lengthy criminal records nonetheless successfully obtain handguns through conventional over-the-counter transactions.[3]

OTHER CHARACTERISTICS OF THE CRIMINAL-HANDGUN MARKET

Table 9.1 contains some additional descriptive details about the nature of the criminal-handgun market. Given what has already been said, it comes as no surprise to learn that the market was dominated by used versus new equipment: Among those who answered the question, nearly two-thirds (65%) reported that their most recent handgun was used when they obtained it. Used guns were somewhat more prominent when use in crime was a major or secondary motive for the acquisition than when it was not; new handguns were reported disproportionately by the Unarmed relative to the more predatory groups.

---

[3] This, of course, does not imply that the men in question themselves simply walked into a gun shop and bought themselves a gun, in direct defiance of the Gun Control Act of 1968. In many cases, these purchases would have been made in the felon's behalf by friends or associates with "clean" records, which is, to be sure, still quite illegal. Although we asked these men where and how they had obtained their most recent guns, we did not ask who, exactly, had obtained them.

The illicit-firearms market was also predominantly a local market: More than three-quarters of the sample (77%) reported that they had procured their most recent handgun in-state. In general, there were no important differences in this fraction according to type, or according to the motive for acquisition, or by state.[4]

We also asked these men how long it took them to actually get their most recent handgun once they had decided to do so; overwhelmingly, the answer was "almost immediately."[5] About 60% obtained it within a few hours, and about three-quarters of them within the day. Only about one-tenth reported that it took more than a few days. Clearly, these men encountered not much more difficulty in acquiring a handgun than they would encounter in making any sort of usual retail purchase, their criminal records and felonious leanings notwithstanding.

WHERE AND HOW DO FELONS OBTAIN SHOULDER WEAPONS?

Men in our sample were also asked whether they had ever owned a rifle or a shotgun; 1023 said YES.[6] This amounts to 55% of the total sample and to 78% of those ever owning any kind of firearm. Parallel questions about means and sources of shoulder-weapon acquisition were also asked; marginal results are shown in Table 9.1.

The patterns differed, but only modestly, from what has already been observed in the case of handguns, and so these data can be summarized quickly. Again, outright cash purchase was the most common method of acquisition (42%), followed by theft (23%), followed, interestingly, by gifts (22%). Clearly, felons were more likely to receive shoulder weapons as gifts

---

[4] The confiscation studies usually report much larger fractions of out-of-state handguns than are reported in the text, especially for states with relatively strict gun control laws. Our result addresses only where the felon *obtained* his most recent handgun and says nothing about where that handgun was first sold at retail. It is certainly possible that many of the "in-state" acquisitions reported by the sample involved handguns originating in other states.

[5] Phil Cook (private communication) points out that many of these men would have presumably "decided" to obtain their most recent handgun the moment they were offered one on the street or found one in the dresser drawer of the home they were burglarizing. In these cases, clearly, the "how long did it take" question is without meaning.

[6] It is worth noting that the Gun Control Act of 1968 imposes the same restriction on shoulder-weapon sales to felons as on handgun sales. All these restrictions, incidentally, are for persons with felony convictions. Although every man in our sample had at least one felony conviction when we interviewed him, he need not have had a felony conviction when he was last arrested and sentenced to prison (i.e., his conviction offense might have been his first-ever felony conviction). We lack adequate detail in our criminal-history questions to sort out those for whom the conviction offense was the first felony.

than they were to receive handguns. Borrowing and trading were again fairly minor methods, reported by 6–7% each.

As in the case of handguns, friends were the predominant source of shoulder weapons (33%), followed by family members (22%), followed by gun shops (17%). Conventional retail outlets were clearly more important in the shoulder-weapon market than in the handgun market; in contrast, gray- or black-market sources were less important. Overall, 55% of these men obtained their most recent shoulder weapon from family and friends, 31% from a customary retail outlet, 12% from a gray- or black-market source, and the remaining 2% from a variety of other outlets.

The cross-tabulation of the shoulder weapon "where" and "how" questions is shown in Table 9.5. Outright cash purchase of shoulder weapons

TABLE 9.5. Means by Sources of Shoulder-Weapon Acquisitions (in Percentages)

Sources	Means[a]			
	Purchase	Rent/borrow	Trade	Gift
Family/friends	34	78	59	88
Gray/black market	14	14	30	2
Retail outlet	51	2	8	8
All other	1	5	3	2
(N) =	(396)	(58)	(63)	(200)

[a] Columns total 100%.

tended to involve customary retail outlets (51%) or family and friends (34%); borrowing long guns and receiving them as gifts were overwhelmingly from family and friends; trading was primarily with family and friends (59%) but sometimes with gray- or black-market outlets as well (30%). (Men who had stolen their most recent shoulder weapon were not asked from whom it had been stolen.) The major differences between the criminal-handgun and shoulder-weapons markets were that (1) customary retail outlets were a more important source of shoulder weapons than handguns, and (2) gifts were a much more important source of shoulder weapons than handguns. Otherwise, the two markets appeared to be rather similar.

SUMMARY

The illicit firearms market as exploited by the men in our sample was clearly and heavily dominated by informal, off-the-record transactions, either with family and friends or with various gray- and black-market sources. Cash purchase was the principal mode of acquisition, followed by theft. The market was primarily in used guns and was largely an in-state, not out-of-state, market. Once felons decided they wanted (or needed) a handgun, they obtained one almost immediately. Not more than about one in six did so through means and sources that were likely to be concerned about the legality (or perhaps even the advisability) of the transaction. Restrictions on firearms acquisitions by felons at the point of retail sales simply miss the largest share of these transactions and are apparently ineffectual in preventing the remainder.

Shutting off the supply of guns to criminals means, of necessity, shutting off the informal circulation of guns among the friends and associates of these men and, of course, stemming the supply obtained through theft. Both are problematic: It is already illegal to transfer a firearm to a convicted felon (see Footnote 1), yet many of the friends and associates of these men apparently do it just the same. Legislation has not done the trick; perhaps sentencing would work better. (One might consider, for example, stiff penalties for firearms transfers to felons whenever these were detected and, in the same framework, stiff penalties for the crime of gun theft.)

Of the many sources of firearms exploited by these men, theft is perhaps the most difficult to contain. No matter how we attempt to interdict the criminal acquisition of handguns, any handgun that can be legitimately owned for any reason can subsequently be stolen from its legitimate owner and turn up in the hands of a felon. As we have seen, about one-third of the handgun owners in our sample themselves stole their most recent handgun; as we see in the next chapter, many of the handguns obtained through other means were either definitely or probably stolen by other parties. The extensive commerce in stolen firearms among criminals tends to erode beyond all recognition the distinction between the licit and illicit markets; it is thus to the specific topic of gun theft that we now turn.

10

PATTERNS OF ACQUISITION: GUN THEFT

A major source of the firearms used by our felon sample was theft, the means by which 32% of our sample acquired their most recent handguns. Stolen guns pose a serious criminal justice problem: A stolen firearm is, by definition, in "the wrong hands" but under the best of circumstances can only be traced back to the last legal owner if the gun is subsequently used in a crime. As we saw in Chapter Eight, untraceability is an important characteristic that felons look for in handguns, and stolen guns fit that definition very well. Even when other sources of supply are available, it is easy to see that there might be a preference among criminals for stolen equipment.

Our survey included a fairly extensive series of questions on the theft of firearms, results from which are presented in this chapter. Marginal frequencies for the relevant items are shown in Table 10.1.

That theft of guns represents a major source of the firearms used by criminals has long been suspected, and yet, surprisingly little previous research on the topic has been reported. Indeed, there are no more than a handful of studies (so far as we can determine) that have even considered the issue, and only two that have explored the topic in some detail. The first of these is the offender survey conducted in Florida by Burr (1977); the second is Brill's *Firearms Abuse* (1977). Where possible, results from both these studies are compared to our own results throughout this chapter.

HOW MANY CRIME GUNS ARE STOLEN GUNS?

Estimates of the percentage of stolen guns among the firearms used in crime vary widely. The lowest estimate that appears in the literature is 6%, this figure having been derived from the well-known Project Identification study of confiscated weapons. The opinion of Brill and most other observers is that this is almost certainly an underestimate, quite probably a severe one. The follow-up study, Project 300, is also based on a sample of confiscated guns but results in a more credible estimate of 22%. Brill's best estimate is about 19–20% (1977: 103); this too is based on a sample of confiscations. Studies of police-confiscated weapons thus appear to converge on roughly 20% as the fraction of stolen guns among crime guns.

TABLE 10.1. Marginal Frequencies For Items on Gun Theft (in Percentages)

(Total Sample) During any of the crimes you ever committed during your life, did you ever steal a gun?

No	53
Yes	47
(N) =	(1678)

(Asked of those who ever stole a gun): About how many guns would you say you have stolen in your life?

1	13
A few	43
10 or 15	17
Dozens	17
Hundreds	9
Thousands	2
(N) =	(775)

Have you ever gone out specifically looking for a gun to steal, or did you just steal guns when you came across them?

I have looked specifically for a gun to steal	24
I stole guns when I came across them	76
(N) =	(766)

When you stole a firearm, was it usually because you wanted it for yourself, or was it usually because you intended to sell or trade it to somebody else?

Usually to keep for myself	31
Usually to sell or trade	70
(N) =	(765)

Of all the guns you have ever stolen, did you ever keep one for your own personal use?

No	32
Yes	68
(N) =	(774)

(Asked of those who ever kept a stolen gun): Why did you keep the gun(s)?

	Yes	No	(N)
I didn't know what else to do with it	7	93	(515)
It was a nice piece	68	32	(520)
I did not have a gun then	37	64	(513)
A stolen gun could never be traced to me	34	67	(517)
I collect guns	19	81	(513)
I couldn't find anyone else to sell it to	12	88	(509)

(Asked of those who ever stole a gun): Have you ever sold or traded a stolen gun to somebody?

No, never	11
Yes, one time	14
Yes, a few times	41
Yes, many times	32
(Inferred Yes—answered follow-up)	3
(N) =	(774)

(continued)

(Asked of those who sold or traded a stolen gun): Which of the following best describes who you have sold or traded stolen guns to?

	Yes	No	(N)
To a friend	66	34	(677)
To another member of my family	12	88	(676)
To a pawnshop	21	79	(670)
To a fence	49	51	(673)
To a gun dealer	21	79	(674)
To a stranger on the street	25	76	(674)
To people I was in debt to	20	80	(677)
To my drug dealer	31	69	(672)

(Asked of all respondents): Suppose you decided you really needed a handgun for some reason, and that the only way to get one was to steal it. Which of the following best describes where you think you would go to steal a handgun if you really needed it?

	Yes	No	(N)
Directly off a person	10	90	(1599)
From a home or apartment	58	42	(1602)
Out of a car	31	69	(1600)
From a policeman	8	92	(1595)
From a store	28	72	(1602)
From a manufacturer	11	89	(1593)
Off a truck during shipment	13	87	(1592)

There are, to be sure, a wide range of technical difficulties encountered in making inferences from these confiscation samples; Brill (1977) provides a complete description of them. Perhaps the most serious problem is that in order for a confiscated gun to show up in these analyses as a stolen gun, the theft must have been reported to the police, complete with a correct serial number and description of the firearm. No one knows for sure what fraction of stolen guns is ever reported to the police; certainly, the fraction is less than 100% and may be much less than 100%. Indeed, a gun owner would have good reason not to report a theft if there was a possibility that the gun was not possessed legally by that owner. Given the complexity of gun laws in this country and the wide variability in them from place to place, nearly any gun owner might have some concerns on this score. In addition, many gun owners may not have sufficient information about the stolen weapon—especially its serial number—to provide the police with a usable report. For these reasons, many have assumed that a large share of the gun thefts simply go unreported. If so, then all estimates of the fraction of stolen guns among the guns used in crime that are based on traces of police confiscations would have to be taken as lower boundary estimates.

Another approach to the problem is to ask felons themselves whether they stole their gun(s), as, indeed, we have done in our study. So far as we know, the only previous survey of felons to include such a question is Burr's. Among the 176 handguns owned among Burr's sample of felons, 23% were listed as stolen firearms by the felons themselves, roughly in the same range as the estimates based on confiscation samples.

Somewhat in contrast to these findings, all the handgun owners in our sample were asked, "Which of the following best describes how you got [your most recent] handgun?" Results were reported in the previous chapter: About one-third (32%) said that they personally had stolen it, a somewhat higher figure than reported in previous studies.

This, moreover, is obviously an underestimate of the true fraction of stolen guns among the guns used in crime, since a stolen gun need not have been stolen by the felon himself; many of these men, knowingly or unknowingly, will have bought, traded for, or otherwise obtained a handgun that had been stolen by someone else.

To tap what can be called the secondary market in stolen guns, all the handgun owners in the sample were asked, "To the best of your knowledge, was [your most recent handgun] a stolen weapon?" Men who had personally stolen the gun were instructed to circle "definitely stolen" in response to this question, but not all of them did. (Many, in fact, simply skipped the question.) If we treat every handgun that was reported to have been personally stolen as a "definitely" stolen weapon, then, all told, 46% of the most recent handguns possessed by this sample were reported as "definitely stolen," and another 24% were "probably stolen." *Thus, at least four-tenths, and possibly as many as seventh-tenths, of the most recent handguns owned by this sample were stolen weapons.* These data suggest, unmistakably, that stolen handguns are a much more important source of supply to the criminal population than has been suggested in previous studies.

To be sure, these estimates strictly apply only to the felons' most recent handguns; whether they generalize to all the handguns these felons ever owned is, therefore, an open question. Still, we see no reason why these "most recent" transactions would have been atypical of the total population of firearms transactions in which these men have engaged, so we are inclined to take these results as indicative and generalizable. If so, then it is clear beyond question that stolen guns are heavily involved among the firearms used in crime.

Although our estimates of the percentage of stolen guns among crime guns differ considerably from previous ones, the differences are not irreconcilably large. For example, Brill's most extensively studied confiscation sample was a New York City sample of 144 handguns submitted for tracing to the Bureau of Alcohol, Tobacco, and Firearms (BATF). New York City, of course, has very strict controls over the private ownership of handguns; this notwithstanding, the New York City police have guessed that there are 2,000,000 unlicensed and therefore illegally possessed handguns in the city.[1]

---

[1] This is almost certainly a high estimate. If handguns were owned in New York City at the average rate of handgun ownership for the nation, and if, as we have estimated elsewhere, there are about 40 million handguns presently in private hands,

Moreover, New York City has extraordinarily high burglary and robbery rates. From these facts, one can infer that criminals in New York City commonly encounter unregistered and illegally possessed handguns whose theft is not likely to be reported to the police; many of the guns that are stolen in New York City, in other words, would never show up in an ATF search as stolen weapons because their theft would never have been reported.

Clearly, no one knows for sure the rate at which stolen handguns are reported to the police in New York City. If two-thirds are and the remaining one-third are not, then a simple correction of Brill's best estimate (of 20%) would raise it to about 30%. If only one-third of the gun thefts are reported, the same correction would raise Brill's estimate to about 60%, or in roughly the same range as our upper estimate. Whether there is any genuine "discrepancy" between our results and Brill's appears, therefore, to turn entirely on the rate at which handgun thefts are reported to the New York City police; plausible (although admittedly untested) assumptions about this rate narrow the differences between the estimates considerably.

As to Burr's estimate, it is clear that the fraction of his felons who themselves stole their (most recent) handgun (about 23%) is similar to the fraction of our felons who did so (about 32%); the critical point is that this fraction is a clear underestimate of the true fraction of stolen guns among crime guns, since, as we have seen, many of the stolen handguns possessed by our felons (or by felons in general) were not stolen directly by them but were acquired through purchases and trades with other parties. Taking this secondary market in stolen guns into account approximately doubles the estimated percentage of stolen guns among the firearms used in crime.

WHO STEALS GUNS?

Corroborating evidence on the extent of firearms theft among the sample was obtained in the criminal-history section of the survey. All respondents were asked, "During any of the crimes you ever committed in your life, did you ever steal a gun?" Of those who responded ($N = 1678$), 47% said "yes;" among those who had ever stolen a gun ($N = 790$), 86% reported having stolen more than one of them.

The tendency to have ever stolen a gun was related, although not perfectly, to the tendency to have used guns to commit crimes (Table 10.2). About one quarter of the Unarmed Criminals reported having stolen at least one gun; of this one-quarter, one-third reported having stolen more than 10 guns. Among the Improvisers, 45% had stolen a gun; among the Knife

---

then the total number of New York City handguns would be about 1.2 million at the most. The true number is probably even lower since, in general, gun ownership tends to be lowest in large cities, especially in the Northeast (Wright, Rossi, and Daly, 1983: Ch. 6). Realistically, the total number of unregistered handguns in New York City is probably on the order of several hundreds of thousands, not 2 million.

Criminals, 34%; and among the One-Timers, 35%. Thus, among the less predatory felon categories, fractions ranging from about one-quarter to about one half had stolen at least one firearm.

The remaining categories stand in sharp contrast; among the Sporadics and Predators, it was the rare man who had not stolen a firearm sometime in his life. Indeed, in these categories, the fraction who had ever stolen guns runs from 70 to 80%. These, moreover, tend to be high-rate thieves: Among the Sporadics and Predators who had stolen at least one gun ($N = 472$), a mere 5% had stolen only one. As with virtually all other forms of criminality examined in this analysis, then, gun theft is heavily concentrated among the more predatory groups of criminals.

TABLE 10.2. Gun Theft by Type

Type	Percentage reporting ever stolen	$\overline{X}$ stolen/ thief	SD	(N)	Total guns
Unarmed	26	32	136	(160)	5063
Improviser	45	13	24	(31)	407
Knife user	34	30	155	(41)	1228
One-timer	35	47	193	(78)	3624
Sporadic handgunner	70	29	134	(164)	4768
Handgun predator	81	47	144	(239)	11,223
Shotgun predator	75	61	177	(62)	3801
Entire population	47	39	147	(775)	30,114

HOW MANY GUNS ARE STOLEN?

Men who reported having stolen a gun at some time in their careers were then asked how many guns they had ever stolen. Response categories were just one, a few, 10–15, dozens, hundreds, or thousands. Taking "a few" to mean 5 and "dozens" to mean 25, and using the lower limits to all the other categories, we estimate that the gun thieves in our sample had stolen some 30,000 guns in their careers, an average of about 39 stolen weapons per man. This average, of course, is greatly inflated by the small number of men who report thousands of thefts; the median value would be substantially lower.[2] Still, it is clear that at least some of these men had stolen guns in very large numbers.

[2] Admittedly, "thousands" of gun thefts seems a bit unlikely. The question asks, however, for the number of guns ever stolen, not the number of separate thefts. One hijacking of a truck in shipment or one heist from a manufacturer's warehouse would be adequate to produce 1000 stolen guns. As we report later, men who said they had stolen large numbers of guns were also more likely than others to report thefts from potential high-volume sources (see the section on "professional" gun thieves.)

About 13% of the sample of gun thieves reported having stolen a single gun, most of them in the less predatory categories. These "one-time" thieves accounted for less than 1% of the total number of guns stolen. Of vastly greater concern are the 85 men—11% of the gun thieves—who reported stealing hundreds or thousands of guns; these men accounted for nearly 80% of the total volume of stolen guns reported by our respondents. About three-quarters of these "high-rate" gun thieves were from the two Predator categories. The Predators contribute disproportionately to every aspect of the crime problem, the gun-theft aspect clearly included. It is worth mention, however, that 13% of the high-rate gun thieves were Unarmed Criminals, men who had apparently stolen large numbers of guns but had never actually used guns in committing their crimes.

WHY ARE GUNS STOLEN?

The presence of a relatively large group of Unarmed Criminals among the high-rate gun thieves illustrates an important point about gun theft, namely, that the motivation to steal a weapon need not simply be that the felon wants (or needs) a gun for his own personal use. To the contrary, one may assume that many guns are stolen for the same reason that many television sets or stereos are stolen, that is, to fence for cash or otherwise dispose of in the gray or black markets. Indeed, given the evident high demand, potential quick turnover, and easy portability, one can readily imagine that firearms (particularly handguns) are probably among the more desirable things to encounter in burglarizing a residence or a store, even if the thief has no personal use for the weapon.

As we have just seen, guns were stolen by felons who did not use guns as well as by the gun users. The nonusing categories amounted to one-third of the gun thieves and accounted for about one-fifth of the total volume; on the average, in other words, the nonusers stole guns at a lower rate than the gun users stole them, but both groups stole guns with alarming frequency.

That the motivation to steal guns was a mixture of personal and commercial concerns was apparent in the responses to some of the follow-up questions. All the gun thieves were asked, "Have you ever gone out specifically looking for a gun to steal, or did you just steal guns when you came across them?" More than three-quarters (76%) of the gun thieves stole guns when they came across them; thus, going out looking specifically for a gun to steal was a relatively rare behavior. Likewise, we asked, "When you stole a firearm, was it usually because you wanted it for yourself, or was it usually because you intended to sell or trade it to somebody else?" More than two-thirds (70%) of the gun thieves "usually" stole guns to sell or trade to someone else. Clearly, most gun thefts were "opportunity" crimes: Guns were stolen mainly because they were there to steal, not because the felon had decided he needed a gun and that theft was the most convenient or cheapest way to obtain it.

To be sure, a minority of the gun thefts were rather more purposive in character; Table 10.3 shows that these "more purposive" gun thefts were concentrated among the Predator categories. More than one-third of the Handgun Predators (34%), and two-fifths of the Shotgun Predators (41%), reported having looked specifically for a gun to steal—higher percentages than obtained in any of the other categories. The Handgun Predators were also the likeliest, by far, to steal guns to keep for themselves (45 versus 30% in the total sample of gun thieves). Still, even in the Predator categories, opportunity theft was the rule: Looking specifically to steal a gun for one's own personal use was the minority tendency in every category.

TABLE 10.3. Intention and Motive in Gun Thefts (in Percentages)

Type	Percentage who		Percentage who stole	
	Looked for guns to steal	Stole guns when they came across them	For myself	To sell
Unarmed	12	88	16	84
Improviser	10	90	16	84
Knife user	12	88	20	81
One-timer	15	85	37	64
Sporadic handgunner	24	77	29	71
Handgun predator	34	66	45	55
Shotgun predator	41	59	23	77
Entire population	24	76	31	70

The cross-tabulation of these two questions isolated an interesting subgroup, namely, 100 men who reported that they looked specifically for guns to steal, and that they usually stole guns to sell or trade to others. In some sense, these are men who appeared to specialize in gun theft, and so some additional analysis of them is in order.

First, these 100 "professional" gun thieves stole guns in larger than average numbers: Their average number of guns ever stolen was 84, or more than twice the average for all gun thieves. Relative to the others, they were also distinctively more likely to steal from high-quantity sources. Among the total sample of gun thieves, for example, 8% said they had stolen guns directly from a manufacturer; among the 100 "professionals," this was true of 15%. They were also more likely to steal from a shipment (29 versus 16% in the total) and from stores (50 versus 37%). They were also more likely than the others to have stolen a gun from a policeman or "directly off a person." However, gun theft during housebreaks was no more common among the "professionals" than among the total sample.

The "professionals" also differed in how they disposed of the guns they stole. Most sold to fences (64 versus 49% in the total sample of gun thieves); a surprisingly large number sold stolen firearms to gun dealers (32 versus 21% in the total sample). Perhaps the term "gun dealer" was interpreted by many to include persons who traded primarily on the black and gray markets, as well as licensed retailers and wholesalers. Many of them (27%) said they had used stolen guns to settle their debts; nearly two-fifths (of the "professionals" versus 31% of all gun thieves) had also sold stolen guns to their drug dealer.

There was a definite connection between drug abuse and "professional" gun theft as we have defined it here. Relative to the total sample, the "professional" gun thieves were heavy drug abusers and high-rate drug dealers; more than one-half of them (53 versus 27% of the total sample)

TABLE 10.4. Retention of Stolen Guns (in Percentages)

Type	Those who usually stole for self (%)	Those ever keeping stolen gun (%)
Unarmed criminal	16	33
Improviser	16	48
Knife user	20	34
One-timer	37	60
Sporadic handgunner	29	81
Handgun predator	45	90
Shotgun predator	23	81
Entire population	31	68

had made dozens or hundreds of drug deals. They were also more likely than the average man in the sample to have been armed during the conviction offense (about two-thirds versus just over one-half of all respondents); relative to other armed criminals, they showed a preference for sawed-off shotguns (21 versus 13% among the total armed-criminals sample).

We indicated earlier that most of the gun thieves in the sample stole guns because they were there to steal, and that the predominant motive in doing so was to sell or trade the gun to another party. Yet another follow-up question asked, "Of all the guns you have ever stolen, did you ever keep one for your own personal use?" Although less than one-third of the gun thieves *usually* stole guns for themselves, fully two-thirds had kept at least one for their own personal use, at some time, for some reason. Predictably, the tendency to have kept at least one stolen gun for personal use increased regularly as one moves to the more predatory categories of the typology, reaching a peak among the Handgun Predators, of whom 90% had kept a stolen gun for their personal use (Table 10.4).

Men who indicated that they had kept a gun for personal use were asked why. The most frequent answer, given by 68%, was that "it was a nice piece," presumably a nicer piece than the one they were then carrying. Theft, it appears, serves as a mechanism of technological upgrading among the criminal population. The next most frequent reason for keeping a stolen gun, mentioned by 37%, was that "I did not have a gun then." Roughly one-third mentioned that "a stolen gun could never be traced to me"; predictably, this response was especially common among the more serious gun abusers. Other reasons for keeping stolen guns were all cited less frequently, for example, "I collect guns" (mentioned by 20%), or "I couldn't find anyone to sell it to" (12%).

The results just summarized illustrate an important point about the crime of gun theft, namely, that while large fractions of our sample report having stolen guns and report theft as the means by which they obtained their most recent handgun, the need to obtain a gun for one's own personal use was only rarely the principal motivation in stealing them. Recall: just under one-half the sample had ever stolen any firearm; of this one-half, about two-thirds had kept at least one stolen gun for their own use; among this latter group (which comprise about one-third of the total sample), only 37% gave as the reason for keeping the gun that they did not have a gun at that time. In other words, most of the men who reported stealing weapons did not *need* to steal guns in order to arm themselves; virtually every man in the sample who armed himself through theft would also have had other means that could be exploited for the purpose. It therefore does *not* follow from the high volume of gun theft among this sample, or from the apparently major role of stolen guns in supplying the criminal market, that a drastic reduction of gun theft would result in fewer armed criminals. For most, or so it appears, the theft of guns is a redundancy, not the necessary prerequisite for arming oneself.

THE COMMERCE IN STOLEN FIREARMS

All who reported the theft of a gun were asked if they had ever sold or traded a stolen gun; 90% had. Of these, 16% had done so "just once," 47% had done so "a few times," and 37% had done so "many times." "A few times" was the modal response among all categories except the Predators; among the Predators, "many times" was the most common response. About 95% of the Predators (both groups) had sold or traded a stolen gun at least once in their careers.

Men who reported having sold or traded at least one stolen firearm were queried about their customers in these transactions. The most frequent sale was "to a friend," mentioned by about two-thirds overall. This, in fact, was the modal response in all categories, with percentages ranging from 53% of the Unarmed to 73% among the Handgun Predators.

Next to friends, black-market sales predominated, especially to fences (49%) and drug dealers (31%). Sales "to a stranger on the street" were also fairly common, having been mentioned by 25%. Other frequently mentioned outlets included pawnshops (21%), "gun dealers" (21%), "people I was in debt to" (20%), and family members (12%). Three men volunteered the information that they had sold stolen guns to policemen.

The pattern of commerce revealed in these responses is, of course, very similar to the pattern of acquisition noted in the previous chapter. Felons with stolen guns to sell tended to sell them to the same sources that other felons exploited to acquire guns. Some of these men, clearly, were suppliers to the stolen-gun market, and others were consumers in the market; realistically, most of these men were probably both suppliers and consumers at various times.

It is also of some significance that the 693 men who entered the "who did you sell to?" question sequence gave a total of 1670 answers, for an average of 2.4 channels of distribution per man. More than one-third of these channels involved close associates (friends, family, creditors); another one-third involved clearly criminal enterprises (fences and drug dealers). Roughly one-sixth of the commerce in stolen guns involved legitimate or quasi-legitimate businesses (gun shops, pawn shops). Most of the remainder was sold on the street. Of course, not all stolen guns entered these channels of distribution; as noted earlier, about two-thirds had kept at least one gun for their own use.

Perhaps the most important point to emphasize in all this is the extent to which the market in stolen guns is apparently integrated into the more general criminal markets in stolen goods and in drugs. A striking example of this integration was supplied by one of our southern respondents who described the role of stolen guns in the drug operation with which he worked. In this operation, drug dealers would obtain as many guns as possible from their clients—namely, from drug users who had stolen guns in burglaries and who sought to trade them with the dealers for drugs or cash. In these trades, guns with retail values often in the hundreds of dollars were obtained for drugs whose cost to the dealer was perhaps $10 or $20. Once enough guns had been obtained, they would be loaded for shipment to South America, where guns are in high demand to satisfy the armament needs of the "cocaine cowboys" (private armies in the service of the large Colombian and Bolivian drug operators). The shipment cost, of course, is nil, since the planes would be going to South America anyway to run drugs back to the states.

In South America, guns would be traded at high premium for cocaine or other drugs. In adequate quantity, handguns are said to be worth roughly $200–300 each in Bolivia, with even higher prices obtaining elsewhere. In Bogota, to cite an illustration, a kilo of pure cocaine sells for roughly $6000 and could therefore be acquired in exchange for 20 or 30 guns; that same kilo of cocaine would bring perhaps $50,000 in Miami even if sold in bulk, and considerably more than $50,000 if broken down into smaller quantities for street sale. The 20 or 30 guns necessary to broker the deal in Bogota would rarely represent an out-of-pocket expense of more than several hundred dollars (say, 30 stolen guns obtained at the price of $20 worth of drugs each, or $600 in real costs). Over the entire cycle, from initial acquisition of the guns to the street sale of drugs obtained in South America in exchange for guns, one's investment multiplies several hundred times.

As we reported earlier, about 46% of the sample's most recent handguns were definitely stolen (including the ones stolen directly by the felons themselves), and an additional 24% were "probably stolen." A cross-tabulation of this question with the questions on where and how their most recent handguns were obtained gives some additional sense of the commerce in stolen guns. For this purpose, we ignore the direct thefts and focus on the handguns acquired through other means. To illustrate, 70 men reported that they had either rented or borrowed their most recent handgun; of these, 39 (56%) were rated as "probably" or "definitely" stolen. Of the 349 handguns "bought for cash," 52 were "definitely stolen" and 101 were "probably stolen." Thus, about 44% of the cash purchases made by these men involved stolen guns. Even among the 112 guns received in trades or as gifts, 51% were considered likely to have been stolen. Overall, of the 531 handguns our respondents obtained other than through a personal theft, 259 (49%) were judged either definitely or probably stolen. In short, stolen firearms circulated freely through all the mechanisms of exchange exploited by these men.

Percentaging in the other direction: 276 of the most recent handguns owned by the sample are, in their words, "definitely stolen." Only about two-thirds of these (69%) were stolen directly by the felons themselves. About one-fifth of them (18%) were purchased for cash, 5% were borrowed or rented, 4% were received in trades, and another 4% received as gifts. Most of these transactions predictably involved family, friends, and black-market sources, but roughly one in five apparently involved a legitimate or quasi-legitimate business.

It is also worth a note that the category, "probably not stolen," is also somewhat ambiguous and would no doubt include at least a few stolen guns as well. Transactions involving these "probably not stolen" firearms were, to say the least, a little irregular: Only 57% of the "probably not stolen" were purchased for cash versus 73% of the "definitely not stolen" guns; moreover, about one-third of the "probably not stolen" handguns were obtained from irregular sources: fences, black-market hustlers, drug dealers, or "off-the-street."

In sum, a direct theft is only one among several ways that felons come to possess stolen guns; apparently, at least one-third of the stolen guns they possessed were acquired through secondary sources. The commerce in stolen firearms seems to be quite extensive and thoroughly integrated with the criminal markets in drugs and other stolen property.

WHERE ARE GUNS STOLEN?

The preceding notwithstanding, the principal source of stolen guns to our sample was direct thefts that they, personally, had committed; moreover, direct theft is the ultimate source (obviously) of all the stolen firearms that circulate in the illicit-firearms market. Men who told us they had stolen at least one gun in their careers were asked about the sources from which these guns had been stolen. These data show that about one-half the thefts involved street crimes, residential burglaries, or other crimes against strangers, and that about one-third of them involved friends or family of the respondent. In roughly 1 theft in 10, the victim was an ostensibly legitimate firearms outlet—gun shop, pawn shop, department store, or, in a few cases, the military. The remaining thefts, about 7% of the total, involved illicit sources: fences, drug dealers, and black-market operators.

We asked the gun thieves not only about the sources but also about the locations of their gun thefts. The modal response was "from a home or apartment," mentioned by 84%. In other words, 84% of the men who had ever stolen at least one gun had stolen a gun directly from a private residence. This fraction varied little across the categories of the typology.

About one-half the gun thieves (51%) indicated that they had stolen a gun "from a car"; this was especially common among the Handgun Predators. The next most common response was "from a store," mentioned by about one-third of all gun thieves and by one-half the two Predator groups. Stealing a gun "directly off a person" was admitted by 27%; most of these thefts involved the serious gun abusers (Sporadics and Predators).

"Off a truck during shipment" was mentioned by 15%; 14% claim to have stolen a gun directly from a policeman. In both cases, the Predators showed the highest percentages of all groups. About 8% of the thieves reported having stolen from manufacturers; again, the Predators led the list.

In terms of the number of thefts, then, most involved residences and vehicles, although thefts from commercial establishments, shippers, and manufacturers also seem alarmingly common. In terms of the total number of guns stolen, however, it is possible that theft from residences is less important and theft from these other sources more important. The heist of one semitrailer full of guns might well net more equipment than hundreds or even thousands of residential burglaries. Unfortunately, we did not ask the sample just how many guns they had ever stolen from each of the sources, so we can only speculate that thefts from stores, shippers and manufacturers account for a large share of the total volume. Still, the frequency with which these men reported thefts against potential high-volume sources argues in favor of additional research on this aspect of the gun-theft problem.

Brill has reached a similar conclusion on the basis of his confiscation samples. Because of the extremely small sample sizes, Brill concludes that his analysis "cannot be read as evidence than nonindividual thefts (thefts

TABLE 10.5. Respondent's Theft Experiences and Hypothetical Optimal Theft (in Percentages)

Source	Respondents who ever stole from each source (%)	Those who would steal from each source (%)
Directly from a person	27	10
From a home/apartment	84	58
Out of a car	51	31
From a policeman	15	8
From a store	37	28
From a manufacturer	8	11
Off a truck shipment	16	13
Other		
Relative	0.3	0.7
Friend	0.1	0.4
Military	0.5	0.2
Work	0.4	0.1
I'd buy it	NA[a]	4.1
Don't know	NA[a]	0.4
Other	2.8	3.6

[a] NA = not applicable.

from manufacturers, distributors, dealers, or transporters) constitute the majority of firearms thefts, but it does indicate that these non-individual thefts may be a serious problem" (197: 110). Interestingly, officials at BATF disputed this conclusion, claiming that the nonindividual thefts would probably "equal less than 1%" of all stolen firearms. Our results tend to favor Brill's position; at minimum, it is clear that thefts from potential high-volume sources were committed quite frequently by the felons in this sample.

THE OPTIMAL GUN THEFT

Every man in the sample, whether he had ever stolen guns or not, was asked to imagine the following hypothetical situation: "Suppose you decided you really needed a handgun for some reason and the only way to get one was to steal it." They were then asked how they would go about it. The results, shown in Table 10.5, are quite similar to the behavioral reports already discussed: The rank ordering of places where they would go to steal a gun is effectively identical to the ordering of places from which they had in fact stolen guns. "From a home or apartment" leads the list and was noted by 58%, followed by "out of a car" (31%), and "from a store" (28%), with all remaining responses being much less frequent.

Of some interest is the number of volunteered responses we obtained with the question, many of them quite detailed, for example: "Follow a man with a business for a few days and find out where he keeps it, then get it at night," or "Hide in store clothing rack with wire cutter and get one that way." Respondents frequently commented during debriefing that the police were always a good source, since they always carry at least one handgun and frequently two or three. In the total sample, interestingly, 8% mentioned "from a policeman" as the place they would go to steal a handgun; among the Handgun Predators, this response was offered by 14%.

SUMMARY

The principal conclusions to be drawn from data presented in this chapter are as follows:

1. Our best estimate of the fraction of stolen guns among the firearms used in crime is substantially higher than estimates reported in other studies. One-third of the sample's most recent handguns were personally stolen by the felons themselves; an additional 14% were reported as "definitely stolen" weapons and another 24% as "probably stolen." Overall, then, at least four-tenths, and possibly as much as seven-tenths, of the most recent handguns possessed by this sample were stolen guns.

2. About one-half of the felons in the sample had stolen at least one gun in their careers; men who had stolen at least one tended to have stolen fairly large numbers of them. Most guns were stolen simply because they were there to steal; usually, the point in stealing a gun was to sell or trade it for cash, drugs, or other goods. Gun theft, in short, was predominantly an opportunity crime. Still, two-thirds of those who had ever stolen a gun had kept at least one of them for their own personal use, usually because "it was a nice piece."

3. Gun theft was fairly common among all groups of criminals, even among those who did not use guns to commit their crimes, but it was most common among the more serious gun abusers.

4. We estimate that our sample had stolen a total of roughly 30,000 guns overall. About 80% of the total volume was accounted for by roughly one-tenth of the thieves who stole guns in very large numbers (in the hundreds or thousands). Relative to the total sample, the high-rate gun thieves tended to be drug dealers and users.

5. Stolen firearms circulated widely and freely through all the mechanisms of gun commerce exploited by these men. Nearly one-half the cash purchases of handguns involved stolen weapons.

6. Most gun thefts involved private residences or automobiles, but a good sized fraction of them involved potential high-volume sources such as dealers, shippers, and manufacturers. We cannot estimate the fraction of the total number of stolen guns that originated in these high-volume thefts, but the frequency with which high-volume sources were targeted in thefts suggests that the fraction is probably substantial.

11

HANDGUN CONTROLS AND WEAPONS CHOICE: THE SUBSTITUTION ISSUE

In any substantive area, current patterns of human behavior provide important guides to social policy, providing descriptive information on the nature of the problem in question that should be taken into account in whatever policy may be constructed. But current patterns of behavior are an incomplete guide to what might occur if policies were changed. Human behavior is adaptive, and adaptations occur as well to changes in social policy. In the current case, our survey has provided descriptive information on how felons have used guns in the past and possibly some guides about how they might use guns in the future, assuming that social policies concerning guns remain much the same.

What might happen, however, were gun control policies to change in dramatic ways? Is there anything our survey can tell us about the likely outcomes resulting from efforts to reduce the access of criminals to firearms? In particular, suppose that some sort of effective controls were enacted that substantially reduced the ability of criminals to obtained handguns or certain kinds of handguns. What might happen in that event?

SUBSTITUTION THEORY

Key issues are the extent to which criminals can find effective and efficient substitutes for firearms and how such substitutes might affect both crime rates and the total social costs of crime. The arguments that have been advanced run the full range of optimism. For example, in 1968, Zimring published an argument to the effect that gun controls that effectively reduced the availability of firearms to criminals would reduce violent killings. The key premises in his argument were that in the absence of firearms, most of the assaults and attacks now perpetrated with firearms would instead be perpetrated with knives, and that knives are intrinsically less lethal than firearms. The conclusion is that if there were fewer guns, there would be fewer criminal killings—not because criminals would somehow become less violence-prone but simply because the means of violence available to them would be markedly less effective.

For the moment, we will not consider whether the goal of a substantial reduction in the number of available handguns can be accomplished without some considerable social cost. Assuming that this goal can be achieved, there are serious questions that raise doubts about Zimring's arguments. To begin, it is not clear that less lethal weapons such as knives would always be substituted for handguns; some (such as Kates, 1978, and Kleck, 1983; 1984a) argue that the more lethal sawed-off shotgun would be substituted instead, at least in some cases. It is thus possible that the "no handguns" condition would leave us with the same violent-crime problem we now face, or possibly even a worse one, if the fraction substituting sawed-off shotguns rather than knives were substantially large.

Still another possibility, clearly the most desirable, is that in the absence of handguns, criminals would simply go unarmed. It has been argued, for example, that the handgun provides the psychic "strength" necessary to commit crimes, that it supplies the needed "courage." Absent handguns, it is possible that many felons, therefore, simply would get out of the crime business altogether and stop carrying weapons of any sort. This, clearly, would constitute an improvement.

In short, there are several possible criminal adaptations to a world in which handguns were more difficult or impossible to obtain. Data from our survey may not definitively point out which ways may be followed, but the information may help at least to sharpen the question.

POSTRELEASE GUN ACQUISITION

Of course, no one knows for sure just what criminals would do if we could somehow attain a "no handguns" condition or some close variant [i.e., no cheap handguns, no Saturday Night Special (SNS) handguns]. The possibility that a nontrivial fraction would substitute more lethal weapons instead is, however, sufficiently important that an extended inquiry into the matter is in order. Although the felons in our sample may not be the best or most reliable source of information on what might happen under certain future circumstances, their views on these issues are certainly of some relevance.

Under the provisions of existing federal law, it is already illegal for a convicted felon to acquire a firearm. It is of some interest and pertinent to the concerns of this chapter to see how the likely postrelease firearms behavior of our sample would be constrained by this fact.

Interestingly, most (73%) of the men in our sample were aware of this restriction (see Chapter Eight). This notwithstanding, most of them did not anticipate much trouble in acquiring a handgun once released from prison. First, as in polls of the general public, most of the men in our sample (82%) agreed that "gun laws affect only law-abiding citizens; criminals will always be able to get guns." [1] In like fashion, most (88%) also agreed that "a criminal who wants a handgun is going to get one, no matter how much it costs." A more direct question sequence posed the following hypothetical situation: "Suppose now that you have been released from this prison and you have decided that you need to get a handgun for some reason. Let's also suppose you don't already have one. How much trouble do you think it would be for you to get a handgun after you get out of this prison?" Follow-up questions asked for details—how much would it cost, how long would it take, where would you go to get it, etc. Results are shown in Table 11.1.

Overall, the modal response for the "how much trouble?" question was "no trouble at all," the answer given by 59%. Another 16% affirmed that it would be "only a little trouble." Thus, three-quarters of the sample believed they could obtain handguns with little or no trouble subsequent to their release from prison. This, of course, was the result for the total sample. Men who were experienced in using firearms to commit crime anticipated even less difficulties: Among the Predators, for example, more than four-fifths thought they could arm themselves with little or no trouble, and much the same held for the Sporadic Handgun Users as well.

Whether these are realistic judgments or not is certainly an open question, but at the moment, we have no evidence to suggest that they are not. Clearly, many of these men, especially the firearms abusers, had acquired firearms in the past, and given an average of three prior incarcerations, many would have at some previous point been exactly in the situation in question. Therefore, it is likely that these data represent reports of past experience as much as judgments of future possibilities. For this reason, we are inclined to accept them as accurate.

A follow-up question asked how much each man felt he would have to pay to get the handgun he wanted. Many responded "nothing" at this point, adding that they would steal one. Among those who stated a specific dollar price, the modal response was $100, and the overall sample mean response = $114. Acquiring a handgun subsequent to release was neither especially troublesome nor especially expensive, at least as these men saw it. (It is important to bear in mind that given the handgun-acquisition practices of these felons, the prices are not those of the legitimate market but of the gray or black market.)

---

[1] In a 1978 poll conducted by Patrick Caddell (Cambridge Reports, Inc., 1978), 78% agreed that "gun control laws affect only law abiding citizens, criminals will always be able to find guns," a virtually identical result to that obtained among the prisoners. Likewise, a DMI poll (Decision-Making Information, 1978) found 85–90% agreeing that "registration of handguns will not prevent criminals from acquiring or using them for illegal purposes." (Findings from both polls are discussed at some length in Wright, 1981.) Consensus on the point is thus virtually unanimous among felons and the general population alike.

TABLE 11.1. Acquiring Handguns after Release from Prison, by Type

	Total	Unarmed	Improviser	Knife	One-timer	Sporadic	Handgun predator	Shotgun predator
1. How much trouble do you think it would be for you to get a handgun when you get out of this prison? (in percentages)								
A lot of trouble	15	23	21	13	15	6	5	9
Some trouble	10	12	11	11	9	12	6	7
Only a little trouble	16	14	16	20	13	24	15	14
No trouble at all	59	51	51	56	62	58	74	70
(N) =	(1621)	(606)	(70)	(119)	(216)	(234)	(290)	(86)
2. About how much do you think you would have to pay . . . ? (in dollars)								
$\bar{X}$	114	112	166	130	131	100	104	102
SD	150	118	321	142	239	92	112	123
(N) =	(1393)	(481)	(53)	(100)	(186)	(217)	(278)	(78)
3. About how long do you think it would take . . . ? (in percentages)								
Few hours	42	35	36	31	48	45	53	54
Day	16	13	19	16	12	19	19	18
Few days	21	23	19	22	23	19	19	16
Week	6	6	6	13	6	6	3	4
Few weeks	6	7	11	8	5	8	3	4
Month or more	9	16	8	10	6	3	3	5
(N) =	(1527)	(539)	(62)	(115)	(202)	(235)	(291)	(83)

4. How would you go about trying to get one . . . ? (in percentages)

Steal	11	10	8	14	7	12	13	16
Rent	1	1	0	0	1	1	1	4
Borrow	21	18	26	18	19	23	27	20
Trade something	6	8	5	3	6	5	6	6
Buy one for cash	61	63	61	66	67	59	54	54
(N) =	(1521)	(544)	(62)	(114)	(204)	(230)	(286)	(81)

5. Where would you try to get one?

Percentage yes for

Friend	58	45	59	60	53	68	75	73
Gun shop	16	20	12	19	19	10	13	9
Pawnshop	19	21	17	31	18	15	16	17
Family member	15	15	15	16	13	13	19	14
Fence	35	28	39	36	30	41	43	51
On the street	42	37	33	47	39	50	45	53
My drug dealer	20	11	21	17	13	25	34	33
Black market	31	22	27	39	28	36	41	43
Hardware/department store	8	10	8	11	9	5	7	4
Mail order	5	6	8	8	4	2	2	5

213

We also asked how long they thought it would take. The modal response was "a few hours." Nearly 80% of the sample said they could get a handgun in a few days or less; among the Predators, the figure rose to about 90%. Over one-half the Predators said they could arm themselves in a few hours.

The final questions in the sequence asked how and where they would go about trying to obtain a handgun. About three-fifths figured they would simply buy one for cash, another one-fifth thought they would just borrow one, and one-tenth said they would go out and steal one. These patterns were essentially identical across the categories of the typology.

As to where they would go to obtain a handgun, informal sources predominated. Most said they would have attempted to get one from a friend, and this was especially the case for the Predators. In the total sample, the next most likely sources, in order, were "on-the-street" (42%), from a fence (35%), on the black market (31%), "my drug dealer" (20%), a pawnshop (19%), a gun shop (16%), from a family member (15%), from a hardware or department store (8%), and from a mail-order outlet (5%).

It is worth noting that where these men said they would go to get a handgun on release was very similar to where their most recent firearms, in fact, had been obtained (see Chapter Nine); again, the data seem to reflect prior experiences as much as hypothetical possibilities. As in the case of the actual acquisitions, the Predators were especially likely to exploit informal sources. About three-quarters of the Predators, for example, would go to a friend, about one-half would try a fence, the street market, and/or the black market, and about one-third would try their drug dealer. All other possibilities were mentioned by less than 20% of these men. Not more than about one in five of the Predators would have attempted to obtain a handgun from a source likely to be concerned about the legality of the transaction, and even here, one imagines that these "sources" would be mainly back-ups to exploit if the more customary (more frequently mentioned) sources somehow failed to work out.

Summarizing briefly, most of the men in this sample—and especially the more predatory sorts—believed they could acquire a handgun after their release from prison in a matter of a few hours or, at most, a few days, that it would be little or no trouble to do so, and that the out-of-pocket cost for so doing would be on the order of $100. And clearly, many of them had well-articulated plans as to how they would go about it. One man, discussing this question sequence with the field staff, pointed out that he would first have to go to a hardware store and buy a knife (presumably, with his gate money); this would take perhaps a half-hour. Then, knife in hand, he would have to find an open gas station—where, he explained, one will almost always find a handgun on the premises. He would then use the knife to rob the gas station of its handgun: the total elapsed time, he figured, would be perhaps 1 hour, and the total expense would be the price of the knife, let us say, $10. "You see," he added, "no problem!"[2]

ACQUISITION UNDER CONDITIONS OF SCARCITY

The above, of course, pertains to the handgun situation as it now exists. That situation includes, as its most salient features, lots and lots of readily available handguns and at least some (however fitful) efforts to regulate the acquisition of handguns by convicted felons. It is apparent from the above that the weapons behavior of our sample is far more strongly dictated by the ready availability of handguns than by current efforts at control.

The study also explored some alternatives to the existing arrangements, each relevant in one or another way to at least some proposed solutions to the problem of handgun violence. Again, all these questions are highly and unavoidably hypothetical, and one may properly wonder just how many of these men would in fact do what they said they would do if such situations existed. Still, given the nature of this sample, their responses even to hypothetical possibilities are of more than passing interest.[3] Data are shown in Table 11.2.

One much-discussed policy option is to "tax the bottom out" of the handgun market. This proposal is rooted in the belief (but see Chapter Eight) that cheap handguns are overrepresented among the handguns used to commit crimes.[4] Obviously, most of the men in our sample believed that they could get the handgun they wanted for roughly $100. According to Cook (1976), the average "take" in a handgun robbery was roughly $160, some three times the average take in a nongun robbery. (A correction for

[2]One reader of an earlier draft objected at this point, arguing that if it were really that easy, all these men should be rich, since all they would need to do is steal the money. If there were as many rich people to rob in this world as there are gun owners to steal guns from, and if the average rich person took no greater precautions with his or her wealth than the average gun owner appears to take with his or her weapon, we would most certainly agree.

[3]In interpreting the ensuing data, the differences between our sample of prisoners and the total population of street criminals should especially be kept in mind. Our felons, to emphasize, are older, more violent, and with longer criminal careers than the average street criminal would be; in a word, they are more hardened. How these men might respond to some of the options considered, for that reason, is not necessarily indicative of how criminals in general would respond.

[4]Data reported in Chapter Eight do not suggest a predominance of "cheapies" among this sample's most recent handguns; attitudinal data do not suggest that price is much of a concern. Considering the dominant role played by gun theft in the illicit firearms market (Chapter Ten), it is hard to imagine that price would be a concern to the felon market unless the price rose to such a level that ordinary citizens stopped buying handguns for felons to steal.

TABLE 11.2. Weapons Choices under Various Handgun Control Policies by Type (in Percentages)

	Total	Unarmed	Improviser	Knife	One-timer	Sporadic	Handgun predator	Shotgun predator
1. Suppose the cheapest handgun you could find cost more than you could possibly afford to pay for it. What would you do then?"								
Steal a handgun	20	11	12	22	16	26	36	19
Saw off a shoulder gun	11	7	8	12	10	8	13	35
Borrow a handgun	25	17	23	17	27	36	34	29
Carry a knife or club	8	5	15	21	9	7	6	6
Not carry any weapon	36	60	42	28	38	22	10	11
(N)=	(1538)	(563)	(65)	(112)	(207)	(230)	(276)	(85)
2. "Let's suppose that the handgun you really wanted was a small, cheap, low-caliber little handgun, but that there just weren't any of them around for you to get. If you thought you wanted a handgun but found you just couldn't get one, what do you think you would do instead?"								
Get bigger, more expensive	45	30	34	32	47	63	68	38
Saw off shoulder weapon	12	7	6	9	9	9	18	45
Carry knife or club	10	6	19	36	10	10	8	8
Not carry	33	57	40	24	35	18	6	9
(N)=	(1495)	(539)	(67)	(110)	(204)	(218)	(272)	(85)

3. "Some people say that if there were no handguns at all, criminals would carry knives or clubs instead. Other people say that if there were no handguns, criminals would carry rifles and shotguns that had been sawed off so you could hide them: Which of these comes closest to your own beliefs?"

Carry knives or clubs	21	25	39	32	19	17	10	10
Carry sawed-off	64	59	43	53	66	67	75	82
Not carry	7	12	7	4	7	5	2	1
Carry knives and sawed-off	8	5	11	11	9	11	12	7
(N) =	(1644)	(611)	(74)	(119)	(229)	(236)	(288)	(87)

4. "And how about you personally. . . . If you wanted to carry a handgun but you just couldn't get your hands on one, which of the following do you think you would do?"

Carry knife or club	24	18	32	50	26	26	20	14
Carry sawed-off	40	22	27	31	33	51	72	74
Not carry	37	60	41	19	41	23	8	12
(N) =	(1636)	(607)	(71)	(119)	(228)	(233)	(290)	(88)

inflation would raise this figure by quite a bit.) Given these values, it is clearly cost-effective for the would-be robber to buy a handgun at prevailing prices; it is, after all, a rare business venture where one's entire capital outlay can be recouped in the first "transaction." But what, then, might happen if the cheapest handgun available in the market cost more than the typical felon could possibly afford to pay? Would the cost-effectiveness equation then not tip sharply away from obtaining a handgun?

Panel 1 of Table 11.2 shows the responses of the sample to the pricing strategy. In the aggregate, the modal response was not to carry any weapon, mentioned by 36%, seemingly an optimistic finding. Note, however, that this response was heavily concentrated among the less predatory categories, especially among the Unarmed Criminals (60% of whom said they would not carry any weapon under this condition). That those who did not carry firearms in any case said they would continue not carrying in the face of the pricing strategy is hardly surprising. Among the Predators, the number who said they would not carry any weapon in the face of the pricing strategy was on the order of 10%, and for the Sporadics, on the order of 20%. Thus, while at least some of these men would apparently be affected by exceptionally high handgun prices, 80–90% of them clearly would not be.

A few men in all categories said they would respond to the pricing option by carrying knives or clubs—these represented about 8% of the total sample, some 15% of the Improvisers, 21% of the Knife Criminals, and less than 10% of everyone else. The simple expedient of borrowing the handgun one needed was mentioned by 25% of the total sample and by approximately one-third of the three most predatory groups. Among the Sporadics, in fact, borrowing the necessary weapon was the modal response, followed by stealing one (26%), and simply not carrying anything (22%).

Among the Handgun Predators, the pattern was somewhat different: Most (36%) would steal the handgun they wanted, about the same proportion (34%) would borrow it, and 13% would saw off a shoulder weapon. Among the Shotgun Predators, sawing off a shoulder weapon was the modal response to the pricing strategy (given by 35%), followed in turn by borrowing a handgun (29%), then stealing one (19%). Given the above patterns, it is clear that most of these men thought they could readily evade the pricing strategy.

The result for the Handgun Predators is informative. If the cheapest handgun around cost more than they could possibly afford to pay, some 70% would respond by either stealing or borrowing the handgun they wanted. Call this "lateral substitution" (i.e., the "substitute" weapon in these cases is for all practical purposes the same weapon they would have been carrying otherwise). Of the remainder, approximately one-half would substitute something less lethal (i.e., a knife, club, or no weapon at all); and the other one-half would substitute something more lethal—a sawed-off shotgun. The net result, if these responses are creditable, would not constitute any obvious improvement.

The answers given in response to the pricing question, moreover, are not unrealistic, in our opinion. As we saw in earlier chapters, most of our sample, especially the more predatory ones, associated with other men who also owned and carried firearms, so the possibility of borrowing a handgun would usually be open to them. (To be sure, not everybody can borrow; there have to be some owners around to borrow from.) Open, too, would be the option to steal a gun, as we saw in Chapter Ten. We have more to say later in this chapter about the final possibility, sawing off a shoulder weapon, but it, too, turns out to be a real option. Whether these men can actually be counted on to act as they said they would act is not known, but there is a certain consistency between these reports and what they told us elsewhere in the questionnaire.

A proposal similar in many ways to the pricing strategy is a ban on the SNS, the small, cheap, low-caliber little handgun. We saw in Chapter Eight that the characteristics of the SNS are not especially high on the list of things these men looked for in a handgun; indeed, accuracy, quality, and firepower were more important desiderata. Still, a fair amount of the crime that is committed with handguns is committed with cheap handguns, and it is an interesting and policy-relevant question to ask what might happen if no inexpensive handguns were around.

Panel 2 of Table 11.2 shows the response of the sample to the "ban SNSs" strategy. Overall, the modal response was to obtain a bigger and more expensive handgun, mentioned by 45%. Among the handgun Predators, this option was chosen by 68%, among the Sporadics, by 63%, and among the One-Timers, by 47%. The next most frequent response in the aggregate was not to carry any weapon, mentioned by one-third, but again, this response was heavily concentrated in the less predatory categories (especially the Unarmed Criminals, among whom it was chosen by 57%). Among the Predators, the option not to carry in the face of the SNS ban was chosen by less than 10%. About one-fifth of the Handgun Predators said they would shift to sawed-off weapons.

Zimring (1972) has analyzed death from handgun assaults as a function of caliber. The result is straightforward: As the caliber increases, so does the death rate. Since more expensive handguns tend to be larger caliber weapons and since they are typically designed to handle hotter ammunition loads, one may presume that the rate of death would also increase with the quality of the weapon as well. Thus, the possible shift to "bigger, more expensive handguns" in the face of a SNS ban, as reported by our sample, would probably be a shift from less lethal to more lethal firearms. The effect of such a ban on the Handgun Predators (they say) would be, in essence, to shift about 85% of them to more lethal weapons (either bigger handguns or sawed-off shotguns) and to shift the remaining 15% to less lethal weapons (or to no weapons at all). The same was true of the Shotgun Predators. Among the Sporadics, about three-quarters would shift in the more lethal direction. One possible consequence of a SNS ban, one that left all the heavier duty equipment still on the market, is that the rate of death from criminal violence could well increase, perhaps rather dramatically.

A final possibility explored in the survey was a complete ban on all handguns. Responses of the sample to this option are shown in Panels 3 and 4. In the aggregate, the modal response (given by 40%) was to carry a sawed-off weapon, followed by not carrying anything (37%), with the knife or club option being the least popular (24%). As before, the option not to carry was mentioned most often by men who did not carry in any case— by 60% of the Unarmed Criminals, by 41% of the Improvisers, and, inter-estingly, by 41% of the One-Timers as well. Also predictably, the Knife Criminals would continue to carry knives. Among the Sporadics, just about one-half would "move up" to sawed-off equipment, about one-quarter would carry knives or clubs, and about one-quarter would go unarmed.

Among Predators, of course, the result was even worse. Three-quarters of them said they would carry sawed-off shoulder weapons if there were not any handguns around for them to carry instead. If the truly vicious as-saults are as concentrated among our Predator categories as our earlier re-sults suggested them to be (see Chapter Three), and if these men can be taken at their word, then the apparent consequence of a complete ban on handguns would be stark increase in the rate of death from violent criminal assault.

There is at least some reason to take these men seriously when they say they would substitute a sawed-off rifle or shotgun under the various speci-fied conditions. Many of the men who said that this is what they would do also said that they, in fact, had sawed off rifles and shotguns in the past (see Table 11.3). First, most of the men in the sample agreed with the hy-pothetical possibility that "if a criminal wants a handgun but can't get one, he can always saw off a rifle or a shotgun." Agreement with this sentiment ran from 80 to 90%. Again hypothetically, most of the men in the sample thought it would be "easy" (39%) or "very easy" (32%) for them to saw off a shoulder weapon, and in the Predator categories, the fraction thinking it would be easy or very easy ran upward to about 90%. We also asked, "Have you personally ever sawed off a rifle or shotgun?" Overall, 29% of the sample had, a fraction that varied from 9% of the Unarmed Criminals up to about 70% in the two Predator categories.

Perhaps more directly to the point, 50% of the men in the sample who said they would carry a sawed-off weapon in the face of a complete hand-gun ban also said they, themselves, actually had sawed off a weapon at some point in their lives. This was the aggregate result across all seven cat-egories. Among the Handgun Predators specifically, 77% of those who said

TABLE 11.3. Data on Sawing Off Shotguns, by Type (in Percentages)

	Total	Unarmed	Improviser	Knife	One-timer	Sporadic	Handgun predator	Shotgun predator
1. If a criminal wants a handgun but can't get one, he can always saw off a rifle or shotgun:								
Agree	82	80	84	86	82	79	86	88
Disagree	18	20	16	14	18	21	14	12
(N)=	(1651)	(624)	(71)	(118)	(228)	(237)	(287)	(86)
2. Do you think it would be hard or easy for you to saw off a shotgun or rifle so you could conceal it?								
Very hard	12	20	11	8	17	8	2	4
Hard	16	19	23	18	11	22	11	7
Easy	39	34	31	46	42	46	42	35
Very easy	32	27	36	28	30	24	45	54
(N)=	(1505)	(543)	(62)	(113)	(201)	(226)	(278)	(82)
3. Have you personally ever sawed off a rifle or shotgun?								
No	71	91	76	86	74	70	31	28
Yes	29	9	24	14	26	30	69	72
(N)=	(1638)	(616)	(70)	(120)	(223)	(234)	(286)	(89)

(continued)

221

TABLE 11.3. Data on Sawing Off Shotguns, by Type (in Percentages) (*continued*)

	Total	Unarmed	Improviser	Knife	One-timer	Sporadic	Handgun predator	Shotgun predator
4. If YES to 3: About how many?								
Just one	30	58	35	69	55	30	16	14
A few	43	32	35	31	29	51	50	40
5 or 10	17	9	18	0	11	14	21	25
More than 10	10	2	12	0	5	6	14	21
(N) =	(476)	(57)	(17)	(16)	(56)	(71)	(196)	(63)
5. If YES to 3: Did you ever use a sawed-off rifle or shotgun to actually commit a crime?								
No	44	94	88	82	68	49	25	8
Yes	56	6	12	18	32	51	75	92
(N) =	(474)	(53)	(17)	(17)	(57)	(71)	(196)	(63)
6. If YES to 3: About how old were you when you first sawed off a rifle or a shotgun?								
$\bar{X} =$	17.8	19.6	15.8	19.4	20.2	17.5	17.3	16.7
SD =	4.1	4.7	3.3	4.3	5.8	3.4	3.5	4.0
(N) =	(373)	(32)	(13)	(11)	(41)	(56)	(166)	(53)

they would carry sawed-off equipment also said they had sawed off a rifle or shotgun at some time.

Men who indicated that they had sawed off a rifle or shotgun were asked a few follow-up questions. About 70% of those who had ever sawed off shotguns had done so more than once; among the Predators, this was true of about 85%. On average, the men who had ever done so had been about 18 years old at the time. Among those who had ever done so, 56% reported that they had used a sawed-off weapon at least once in committing a crime, a percentage that varied in a remarkably linear manner from 6% of the Unarmed Criminals to 75% of the Handgun Predators and 92% of the Shotgun Predators.

In short, here as in the previous options discussed earlier, there is a certain consistency between what these men said they would do and what they said they, in fact, had done at other times in their lives. Unquestionably, some of the responses obtained in this question sequence have to be discounted as bravado; others, also unquestionably, are genuine.

How much, then, is bravado, and how much genuine? Although we have no data that provide a definitive answer, our feeling is that most of the responses to these questions should be taken quite seriously. The argument that these responses are "bravado"—presentations of the felon's self in the nastiest, most brutal light possible, perhaps to impress our field team—assumes implicitly that these men are short on opportunities to express their essential meanness and thus resort to fabricating "nasty" answers to survey questions. What these men seem to be saying (this, in any case, is our interpretation) is that their predatory designs on other human beings will not be thwarted for lack of the appropriate instruments. To summarily dismiss this message on the grounds that the responses of felons to survey questionnaires cannot be taken too literally is, in our opinion, unwise.

In summary, evidence assembled in this chapter is not consistent with the argument that the likely substitute weapons that would be used in the face of various partial or total handgun bans are less lethal than the weapons felons currently carry. In all cases, the fractions who said they would "move down" to less lethal equipment are more than offset by the fractions who would move up—to bigger and more expensive handguns in some cases, to sawed-off shoulder weapons in others. None of the options considered here produces a net shift in a less lethal direction.

12

"THE GREAT AMERICAN GUN WAR": SOME POLICY IMPLICATIONS OF THE FELON STUDY

INTRODUCTION

In an oft-quoted article published in 1976, Bruce-Biggs (1976) characterized the perennial debate in American political life over what to do about firearms as "The Great American Gun War," suggesting, correctly in this case, a rather more rancorous and hotly contested arena of public policy than one normally might expect to encounter. There may be some issues in American politics where feelings run more strongly (abortion being one, nuclear power perhaps another), but not many; few issues evoke such passion or have had a longer run on the political playbill than what to do about crime and the guns with which crimes are committed.

A session of the Congress seldom passes without at least a few new "gun control" measures being introduced, be they amendments to existing regulations or proposals for entirely new policies. Almost invariably, these initiatives are warmly received in some quarters and bitterly denounced in others. What seems to one group a reasonable method of reducing criminals' access to guns seems to another an unconscionable infringement upon the legitimate rights of the American gun-owning public.

It is worth stressing at the outset of a discussion of the policy implications of our results that the key issues in "The Great American Gun War" rarely turn on matters of empirical fact. As Bruce-Biggs correctly observed, the policy debate concerns styles of life and corresponding value systems as much as it concerns the equipment of crime and how to control it. In some segments of American society, guns of all sorts are loathesome objects utterly devoid of redeeming social value; in other segments, guns and the activities that guns make possible are an integral and highly valued aspect of day-to-day existence. Neither segment will be dissuaded from its views by the results of empirical research, no matter how sound or well-conducted.

Although there is no love lost among the contestants in this particular public policy arena, there is at least some agreement among all contending groups that one policy goal should be to reduce significantly the use of

225

firearms in crimes of all sorts. No one denies that the American crime rate is unacceptably high or that the use of firearms to commit crimes is a pressing national problem. The issues at the heart of contention are whether and how this goal can best be reached.

Broadly speaking, the methods available to achieve the agreed-upon goal fall into two categories: (1) reducing the ability of criminals to obtain firearms in the first place; and/or (2) reducing the criminals' use of guns in committing crime once guns have been obtained. Clearly, the issues are closely related: if we could accomplish (1), (2) would then be moot. Hence, the second issue is only an issue because of the presumption that complete success at preventing criminals from obtaining firearms will probably not be possible.

Both available methods are rife with considerable complexity, even ambiguity. It is easy to agree, for example, that one goal of policy should be to "keep guns out of the hands of criminals." Indeed, other than the criminals themselves, it is hard to imagine anyone who would not agree. But this presumes that criminals can somehow be easily identified before the fact, a task that has occupied criminologists for a century with little notable success. It is, of course, very easy to identify criminals after they have committed crimes and have been convicted and sentenced for them; thus, after the fact, it is always easy to say that "that man should not have been allowed to own a gun." Identifying the people who "should not be allowed to own a gun" before they have acquired one and inflicted harm on others is an immeasurably more difficult and perhaps intractable problem.

It is of some interest that partisans on both sides of the gun debate, or some of them at least, both recognize and accept the fact just noted (namely, that criminals are hard to identify in advance of their actually committing crimes). One side infers from this that the appropriate strategy, therefore, is to keep guns (or at least handguns or certain kinds of handguns) out of everybody's hands, which would assure (assuming a 100% success rate) that they were being kept from criminal hands in the process. The other side infers that the appropriate strategy, therefore, is to forego any effort to interdict before the fact and simply punish abuses as they occur. In the interpretation, in other words, the same fact subtends two entirely different implications. It should be noted that this area of social policy is no different in this respect from others: The same empirical facts can be accommodated within a variety of widely differing policies.

Other complications are introduced by the unintended side consequences of policies that are or may be enacted. The best of all imaginable firearms policies enacted to reduce gun crime would clearly be ones that somehow impacted only on criminals and on no others. Furthermore, such policies would be ones that had only the intended effect on the target population and no other effects. The ideal policy, in short, complicates the life of the gun-wielding felon but not the lives of legitimate firearms users, at least not unduly.

Unfortunately, it is hard to target any social policy with a high degree of accuracy; serious definitional questions arise, particularly at the margins. To illustrate, the United States Olympic pistol shooting team represents an obviously legitimate body of handgun owners whose right to own and use handguns can be taken as given; likewise, an urban street thug with a lengthy criminal record and overt sociopathic tendencies is obviously a person who has long since foregone any claim to legitimate handgun ownership. At the extremes, the categories of legitimate and illegitimate are easy to recognize. But what of the adolescents who may someday grow up to become either Olympic shooters if all goes well or street thugs if all does not? Or of young men in urban slums who today may feel they need a gun to defend against the thugs but who tomorrow might be thugs themselves? What, for that matter, of the outwardly placid and upstanding citizen who buys a shotgun to hunt quail but who, in an alcohol-induced fit of psychotic anger, barricades himself in his house and kills everything in sight?

Unacceptably adverse consequences to noncriminal gun owners represent the single greatest barrier to the design of effective policy in the "gun crime" area. A stiff tax on handguns imposed at the point of production would no doubt raise the price of handguns enough to drive some criminals out of the handgun market, but it would also drive millions of noncriminals out of the market as well. The cheap, low-quality handgun that is not available for use in crime is also not available to impoverished families in high-crime neighborhoods who feel (correctly or otherwise) that they need a gun to defend against the predation rampant on their streets. A jurisdiction that requires a week-long waiting period to obtain a handgun while the police run the appropriate criminal records check will come across an occasional criminal attempting to obtain a handgun through customary channels and enormous numbers of other people for whom both the waiting period and the records check were altogether immaterial.

Aside from the spill-over of effects onto the noncriminal population, there is also the problem of unintended effects on the target (criminal) population. A policy designed to prevent the transfer of firearms to felons through customary retail channels (such as the Gun Control Act of 1968) might only result in an increase in the rate of gun thefts by felons from nonfelon owners or an increased level of activity in the informal nonretail market. As we saw in the previous chapter, a policy intended to prevent criminals from carrying small, cheap handguns might cause them to carry big, expensive, and more lethal handguns instead.

The intended effect of virtually every piece of "gun-crime" legislation enacted in the twentieth century has been along one or the other of the lines suggested earlier: to prevent criminals from obtaining guns or to prevent them from using guns once obtained. And yet, the number of armed criminals and the amount of armed crime has tended to increase, not abate. What has happened is not what was intended. We do not mean to suggest that gun-control legislation has caused crime, in some way, to increase, only that the hoped-for reduction in armed crime has not occurred.

One final and long-standing complication, of course, has been the well-known Second Amendment to the Constitution of the United States and the apparent ambiguity about what rights it grants to whom. In the current epoch of nuclear weaponry, for example, what meaning should be construed for the phrase, "an armed militia?" Does the "right to keep and bear arms" include the right to target practice? To own a gun for self-defense? To keep loaded firearms in the home with children present? Surely, in a democratic society, every right comes with certain corollary obligations. But what, then, are the obligations that come with the right "to keep and bear arms?"

The last few pages are not intended to create despair, and much less to enumerate exhaustively all of the complications that are inherent in this particular public-policy area. Our point, rather, is to illustrate that the issues involved go well beyond anything that can be learned from data supplied by a sample of state prisoners. Much, in fact, goes well beyond what could be learned from any study; and many relevant empirical questions cannot be answered with data on prisoners alone.

This study, of course, was not designed to answer all the relevant empirical questions, only to provide baseline information about the acquisition, ownership, and use of guns among a criminal population, information that could be useful in discussing the appropriate policy issues. Although seldom in an explicit fashion, all policies and policy recommendations make assumptions about the "facts" concerning the area of human behavior in question. Clearly, the chances of successful policy are higher the more accurate these assumptions turn out to be. A policy based on the assumption that criminals prefer small, cheap handguns can hardly be successful if in fact they do not. Our point in undertaking this study, in short, was to test some common assumptions and provide useful descriptive data, assuredly not to evaluate the wisdom of one or another "gun-control" measure.

Research of the sort reported in this volume is often very good in describing the nature of a problem and rather poor in suggesting adequate solutions. This study is no exception: We have tried to obtain reasonably accurate readings on certain facets of the criminal acquisition and use of guns, but by themselves, the findings of the research do not immediately suggest any effective solutions. "Policy implications" are just that: implications that derive from one particular interpretation of a set of research findings, certainly not policy conclusions or recommendations whose wisdom is self-evident now that the findings are in hand. Policymaking is the rightful domain of policymakers: Our intention is that policymaking be informed, but not overly constrained, by the results and interpretations we have reported.

In order to prevent criminals from obtaining guns, we need to know where and how their guns are obtained; to prevent them from carrying guns and using them in crime, we need to know why they carry and how they use them, or in short, the roles that firearms play in the lifestyles of the felon population. Most of the policy implications of this study derive from the information we have assembled on these topics.

THE NATURE OF THE ILLICIT FIREARMS MARKET

Firearms manufacturers are, of course, the ultimate source of virtually all the guns that are ever used for any purpose, since the home manufacture of firearms is apparently rare. This obvious fact means that guns come into the hands of criminals by means of a system of distribution that connects manufacturers and criminals through a chain of transfers. The early links in this chain ordinarily involve firearms wholesalers and retailers, a fact that tempts policymakers to consider using these intermediaries as points to detect potential firearms abusers and thereby to prevent firearms from falling into improper hands. The ultimate efficacy of such an approach depends to a considerable extent on the length of the chain of transfers and the location of retail outlets within the chain.

The findings from our study cast some light on the nature of the transfer chain: We cannot reconstruct the complete chain from manufacturer to criminal consumer, but we have considerable detail on the last link in the chain, the transfer of a firearm into criminal hands. From the viewpoint of policy, two features of these data stand out, and these are discussed in the next sections.

Deterring the Acquisition of Firearms

Legitimate firearms retailers play a minor and unimportant role as direct sources of the criminal handgun supply. Not more than about one in six of the most recent handguns acquired by our sample was obtained through a customary retail transaction involving a licensed firearms dealer; the market into which criminals are tied, rather, is dominated by informal, off the record, transactions, mostly involving friends and associates, family members, and various black-market sources. The means of acquisition from these informal sources include cash purchase, swaps and trades, borrowing and renting, and often theft. (Indeed, our impression is that the verbs, "borrow," "take," "steal," and "rent" were blurred and indistinct in the vocabularies of our respondents.) Whatever the verbal ambiguities, however, it is clear that our sample was enmeshed in a largely informal market in firearms that served as the immediate source of their supply.

The implication of this result is probably not that we should simply give up on our efforts to interdict criminal acquisition of handguns at the point of retail sale. To so argue would be equivalent to arguing that we should stop the airport metal searches because they only rarely detect a weapons-carrying passenger. Restrictions at the point of retail sale, that is, may serve a useful preventive function; at minimum, the acquisition of a firearm by a felon should be somewhat more complicated than just walking into a gun shop and buying one. The implication, rather, concerns the ultimate effect of such efforts, which is not to prevent the acquisition of guns by criminals but rather to force them out of the retail market and into other, less formal channels of distribution.

One tempting way to intervene between the manufacturer and the criminal end-user is to raise the price of weapons entering the market, perhaps by taxing handguns heavily. Eventually, a sharp rise in handgun prices would be reflected on the gray and black markets as well as in the retail stores. Our data do not allow any calculations of how high prices on the legitimate market would have to go to affect those on the gray and black markets, but we suspect that a dollar increase on the former most likely means considerably less on the latter. Furthermore, it is not at all clear how price-elastic the criminal demand for handguns is; price increases may affect criminal gun acquisition only once they reach very high levels.

Moreover, although exceptionally high prices might drive some criminals out of the handgun market altogether, it would also increase the attractiveness of gun theft and, therefore, might draw some criminals *into* the market, as procurers of stolen handguns. Furthermore, there would also be a large price burden placed on literally millions of legitimate handgun users, some of whom might then be tempted to become buyers on the gray and black markets.

The further implication of our results, of course, is that if we do intend seriously to complicate the acquisition of guns by felons, then methods must be found for intervening in the informal firearms market. As we have already noted, the transfer of a firearm to a felon, whether formal or informal, is already illegal, so legislation to make it illegal is clearly not the answer. By their very nature, such transactions are difficult or impossible to detect, so "stricter enforcement" of existing laws is also probably chimerical. One might require, as a matter of federal policy, that every firearms transaction be reported to the cognizant authorities and the appropriate criminal records check undertaken; but one quickly senses that this measure would have virtually no effect on the criminal users we are trying to interdict and a considerable effect on legitimate users among whom a large informal market also exists.

There is, in short, some reason to doubt whether any politically acceptable, implementable, effective, and Constitutional method of intervening in the informal market can be found; the implication of our results is not a method by which this could be done but rather the information that it must be done if we are to prevent or even seriously hamper the acquisition of firearms by criminals.

The Role of Gun Theft

Our study also confirms beyond serious doubt the important role that gun theft plays in connecting the criminal market to its firearms supply. One-half the men in this sample had stolen at least one gun at some time in their lives; many had stolen more than one; a few had stolen guns in extremely large numbers. At least 40%, and perhaps as much as 70%, of the most recent handguns owned by this sample were stolen weapons.

We indicated earlier that the ideal "gun-crime" policy is one that impacts directly on the illicit user but leaves the legitimate user pretty much alone. This presupposes a sharp distinction between the licit and illicit markets, a distinction that is made tenuous by the apparently heavy volume of gun theft. To leave the legitimate user "pretty much alone" at least implies a guarantee of the right to acquire firearms under some set of prescribed conditions; and yet, all else equal, any gun that can be legitimately possessed by a legal and law-abiding owner can be stolen from its owner and subsequently fall into criminal hands.

Again, our data suggest little by way of a method through which the gun theft problem could be attacked. In terms of the total number of thefts, thefts from homes and apartments are clearly the most numerous, which suggests, as one approach, that legitimate gun owners be made more aware of the problem and the strategies available to them to prevent theft of their weapons. Police chiefs who are empowered to issue permits to own or purchase firearms might be one point at which this information could be imparted; information booklets produced by the manufacturers for inclusion with shipped weapons would be another.

Legitimate gun owners might also be induced to exercise greater caution in storing their weapons in relatively theft-resistant ways—for example, by tax credits or insurance discounts similar to those given for energy conservation measures or the installation of home fire detectors.

Finally, some jurisdictions have begun to consider the liability of a legitimate owner whose gun is stolen and subsequently used to commit a crime. Our data do not speak to the advisability or likely consequences of such measures, but certainly, as we have already said, the right to own guns must be accompanied by certain corollary responsibilities, and perhaps these responsibilities include all *reasonable* precaution in storing one's weapons in relatively theft-proof ways. (To be sure, one would still want to insist that the liability of the thief greatly exceeded the liability of his victim.)

Although house and apartment break-ins appear to account for the largest number of thefts, they may not account for the largest number of stolen weapons that enter the illicit market. A distressingly large number of our respondents also reported having stolen guns from potential high-volume sources: manufacturers, shippers, wholesalers, retailers, and even military establishments. Our impression is that security measures in these quarters are already pretty tight, but perhaps they could be increased even further.

The "scale" problem is pertinent in this case: One successful hijacking of a truck during shipment could well net as many total firearms as would be netted in a few thousand household thefts; consequently, the prevention of one hijacking is as useful to society as a whole as the prevention of a few thousand household thefts. All else equal, then, resources might be directed disproportionally to preventing thefts from high-volume sources. Unfortunately, our data do not show that high-volume sources account for more of the total volume than housebreaks, only that they may; this, therefore, is an area that requires further research before the policy implication is obvious.

At minimum, of course, society as a whole could increase the penalty for the crime of gun theft, perhaps by making gun theft a felony whatever the other circumstances of the crime. In most jurisdictions at present, the theft of a gun from a household or store is considered to be a no more serious crime than the theft of any other object of equivalent value.

Whatever the methods one might imagine, however, the nature of the task that society confronts is made reasonably clear by our results: If we are to make headway in preventing the acquisition of guns by criminals, we must find some way to intervene in the informal gun market, a market that, under present conditions, is supplied in substantial part by firearms obtained through theft.

CRIME GUNS: QUALITY AND PRICE

Many "gun crime" proposals that have surfaced in recent years have been targeted to particular classes of firearms: to handguns in general or, somewhat more commonly, to certain restricted classes of handguns, particularly those of the small, cheap, low-quality variety: the "snubbies" or the so-called "Saturday Night Specials." The rationale for such proposals is twofold: (1) legitimate owners have little or no need for such firearms and (2) illegitimate owners do.

To assess the nature of the criminal demand for these kinds of handguns, we asked for considerable information both on the characteristics our sample preferred in a handgun and on the characteristics of the most recent handgun they had actually possessed. Neither of these sources of information represents perfect data on the nature of the criminal handgun demand: The "preferred-characteristics" questions may tell us more about our sample's fantasies concerning the "perfect" handgun than about the true nature of their demand; the characteristics of the most recent handgun may or may not generalize to the typical handgun that felons own, carry, and use to commit crimes. Still, neither source of data suggests much interest among felons in small, cheap handguns; such interest as we observed was concentrated primarily among felons who had never used firearms to commit crimes. The criminals in our sample both preferred to own, and actually owned, relatively large, well-made weapons.

The average price paid by our felons for their most recent handguns was not especially high, falling in the $100–150 range; still, the average quality was well beyond the level of the "cheapies." The most common among the recent handguns was a Smith and Wesson .38 equipped with a 4-inch barrel; no more than about 15% of the most recent handguns would qualify as SNSs. A comparison between the average dollar cost and the average apparent quality suggests that prices in the informal, gray, and black markets are heavily discounted, in all likelihood because of the predominance of stolen weapons in these markets.

Whatever the price paid or the mode of acquisition, however, one result is clear: The more a felon used his guns in crime, the higher the quality of the equipment he possessed. Among the truly predatory criminals in the sample, the small, cheap handgun was not the weapon of choice.

Given the rate of gun theft reported by the sample, it is also of no surprise that price was not a very important consideration. Our interpretation of a question on how much they would be willing to pay for a suitable handgun is that felons are willing to pay the going rate. For what it is worth, far more interest was shown in matters such as accuracy, firepower, untraceability, and quality of construction than in price.

The implication of these findings is that the strategy of purging the market of small, cheap weapons may simply be irrelevant, most of all to predatory felons who are more likely to use their guns to commit crimes. In addition, the apparent price insensitivity argues against a policy that stresses raising the price of guns to keep them from criminal hands. Either or both of these strategies may well prove advisable for other reasons; it is possible, for example, that small, cheap handguns are much more important to first offenders, juveniles, or other classes of criminals who are on average younger, less hardened, and less violent than the men in our sample. So far as the sorts of men who end up doing time in state prisons are concerned, however, it is fairly clear that they do not have much interest in small, cheap firearms in the first place.

WHY CRIMINALS CARRY AND USE GUNS

As long as you got a lot of fire power, you're all right. There was a rule with me that I always have a gun at all times, 'cause sometimes you'd be out in the street and the opportunity just present itself where you see a lot of money. Then you want to be armed. (. . .) So I had the gun always on me to take advantage of opportunities—and to protect myself. A gun is like a part of me. I could wake up in the morning, and before I get out of the bed to go into the bathroom, I strap my shoulder holster over my shoulder. I never would go out of the house without it.

The preceding is not a quotation from one of our respondents, although it certainly might have been. It is, rather, a passage from John Allen's *Assault with a Deadly Weapon: The Autobiography of a Street Criminal* (Allen, 1977: 179–180). John Allen is typical of the predatory felons in our sample in many ways: He is urban, black, and uneducated, commenced his life of crime in his early teens, acquired his first firearm at age 13 by stealing it from his grandfather, was a heroin addict on several occasions and a heavy abuser of drugs, had a lengthy criminal record as both a juvenile and an adult, spent much of his life in prison, was prone to fits of violent rage, and seldom passed by an opportunity to commit a crime, be it armed robbery, car theft, drug dealing, pimping, housebreaking, or whatever. His motives for owning and carrying guns, as expressed in the above passage, are also typical of the motives expressed by our sample: When armed, one is prepared "for anything that might happen"—an opportunity to commit a crime or a need to defend oneself against the assaults or predations of others. His behavior in regard to the weapon is also perhaps typical: As his comment concerning the morning regimen indicates, carrying a gun was an habitual part of his daily routine.

The possession and carrying of handguns (and other weapons: John Allen also kept a sawed-off shotgun at hand for truly serious work) by felons is part and parcel of their day-to-day existence, no more unusual in their circles than the carrying of wallets or purses would be in others. The motivation to do so goes well beyond the instrumental use of guns in committing crimes, although as Allen's testimony and our data make clear, this is assuredly one important motive. Survival in an uncertain but hostile and violent world is, with equal assurance, another.

Most of the gun-owning felons in our sample grew up around guns, were introduced to guns at an early age, and had owned and used guns ever since. Most also hung around with other men who owned and carried guns. In such circles, a handgun is at least an acceptable article of attire, if not a *de rigeur* requirement. Not to suggest that these handguns are strictly ornamental: Our felons tended in the majority to keep their guns loaded at all times and to fire them at a fairly regular rate, often enough at other people: One-half the men in our sample claimed to have fired a gun at someone at some time; one-half also claimed to have been fired upon.

It is, therefore, no surprise that one of their major acknowledged motives for acquiring and carrying guns was for the purpose of self-protection. In an environment where crime and violence are pervasive, and where many of one's friends and associates routinely carry guns, there is plenty to "protect" oneself against. "Self-protection," in this context at least, must be interpreted with some caution, of course. Part of it no doubt implies protection against being preyed upon or continually hassled by others who are better armed; another part, perhaps the larger part, means protection against armed innocents, against the police, against the prospects of apprehension during a crime, etc. The "insurance" that many of these men seek in carrying a gun is only the insurance that they will always be the perpetrator and not the victim of the sorts of crimes they so regularly commit.

A third of our sample (of Gun Criminals), like John Allen, make it a practice to carry a gun more or less all the time; one-half carried whenever the circumstances seemed to suggest it: when doing a drug deal, when going out at night, when they were with other men who were carrying guns, or more generally, whenever their ability to defend themselves might be at issue. Only one in five of the Gun Criminals in our sample carried just when they intended to commit a crime.

Since it follows directly from this finding that most of the guns used to commit crime are not carried *specifically* for the purpose, the implication is that the decision to carry is the critical decision point, not the decision to use the gun in a crime. This is to suggest only that the decision to carry guns regularly by men prone to criminal acts is causally prior to the actual uses of these weapons on victims and, therefore, may represent the theoretically most effective point of intervention.

How one might intervene in the decision to carry, however, is a rather depressing question to contemplate. Unlicensed carrying of concealed weapons is already illegal everywhere. Stricter enforcement of the relevant laws prohibiting concealed carrying of weapons—for example, by periodic shakedowns of people on the streets or in the bars—is a theoretical possibility but raises obvious Constitutional issues; such dragnets would also net large numbers of otherwise legitimate people who are carrying a weapon out of fear. The largest handguns, and even some sawed-off shoulder weapons, can be carried more or less unobtrusively; the smaller the weapon, the more true this becomes. A patrol officer might have some suspicions about a particular person, but anything short of open display might fail the criterion of probable cause.

If one accepts the idea that self-protection in a hostile and dangerous world is a principal motive for the ownership and carrying of guns among felons, then it follows that relevant policies to discourage the practice are those that would reduce the hostility and danger endemic to the social worlds inhabited by these men, that is, poor, urban neighborhoods in the main. As is well known, these neighborhoods produce not only most of the perpetrators but also most of the victims of crime; crime, violence, and routine handgun carrying are distinguishing features of urban slum existence. Unfortunately, there are few issues in law enforcement that seem more intractable than that of substantially reducing violent crime in high crime areas:

It is not at all clear just how such a goal might be attained, nor is it clear that communities would support the effort by paying the added taxes that would be required.

Outright neglect is, of course, one possibility, one that, in fact, has been followed in at least some of our major cities from time to time. Here, the strategy is for the police to withdraw in force, hoping to contain the crime problem within certain boundaries. (Some have also charged, perhaps with reason, that a second hope is that the criminals within the boundaries will kill or maim each other in sufficient numbers that the rest of us could walk our own streets in peace.) "Containment" has not proven to be a very effective strategy, however; crime has a habit of spilling over into the more affluent (and politically powerful) communities. A humane society should also not be indifferent to the victimization by crime of those who can least afford it and who are also victimized by many of society's other institutions and practices as well.

We conclude that a viable policy designed to reduce the criminal use of guns will have to find means of reducing the violence that is characteristic of many urban neighborhoods. We recognize the circularity of this reasoning: What we are suggesting is that the way to get criminals to stop carrying guns is to get criminals to stop carrying guns! Our point, however, is not entirely tautological: What we are suggesting is that the reduction of crime in high-crime neighborhoods has to be as much in the center of law enforcement concern as protecting middle-class citizens from the incursions of predatory criminals.

One might also simply give up dealing with the causes of gun carrying among felons and deal directly with the behavior itself, for example, through policies designed to encourage criminals to leave their weapons at home when they "go to work." Here, the effort would be concentrated on making the carrying and use of guns as difficult and as costly to the felon as possible.

One strategy presently in use in many jurisdictions, one that also enjoys overwhelming popular support (Wright, Rossi, and Daly, 1983: Ch. 12) is to provide enhanced (mandatory "add-on") penalties for the use of a gun (or other weapon) in committing crime (or, as in the Massachusetts case, a mandatory penalty for unlicensed carrying, whatever the actual usage or intent).

How successful this tactic has been in reducing the use of guns in crime has yet to be assessed definitively. Often, or so it appears, judges working with mandatory add-ons reduce the sentence for the main charge by an equivalent number of years, so that the total penalty remains much the same. Moreover, the add-on is often a small fraction of the main charge: A typical sentence for an armed robbery (assuming a lengthy prior record) might be 10–30 years; a 1- or 2-year mandatory sentence enhancement might

not alter the sentence enough to make any difference in the subjective calculations of the criminal. Ultimately, increased sentencing runs up against
prison overcrowding as the limiting condition: It does no good to add additional years to a felon's sentence when the state corrections system has
no prison space for him in any case. The overcrowding situation is such
that many prisons now find every reason for early release (e.g., time off for
good behavior, lenient parole) simply to make sufficient room for the "new
arrivals" from the courts.

Another problem in using mandatory add-ons for felonious gun use as a
deterrent to the practice of carrying weapons is that most criminals do not
expect to be caught in any case; what might happen to them once they are
caught, therefore, cannot be much of a concern. (It should be added, nonetheless, that many of the non-gun criminals in our sample mentioned the
prospect of a stiffer sentence when caught with a weapon as a very important reason not to carry one.)

A final problem in deterring the routine carrying of guns (whether through
sentencing or through other measures), at least among the more predatory
men in our sample, is that many of the crimes these men commit are directed toward victims who may be armed themselves. John Allen notes:
"During the times when I was down, though, I would mainly rob the other
dealers to get the drugs or the scratch I needed to buy my drugs" (1977:
176). Why an addict would rob his own dealer (or fellow dealers) is not
hard to fathom: They have the drugs, and they carry a lot of money. But to
do so unarmed would be the height of folly, since the dealer being robbed
doubtlessly will be armed himself. [In discussing one robbery of a fellow
dealer, Allen notes, "This was a way we often got weapons—we'd take
people's guns when we robbed them" (p. 177).]

More generally, the presence of firearms among a felon's associates and
potential victims is probably a much greater threat to his well-being than
the prospect of an extra 1 or 2 years in prison. It would be sensible, therefore, to run the risk of an enhanced prison term by carrying a firearm oneself. In this sense, the predatory gun-wielding felon must be considered to
be largely indifferent to deterrence through after-the-fact punishments; relative to what might happen if he needed a gun but did not have one, most
after-the-fact punishments would pale to relative insignificance.

SUBSTITUTION AND OTHER NEUTRALIZING SIDE EFFECTS

Data presented in the previous chapter raise the possibility that some of
the more commonly advocated "gun-crime" policies could well prove to
have negative and unwanted side consequences. Bans on certain kinds of
weapons, assuming a reasonable success rate, will cause some criminals
not to commit the crimes they would have committed otherwise and will

cause other criminals to commit the same crimes but armed with different weapons. The relative sizes of these two groups is a pertinent issue; so, too, is the question what these "different weapons" would be.

All the data we have presented on this issue are conjectural, and so their implications are even "iffier" than usual. Still, the large majority of the more predatory felons in our sample told us they would respond to various partial or total handgun bans with either lateral or upward substitution—the weapons they said they would carry under these hypothetical conditions were either just as lethal as, or more lethal than, the weapons they would have otherwise carried in any case. One may properly quarrel with some of the details, doubt the practicalities, or debate the probity and realism of these responses, but the major message comes through clearly: The felonious activities of these men will not suffer for lack of the appropriate armament; their intent, so far as we can tell, would be to find substitutes that may be somewhat inconvenient but nevertheless highly effective.

Given our results, we think it likely that the major effects of partial or total handgun bans would fall more on the shoulders of the ordinary gunowning public than on the felonious gun abuser of the sort studied here. The people most likely to be deterred from acquiring a handgun by exceptionally high prices or by the nonavailability of certain kinds of handguns are not felons intent on arming themselves for criminal purposes (who can, if all else fails, steal the handgun they want), but rather poor people who have decided they need a gun to protect themselves against the felons but who find that the cheapest gun in the market costs more than they can afford to pay. Given the materials presented in Chapter Seven on confrontations with armed victims, it is therefore also possible that one side consequence of such measures would be some loss in the crime-thwarting effects of civilian firearms ownership.

Perhaps the most telling implication of our data on weapons substitution is not in the substance of the results but in the more general lesson that any social policy can have consequences that no one foresaw, intended, or wanted—consequences that, under the right conditions, worsen rather than improve the problem being addressed. Anticipating these untoward side consequences, and avoiding them, requires above all else a detailed empirical understanding of the nature of the problem; "solutions" that are implemented before the problem is reasonably well understood rarely solve anything.

Clearly, this study has not "solved" the problem of gun crime in American society; indeed, it has not even exemplified what the solution would look like. But it has provided some information about the nature of the problem itself, information that we hope others will use to formulate workable solutions to the problem of gun crime, thereby improving the collective existence of us all.

BIBLIOGRAPHY

Allen, John
  1977   *Assault with a Deadly Weapon: The Autobiography of a Street Criminal.*
         New York: McGraw Hill.
Anderson, Andy B., Anthony R. Harris, and JoAnn Miller
  1983   "Models of deterrence theory." *Social Science Research* 12(3) (September): 236–262.
Balkin, Steven, and John MacDonald
  1984   "A market analysis for handguns and gun control issues." In *Firearms and Violence: Issues of Public Policy,* ed. Don B. Kates. Cambridge, MA: Ballinger.
Becker, Gary S.
  1968   "Crime and punishment: An economic approach." *Journal of Political Economy* 76: 169–217.
Beha, James A.
  1977   " 'And *Nobody* Can Get You Out.' The impact of a mandatory prison sentence for the illegal carrying of a firearm on the use of firearms and on the administration of criminal justice in Boston." Parts I and II. *Boston University Law Review* 57:1 (January), 96–146; and 57:2 (March), 289–333.
Brill, Steven
  1977   *Firearms Abuse.* Washington D.C.: The Police Foundation.
Bruce-Biggs, B.
  1976   "The great American gun war." *The Public Interest* 45: 37–62.
Bureau of Alcohol, Tobacco, and Firearms
  1976a   *Project Identification: A Study of Handguns Used in Crime.* Washington, D.C.: Bureau of Alcohol, Tobacco, and Firearms.
  1976b   *Project 300.* Washington, D.C.: Bureau of Alcohol, Tobacco, and Firearms.
Bureau of Justice Statistics
  1985   *Bulletin: Household Burglary* (Washington, DC: U.S. Department of Justice), January.
Burr, D. E. S.
  1977   *Handgun Regulation.* Orlando, FL: Florida Bureau of Criminal Justice Planning and Assistance.
Caddell, Patrick
  1978   *An Analysis of Public Attitudes Toward Handgun Control.* Cambridge, Mass., Cambridge Reports, Inc.
Caetano, Donald F.
  1979   "The domestic arms race." *Journal of Communication* 29:2 (Spring): 39–46.

Cambridge Reports, Inc.
   1978   *An Analysis of Public Attitudes Toward Handgun Control.* Cambridge, MA:
           Cambridge Reports, Inc.
Chaiken, Jan M., and Marcia R. Chaiken
   1982   *Varieties of Criminal Behavior.* Santa Monica, CA: The RAND Corpora-
           tion.
Cook, Philip J.
   1976   "A strategic choice analysis of robbery." In *Sample Surveys of the Victims
           of Crime,* ed. Wesley Skogan. Cambridge, MA: Ballinger, pp. 173–187.
   1979   "The effect of gun availability on robbery and robbery murder: A cross-
           sectional study of fifty cities." In *Policy Studies Review Annual,* eds. Rob-
           ert Haveman and Bruce Zellner. Beverly Hills, CA: Sage, pp. 743–781.
   1980   "Reducing injury and death rates in robbery." *Policy Analysis* 6(1) (Win-
           ter): 21–45.
   1981   "The role of firearms in violent crimes: An interpretative review of the
           literature. . . ." Duke University: Institute of Policy Sciences and Public
           Affairs. Pp. 91 (mimeo'd).
   1982   "Research on robbery: An analysis of existing literature and an assess-
           ment of future research needs." Washington, D.C.: National Institute of
           Justice. Pp. 65.
   1983   "Robbery in the United States: An analysis of recent trends and patterns."
           Duke University: Institute of Policy Sciences and Public Affairs. Pp. 49
           (mimeo'd).
   1984   "Is robbery becoming more violent? An analysis of robbery murder trends
           since 1968." Duke University: Institute of Policy Sciences and Public Af-
           fairs.
   1985   "The etiology of robbery violence." Paper presented at the meetings of
           the American Society of Criminology, San Diego.
Cook, Philip J., and Daniel Nagin
   1979   *Does the Weapon Matter?* Washington, D.C.: Institute for Law and Social
           Research.
Curtis, Lynn A.
   1974   *Criminal Violence.* Lexington, Mass.: D. C. Heath.
Decision-Making Information, Inc.
   1978   *Attitudes of the American Electorate Toward Gun Control.* Santa Ana, CA:
           DMI, Inc.
Deutsch, Stephen J., and Francis B. Alt
   1977   "The effect of Massachusetts' gun control law on gun-related crimes in
           the city of Boston." *Evaluation Quarterly* 1 (March): 543–568.
DeZee, Matthew R.
   1983   "Gun control legislation: Impact and ideology." *Law and Policy Quar-
           terly* 5(3) (July): 367–379.
Flanagan, Timothy J., David J. van Alstyne, and Michael R. Gottfredson
   1981   *Sourcebook of Criminal Justice Statistics.* Washington, D.C.: U.S. Gov-
           ernment Printing Office.
Fleisher, B.
   1966   *The Economics of Delinquency.* Chicago: Quadrangle Books.
Geisel, Martin S., Richard Roll, and R. Stanton Wettick
   1969   "The effectiveness of state and local regulation of handguns: A statistical
           analysis." *Duke University Law Journal* 4 (August): 647–676.
Hindelang, Michael, Michael Gottfredson, and James Garofalo
   1978   *Victims of Personal Crime: An Empirical Foundation for a Theory of Per-
           sonal Victimization.* Cambridge, MA: Ballinger.

Inciardi, James A. (ed.)
   1981   *The Drugs-Crime Connection.* Beverly Hills, CA: Sage.
Jones, Edward D.
   1981   "The District of Columbia's 'Firearms Control Regulations Act of 1975:'
           The toughest handgun control law in the United States—Or is it?" *Annals
           of the American Academy of Political and Social Science* 455 (May): 138–
           149.
Kates, Don B.
   1978   "Some remarks on the prohibition of handguns." *St. Louis University Law
           Journal* 23(11), 11–34.
   1984   *Firearms and Violence: Issues of Public Policy.* Cambridge, MA: Ballin-
           ger.
Kleck, Gary
   1983   "Policy lessons from recent gun control research." To appear in *Law and
           Contemporary Problems.*
   1984a   "Handgun control only: A policy disaster in the making." In *Firearms
           and Violence: Issues of Public Policy,* ed. Don B. Kates. Cambridge, Mass.:
           Ballinger, pp. 167–199.
   1984b   "The relationship between gun ownership levels and rates of violence
           in the United States." In *Firearms and Violence: Issues and Public Pol-
           icy,* ed. Don B. Kates. Cambridge, Mass.: Ballinger, pp. 99–132.
Kleck, Gary, and David J. Bordua
   1983   "The factual foundation for certain key assumptions of gun control." *Law
           and Policy Quarterly* 5:3 (July), pp. 271–298.
   1984   "The assumptions of gun control." In *Firearms and Violence: Issues of
           Public Policy,* ed. Don B. Kates. Cambridge, Mass.: Ballinger, pp. 23–
           48.
Lizotte, Alan J., and David Bordua
   1980   "Firearms ownership for sport and protection: Two divergent models."
           American Sociological Review 45(2) (April): 229–244.
Lizotte, Alan J., David Bordua, and Carolyn White
   1981   "Firearms ownership for sport and protection: Two not so divergent
           models." *American Sociological Review* 46(4) (August): 499–503.
Loftin, Colin, and David McDowall
   1981   " 'One with a gun gets you two': Mandatory sentencing and firearms vio-
           lence in Detroit." *The Annals of the American Academy of Political and
           Social Science* 455 (May): 150–167.
Magaddino, Joseph P., and Marshall H. Medoff
   1984   "An empirical analysis of Federal and state firearm control laws." In *Fire-
           arms and Violence: Issues of Public Policy,* ed. Don B. Kates. Cambridge,
           MA: Ballinger, pp. 225–258.
Marks, Alan, and C. Shannon Stokes
   1976   "Socialization, firearms, and suicide." *Social Problems* 23(5) (June): 622–
           629.
Marquis, Kent H.
   1981   *Quality of Prisoner Self Reports: Arrest and Conviction Response Errors.*
           Santa Monica, CA: The RAND Corporation.
Miller, Walter B.
   1958   "Lower class culture as a generating milieu of gang delinquency." *Journal
           of Social Issues* 14: 5–19.
Moore, Mark
   1981   "Keeping handguns from criminal offenders." *The Annals of the Ameri-
           can Academy of Political and Social Science* 455 (May), 92–109.

Murray, Douglas
  1975   "Handguns, gun control laws and firearms violence." *Social Problems* 23(1)
         (October): 81–93.
National Bureau of Standards
  1977   LEAA Police Equipment Survey of 1972. Vol. VI: Body Armor and Con-
         fiscated Weapons. Washington, D.C.: U.S. Department of Commerce.
Newton, George D., and Franklin E. Zimring
  1969   *Firearms and Violence in American Life.* Washington, D.C.: U.S. Govern-
         ment Printing Office.
Pierce, Glenn L., and William J. Bowers
  1981   "The Bartley-Fox gun law's short term impact on crime in Boston." *The
         Annals of the American Academy of Political and Social Science* 455 (May):
         120–137.
Rossi, Peter H.
  1983   "On crime and criminal justice." Chancellor's Lecture: University of
         Massachusetts, Amherst.
Rossi, Peter H., Richard A. Berk, and Kenneth Lenihan
  1980   *Money, Work, and Crime.* New York: Academic Press.
Suttles, Gerald
  1968   *The Social Order of the Slum.* Chicago: University of Chicago Press.
Thrasher, Frederick M.
  1927   *The Gang.* Chicago: University of Chicago Press.
Tonso, William R.
  1982   *Gun and Society: The Social and Existential Roots of the American At-
         tachment to Firearms.* Washington, D.C.: University Press of America.
Weber-Burdin, Eleanor, Peter Rossi, James Wright, and Kathleen Daly
  1981   *Weapons Policies: A Survey of Police Department Practices Concerning
         Weapons and Related Issues.* Amherst, MA: Social and Demographic Re-
         search Institute (mimeo'd).
Wolfgang, Marvin
  1980   *National Survey of Crime Severity.* University of Pennsylvania: Center for
         Studies in Criminology and Criminal Law.
Wright, James D.
  1981   "Public opinion and gun control: A comparison of results from two re-
         cent national surveys." *The Annals of the American Academy of Political
         and Social Science* 455 (May): 24–39.
Wright, James D., and Peter H. Rossi
  1985   *The Armed Criminal in America: A Survey of Incarcerated Felons.* Wash-
         ington, D.C.: U. S. Government Printing Office.
Wright, James D., Peter H. Rossi, and Kathleen Daly
  1983   *Under the Gun: Weapons, Crime, and Violence in America.* Hawthorne,
         N.Y.: Aldine.
Yeager, Matthew G., Joseph D. Alviani, and Nancy Loving
  1976   *How Well Does the Handgun Protect You and Your Family?* Washington,
         D.C.: U. S. Conference of Mayors.
Zimring, Franklin E.
  1968   "Is gun control likely to reduce violent killings?" *The University of Chi-
         cago Law Review* 35: 721–737.
  1972   "The medium is the message: Firearm caliber as a determinant of death
         from assault." *Journal of Legal Studies* 1(1): 97–123.
Zimring, Franklin E., and G. Hawkins
  1973   *Deterrence: The Legal Threat in Crime Control.* Chicago: University of
         Chicago Press.

INDEX